Jenny Diski was born in 1947 in London, where she lived and worked for most of her life. She is the author of eight novels, including *Only Human* and *Nothing Natural* which are published by Virago; a collection of short stories and a book of essays as well as two bestselling memoirs, *Stranger on a Train*, published by Virago, and *Skating to Antarctica*. She now lives in Cambridge.

Also by Jenny Diski

A View from the Bed

And Other Observations

JENNY DISKI

Virago

A *Virago* Book

First published by Virago Press 2003

Copyright © Jenny Diski 2003

The moral right of the author has been asserted

A CIP catalogue record for this book
is available from the British Library

ISBN 1 84408 098 6

Typeset in Horley by M Rules
Printed and bound in Great Britain
by Clays Ltd, St Ives plc

Virago Press
An imprint of
Time Warner Books UK
Brettenham House
Lancaster Place
London WC2E 7EN

www.virago.co.uk

CONTENTS

CONTENTS

To Ian with love

PREFACE AND ACKNOWLEDGEMENTS

For the most part the longer essays in this collection were originally published in the *London Review of Books* over the past
five years. The other articles were variously printed in the
Observer, the *Independent on Sunday*, the *New Statesman*, the
Jewish Chronicle, the *LA Times Book Review* and the *American
Scholar*. The section called . . . AND SHOPPING consists of
a year's worth of columns in *The Sunday Times* on my thoughts
as a supermarket shopper. One or two pieces here are previously
unpublished.

I am very grateful to all the editors who asked me to review
books or write articles, not just because the extra income is welcome but because of the pleasure of being charged to think about
things I hadn't much thought about thinking about. This is the
same kind of gratitude I felt towards English teachers at my
schools who set essays. For a novelist in particular a small defined
task is a treat. For once someone else is thinking up the topic, and
there is the fun and good exercise of writing to outside constraints
of subject matter and length. Even so, reading them in bulk, it's
clear that they are of a piece with my other fictional and non-
fictional writing. Concerns that are recognisably mine (even when
they are not those of the authors of the books reviewed) flit

through the articles like ghosts – sometimes I think I only know my own obsessions because I have to read them in proof. That the pieces are largely grouchy and opinionated is entirely to do with my own bad character and not at all related to the nature of the journal for which they were written. Again I thank those who have published me for letting it be so – not all editors have put up with it and although I delight in the message-in-a-bottle aspect of the kill fee, it's still preferable to have work published.

All reviews are a single opinion and should never be taken as more than that. What I like and don't like is as arbitrary as the style of clothes I choose to wear. Please read these essays as the beginnings of an argument you might like to have.

A VIEW FROM THE BED

A View from the Bed

It isn't often that I wake in the early hours of the morning to find a happy ending squatting in the corner of my bedroom. Mostly I wake in the middle of the night to the sound of the cat being sick under the bed, or the thud of trainers pounding the pavement outside to escape the alarmed wailing of a car that has just been broken into. Occasionally a dream that would have been the perfect novel rouses me, before disappearing round the corner of my mind. But never until the other night have I been woken up by a frog repeatedly hurling itself against the skirting board, apparently trying in its small-brained fashion to batter its way to the sort of place a frog would more like to be.

As a general rule I try to maintain a balanced and realistic approach to life. I don't have wistful thoughts about pots of gold when I see a rainbow. It never crosses my mind to check stray bottles on the beach for genies. I'm convinced that the best place for a rabbit's foot is at the end of a rabbit's leg. And if there are fairies at the bottom of my garden, they go about their business and I go about mine. But although this approach keeps life on an even keel and prevents the stress of both over-excitement and grave disappointment, I do find that the perfectly mundane existence that I strive for and attain can occasionally seem a little flat, a bit lacking in absurdity. So from time to time, when a rattling good cliché, or a thumping banality presents itself, I'm inclined to give it a run for its money. Hand me a candle and I'll burn it at both ends, give me a cart and I'll put it before the horse. Rationalist though I may be in the bright daylight hours, now here I was with a small amphibian in my bedroom, offering me the opportunity of a lifetime. I was trembling on the very brink of living happily ever after. The frog moment had arrived, and, really, it was irresistible.

I switched on the light, got out of bed and cupped the little creature, along with its fate and mine, in my hands. The frog, once I had scooped it up, sat still as a statue between my palms, seeming to wait, as if it had suddenly dawned on it that there might be another way out of the situation apart from beating its brains out on the skirting board. Well, of course there was. Frog salvation was at hand. I had only to bend my head, purse my lips and plant the mandatory kiss on its lumpy green head and it would become transformed in an instant into the sort of handsome prince for whom the environment of my bedroom would hold no terrors. Probably frogs have daydreams too. In that moment the frog and I gazed frankly into each other's eyes and saw the possibility of eternity in our respective limpid pools.

I was about to perform the decisive deed when I was suddenly struck by a series of troubling questions. Handsome princes were all very well in fairy stories, but I was in the middle of a good night's sleep, the sheets were clean and crisp, I had the whole expanse of the bed all to myself. Did I actually want it messed up by some prince I didn't know from Adam? Did I want to live happily ever after, or would I rather have the bed to myself for the rest of the night? Would he get up and go or demand

4

breakfast and small talk the next morning – to say nothing of ever after? It only took a moment's thought. I carried my little frog out to the garden and wished it godspeed as I released it. So much for fairy tales.

Every Mother Prays

*Hairstyles and Fashion: A Hairdresser's History of Paris
1910–1920, edited by Steven Zdatny. Berg 1999*

At 17 I was (let me be bold, let me put it on record) gorgeous, and gorgeous in exactly the way a person was supposed to be in 1964. Thin as a leaf, a Biba size eight, hips that held hipsters perfectly in place, and legs that were designed for emerging from skirts that were little more than a pelmet. But – oh what a waste of temporary good fortune – none of that mattered. My 17th birthday present was a haircut at Evansky's, as stylish a hairdresser as Vidal Sassoon at the time; the place where hair was cut into the essential knife-sharp meticulous geometric shapes that swung like chain mail as you walked. I sat in the chair while behind me Robert, the senior stylist, cast his professional eye over me, lifting hanks of my long hair with a comb and letting them drop, flicking sections this way and that to see how they fell, examining its possibilities. Finally, he pocketed his comb and with a sigh that would have broken a Mock Turtle's heart intoned to my mirror image: 'Every mother prays that their daughter will have straight hair.' I shrank down in my chair with shame, but I didn't need to be told. I knew my case was hopeless. My hair curled, it was thick and wiry; in a million years and with all the hairdressing talents in the universe I could never have that sleek hair that fell of its own accord straight and shiny into an immaculate bob as soon as I got out of bed in the morning. Hair then, as Vidal explains in the current edition of the *Hairdressers' Journal International*, had to 'make a statement rather than just make someone look pretty'. All my hair ever said was 'sorry'. Robert did what he could, he cut it as if I had the right kind of hair and then blow-dried it with agonising tugs of the brush, pulling it away from my scalp to straighten it. I didn't mind, I deserved the pain. I used an iron and ironing-board myself. He made it look wonderful, right, just like those women who had been blessed with proper hair. I had the style, it made the statement. I looked as I was supposed to look when I left, but then it rained, and by the time I got home my hopeless hair had sprung back into frizz, the knife edges serrated, the weighty slab of fringe corkscrewed. Whatever else was right about me didn't count. My hair was wrong, and in the 1960s if your hair was wrong, nothing could be right.

I saw Robert once again, though not at the hairdresser. Some time later he heard from a friend of mine who was a regular customer that I was in a psychiatric hospital. One day he walked into the day-room, looking dreadfully uncomfortable. We sat at a table, but he was ill at ease, not clear, I think, why he'd come, and it was hard to know exactly what to talk about. He would begin to ask, 'Why . . .?' and then stop, perhaps for fear of upsetting me, perhaps because he couldn't formulate the question. After a little while, and several awkward silences, he left, still troubled, squeezing my shoulder and saying he'd be back. He wasn't, but I was moved that he had come at all. Still, in retrospect, I wonder if he thought my insoluble hair was the root of my problem. And, I don't know, who can say for certain what strength of psyche I might have developed if only my hair had conformed to the necessity of the time?

And this is what happens. If I'd been asked to review a book of essays by a zoologist or a literary person, I might have controlled the upwellings of personal reminiscences, the heartache and pleasure of books I've read or animals I've known, but show me a series of articles by a hairdresser and I'm lost in the history of my own hair. I could go on to the 1970s and the need for perms (my curly hair was not even curly in the right way), or to the hennaings, the cropping to half an inch all over, or the moment when my daughter came out of infant school and walked straight past me because that morning her mother's hair had not been purple.

Given my history as a person with socially unacceptable hair, I have always thought of hairdressers as one of the caring professions, like doctors or psychiatrists, but now I learn, from a Paris coiffeur's 'letters' to his British colleagues in the *Hairdressers' Weekly Journal*, that hairdressers have concerns of their own. Like, I suppose, doctors and psychiatrists, when they talk to each other, their vital interest is in using their skills to make a living. Steven Zdatny offers the articles of Emile Long as a particular view of the social history of the early years of the 20th century, and it is a very particular view indeed. The years from 1910 to 1920 were not uneventful in Europe, but for Emile Long writing in a trade magazine, everything that happened was of concern for the effect it had on the business of hairdressing. What did the First World War mean to M. Long and his fellow professionals? It meant a threat to their customary business, the need to find a way of 'counteracting the trade crisis occasioned by this terrible war'. He writes in 1915:

In times of peace the weather generally forms the topic of conversation, but at the present time it is out of place to indulge in such small talk, and opinions are generally exchanged in regard to the latest news from the Front. This gives the coiffeur an excellent chance of making a remark something to the effect:

8

'Did you know that it has become the custom in Paris for people who are fond of one another to exchange locks of hair before parting?'

'–?–'

'– Yes, the men present the women with a small strand of hair, which is artistically worked up and then preserved inside a medallion. For their part the ladies offer the men who are about to leave for the Front, or to visit some distant land, a bracelet, ring or neck band skilfully plaited with some of their longest hair. This custom brings good luck . . . Here are a few of the various but more simple models.'

Long's other suggestions for keeping the business going during these testing times were to diversify into the dressing of little girls' hair and, given that 'the European War continues with unabated severity, and until it ceases all industries, and especially business de luxe, will suffer from stagnation', the making of wigs for the dolls of the little girls whose hair is now, perforce, being dressed. The everyday concerns of a hairdresser trying to make a living in 1915 offer as vital an insight into the pulse of history as Owen or Sassoon's poetry from the Front.

Long is a businessman wishing to share his years of experience with others of his trade. There is always satisfaction in discovering the details of specialist worlds, and the quotidian life of the hairdresser expands into a social drama of heartache and struggle equal to the torments and terrors of Arthur Miller or David Mamet's salesmen. As Zdatny explains and Long complains, hairdressers were at the bottom of a hierarchy of fashion, helpless in the face of the couturiers of the great fashion houses who kept their models' hair short and simple so as not to distract from the clothes. But at a time when hats were compulsory items of dress, the battle raged most directly, and therefore most fiercely, between the hairdressers and the milliners, whose styles each season determined the degree of complexity and therefore the profitability of hairdressing. 'The coiffeur is lamenting,' Long laments, 'because he is ruined by the modiste; by creating a demand for bee-hive hats, which reach down to the shoulders, the milliner has killed waving, hairdressing and postiche.'

But Zdatny warns against putting too much faith in the semiotics of fashion. The milliners, too, were at the mercy of others. In 1910 Long did a tour of the milliners to determine what the fashion was to be for the next season. 'Toques,' they told him, one and all. 'Toques in velvet and furs of all kinds.' When Long asked why, he was told: 'We do not make toques out of preference but simply because our hat shapers have been on strike for four months and we cannot procure felt shapes.' Could Marx or Engels, Weber or Durkheim have explained man's interdependency better?

Long is a model of the bourgeois businessman, single-lensed but commercially passionate, and with an elder's desire to bequeath his wealth of knowledge. He knows about hair – his master was Marcel of the Marcel wave – and he knows about profitability. The weekly cut and set was no more than a hairdresser's dream in 1910. The coiffeur's livelihood depended on the luxury end of the market, dressing long hair as complicatedly and therefore unmanageably as possible. But in the end, like any good businessman, he accedes to his customers' wishes. Elaborate styles and complex postiches might represent the good times for hairdressers, but if the clients want short, simple styles, it is better to take a cut in profits than see your customers go elsewhere. Technology was changing, newer methods made waving and tinting accessible to customers at the less exclusive end of the market, and it became possible to make postiches on a scale that allowed them to be sold over the counter at drapery establishments and department stores. Long's distaste is not merely commercial, he is exquisitely snobbish. The mass-market postiches were 'too frizzy and waved to please the elegant Parisiennes. Nevertheless there is a demand for such work, as there are many coquettes possessing no personal taste and to whom it would be impossible to sell a postiche of the latest design and make.' Though the snobbery, too, is commercial at base, popularisation rebounds on profit, and grand ladies, seeing every flibberty-gibbet on the street with a frizzy postiche, were soon rejecting them. Long did not have a very high regard for women: 'The more civilised and cultured a woman becomes, the more she resembles the savage of the Pacific Islands in her taste for showy colours and glittering ornaments.' But his misogyny, like everything else, is at the service of commercial concern. If women refuse to buy expensive, exclusive postiches, there will always be something, fancy barrettes and decorations, that they can be persuaded to buy. He sounds increasingly nervous, and by 1920, when he stopped writing, women were beginning to get a taste for the simplicity that he feared would do the hairdresser's business accounts no good at all.

Emile Long need not have worried, because there I was, back in 1964, cringing in my chair, and wishing fruitlessly that hats would become de rigueur so that I might conceal my tragic hair. The hairdresser finally won out against the milliners, and short hair, especially precision-cut short hair, needs cutting regularly. Long's fear of mass production was ill-founded. Still, business is business in the hair trade, as the editorial in the February issue of *Hairdressers' Journal International* makes clear:

> We need to know who our audience is and then make sure we tell them what we can do for them – if you're a salon whose clients are young and funky, there's no point in sending flyers to the local old people's home. Getting the right message to the right people is what created some of today's most successful businesses – and there's no reason why hairdressers can't mirror that success.

11

And haircutter to the stars Trevor Sorbie speaks the eternal commercial truth in his advice to present-day hairdressers: 'The future of the industry has nothing to do with hairdressing but the art of business, learning new things like computers, presentation skills, marketing ideas – these are the ingredients to becoming successful. The new medium for hairdressing is the media.' Wouldn't Emile Long's heart sing?

Not long ago I did a reading at a literary festival. I stood in front of the audience and read from a work in progress. They listened, showed no sign of restlessness, clapped appreciatively, and seemed well enough satisfied. At the end a woman came up to me without the usual book in her hand for me to sign, but with a look of sincere admiration. Since childhood I had wanted to be a writer, and such moments, I suppose, were fantasies come true. Yet like most fantasies come true, writing is now a normal thing and the public stuff performed more as a duty than for self-satisfaction. The woman stood in front of me and I prepared my face to receive her compliments on my writing with appropriate humility. 'I just want to tell you that I really love your hair,' she said. I melted.

Being 50

Welcome to Middle Age! (and Other Cultural Fictions),
edited by Richard Shweder, Chicago 1998

I'm nine years old, in bed, in the dark. The detail in the room is
perfectly clear. I am lying on my back. I have a greeny-gold quilted
eiderdown covering me. I have just calculated that I will be 50
years old in 1997. 'Fifty' and '1997' don't mean a thing to me,
aside from being an answer to an arithmetic question I set myself.
I try it differently. 'I will be 50 in 1997.' 1997 doesn't matter. 'I *will*
be 50.' The statement is absurd. I am nine. 'I will be ten' makes
sense. 'I will be 13' has a dreamlike maturity about it. 'I will be 50'
is simply a paraphrase for another senseless statement I make to
myself at night: 'I will be dead one day.' 'One day I won't be.' I
have a great determination to feel the sentence as a reality. But it
always escapes me. 'I will be dead' comes with a picture of a dead
body on a bed. But it's mine, a nine-year-old body. When I make
it old, it becomes someone else. I can't imagine myself dead. I
can't imagine myself dying. Either the effort or the failure to do so
makes me feel panicky.

Being 50 is not being dead, but it is being old, inconceivably
old, for me, that is. I know other people are old, other people are

13

50, and I will be 50 if I don't die beforehand. But the best I can do is to imagine someone who is not me, though not someone I know, being 50. She looks like an old lady; the way old ladies currently look. She looks like someone else. I can't connect me thinking about her with the fact that I will be her in 41 years' time. She has lived through and known 41 years to which I have no access. I can't believe I will become her, though I know, factually, that I must. I can't dress myself in her clothes and her flesh and know what it feels like being her. This is immensely frustrating. I do the next best thing. I send a message out into the future, etch into my brain cells a memo to the other person, who will be me grown to be 50, to remember this moment, this very moment, this actual second when I am nine, in bed, in the dark, trying to imagine being 50.

I was 50 in the summer of 1997 and for the past year I have been recalling the nine-year-old who tried to imagine me. I mean, I have been recalling her trying to imagine me, at that moment, in bed, in the dark, some 41 years ago. I have finally received the memo. It is easier for me to acknowledge her than the other way round, for all that I have learned about the unreliability of memory, because I have lived the missing 41 years she could know nothing about. There is a track back. The vividness of her making a note to remember the moment when she is 50 is startling. But it's not a simple, direct link. I have the moment, but the person I connect with is someone whose future I know. I do not know the nine-year-old as she was then, at all; the one who had not yet experienced the life I led between her and me. I can't imagine her as a reality, in her striving to understand what kind of 50-year-old woman she would be, because she doesn't exist anymore except as a pinpoint in time. She now has an indelible relation to me back through time, that I could not have for her aiming forward. There is a sense of vertigo, something quite dizzying about having arrived at the unimaginable point she reached out towards, at recalling her message and being in a position – but not able – to answer it: here I am, it's like this.

It is not just the nine-year-old's illusive reality that prevents me from responding, it is also my own present inability, aged 50, to imagine what it is like to be 50. I've heard a lot about it, read plenty, seen numbers of 50-year-olds, both depicted and in real life, but that seems to be no help at all. This isn't surprising. The 50 that I seek to understand is the same 50 I wondered about as a child, it has nothing much to do with having lived for 50 years or more. It is, as Richard Shweder and the other anthropologists insist in the coyly named collection of ethnographical essays *Welcome to Middle Age!*, a 'cultural fiction'. Faced with the label, I find it hard not to wonder what use such a designation could be. Presumably everything cultural is a fiction by definition, and come to that everything natural is fiction too since it is named as such and viewed always by acculturated eyes. 'Fictional', Shweder explains, does not mean 'unreal'; he uses the term, he says, in an (oh dear) 'affirmative Post-Modern sense'. Things that are fictions are 'fabricated, manufactured, invented or designed, but they are not necessarily false'.

It's funny how, when social theory is teased out for the unspecialised reader, it splats to earth like a water bomb. The term 'cultural fiction' is manufactured, but it's not necessarily false, it just returns us to the knowledge we started with. The designation of middle age as a cultural fiction is necessary, however, to make this book of essays more than a Disney travelogue of just so stories. 'Middle age', we learn, is simply the story we tell ourselves in this part of the world at this time about a stage in life that has an alternative narrative in other places. That is the premise. 'There are alternative ways of representing the temporal dimension of life without relying on the idea of middle age. For example, in some cultural worlds described in this book, the stages of life (including mature adulthood) are represented in terms of a social history of role transitions within the context of a residential kinship group.' The last phrase, far from radically resetting notions of middle age, seems to describe our current Western point of view quite as well as it describes any alternative cultural formulation of the middle years of life. But there is a real sense of a crusade from Shweder and other contributors to enlighten us, and show how we could have other, better ways of designating mature adulthood. Those better views ('better fictions', if we are using Shweder's terminology) are, of course, to be found in far-away places with strange-sounding names.

A definition of the current Western discourse on middle age is offered by Margaret Morganroth Gullette, who opens the debate with an evangelically strong social-constructionist approach in which she calls for 'critical age studies', which start with the assumption that 'little in midlife ageing is bodily and that nothing considered "bodily" is unaffected by culture'. It's radical stuff, demanding a new negative category 'middle-ageism', born of power, hierarchy and resistance; familiar to readers of Foucault everywhere. Middle age in our culture is a decline narrative that begins at adolescence and peaks in the forties and fifties as mid-life crisis. Since it is taken to be a cultural category, there appears to be no way out of this discourse; the 'ideology of "decline" raining over us' includes those who claim to experience no such thing: 'there may be some people for whom life-course optimism or pessimism is a solid and relatively unshakeable given, so that they infallibly pick out only those elements of the available discourses that support their chosen worldview.' The counter-discourse is dependent on the prevailing discourse. There's no wriggling out of it, Gullette informs us. Those who refuse the narratives of 'crisis-and-fall or crisis-and-cure' are 'also, but unwittingly, taking a stance toward midlife decline ideology: they are supporting it.'

For most of my life, I've felt quite cheery about ageing. It always seemed to me to be better to be older, and on the whole my experience has borne this suspicion out. I have, with each decade, better liked the way my life was; there has been increasing real autonomy, less anxiety, more confidence, greater physical pleasure, fewer physical pressures. This, of course, is all predicated on good luck and relative affluence. I don't feel clever about it, only remarkably fortunate. Even so, I have to report, among other signs, a certain loss of muscle tone, an alarming decline in the ability to recall names and the reason I have just walked into the living-room, and the arithmetical certainty that I am nearer to inescapable death than I have ever been before. As a woman on a plane bound for sun and sea said to her friend to explain her anxiety about wearing bikinis, 'My gravity's going.' Of course, we might rejoice in the new sensuality of soft, pliable flesh, and be grateful for the opportunity to let go of names that no longer concern us. We could look on short-term absent-mindedness as a new-found advantage: the excitement and infinite possibilities of arriving in a room without a clue why you are there are surely more interesting than just going to the cupboard to get a new roll of lavatory paper. Certainly, there are culturally imposed feelings about the bodily changes of ageing, and let's suppose it's possible consciously to alter our attitudes to them. But, for those lacking a conventional religious faith, how are we to celebrate the increasing proximity of death, which includes the loss of all these new advantages we've discovered? When we feel concern about ageing, we are not just kowtowing to received opinion, we are also gripped by panic at the remorselessness of time. Things are not going to get better, there is a definite direction to the physical changes those in middle age experience, from softening flesh and forgetfulness to arthritic immobility and oblivion. We might be lucky and stay relatively fit and mentally alert until the end, but the end is getting closer faster, and the end is foreordained. What exactly is there to look forward to? How do these other cultures avoid the glummest of conclusions?

The answer in almost all the essays is that they replace a decline

narrative with one about life stages. In this view, middle age is a
time of authority, less work and higher social standing. What is
common to the alternative view is a strong sense of hierarchy. In
Samoa, Kenya and rural India, middle life is a time when maximum political power, social status and family responsibility
(though I'm not sure this follows) are achieved. Those at this
stage are functioning at the centre of life and therefore are not
much given to introspection. In Samoa, the physical movement
and hard graft of the young are replaced with passive authority.
Birthdays are insignificant, what matters is where you have got to
in the life plan. 'In age my parents are only 55 and 45, but I call
them "old" because I am in a stage of being responsible for taking
care of them,' one informant explains. In Hindu families in rural
India, people live in three or four-generation families. Parents
cease sexual activity when their firstborn son brings home a wife.
The youngest daughter-in-law is entirely subservient to the
mother-in-law, who rules and runs the house. A 23-year-old
daughter-in-law cooks and cleans for a household of 12 and, after
washing the feet of her parents-in-law, drinks the water.

We are warned by the authors of this essay, Usha Menon and
Richard Shweder, not to make cultural assumptions about this,
nor to take a dim Western feminist view of the life of young
women. What we see as an appalling daily grind has moral
meanings of service to the family. They report relative contentment in their informants: well-being scores an average of 8 on a
scale from 0 to 16. Mothers-in-law, of course, report high levels of
well-being. But time passes not just for the daughters-in-law who
will progress to higher and lighter duties. Mothers-in-law become
grandmothers who are marginalised, lonely and feeble. A sense of
community may have avoided mid-life crisis, and a belief in the
hereafter apparently prevented a premature despair at a blank
end, but it seems to be replaced by a miserable youth and old age.
We are told it is inappropriate to judge these lifestyles negatively,

but at the very least my culturally conditioned eyes look without envy on the culturally conditioned contentment described in these pages. These other ways reject the individualism, the narcissism of Western attitudes to the life course. Instead, they embed it in social relations hedged with rigid rules about appropriate ageing and duty. This may be a more comfortable way to live, it may even be more virtuous, but we've lost it, for better or worse, and the tales of middle age in other places are not alternative ways of being that we can slip on like a kimono; they are no more than interesting ethnographical data.

So we're stuck with where we are. A notional 50 that is related to but not coterminous with our experience of ourselves. A cultural fiction, but in our present culture, lacking firm rules. In all probability everyone is startled by the fact of their having aged and has to align inner confusion with social perceptions, but in our society the signs are unclear. Beyond the notion of '50' that I had as a child, that I have now, there are no guidelines. *How* is one supposed to be 50? There used to be a dress code, as clear as Greeks swathed in black, or white-haired old ladies in shawls who were 'mothers' in old movies. The nearest thing we have now is people who have stuck to whatever style was fashionable when they were young: the middle-aged in mini-skirts, too black eye make-up and the wrong kind of jeans. 'Turn your collar down,' I'm warned by my young. 'You look Sixties.' There are specialist shops. Invisible for most of my life, there is a shop in Kentish Town which, even now, I think of as always closed. When should I begin getting my clothes from here? Inspired by the fieldwork of *Welcome to Middle Age!*, I took a trip to Burston's Jackets and Gowns. It has a permanent window display of shapeless pleated skirts, floral frocks, cardigans and fully fashioned jackets in 100 per cent polyester and crimplene and nylon. I toured the double-fronted windows. Middle age isn't expensive. Even the 'Model Coat' was just £52, while 'Latest' dresses could be had for as little

19

as £12. I hovered at the door. Inside, clothes were neatly racked and under polythene wraps. Two women I could easily identify as middle-aged were sitting chatting to some children who called one of them Granny. It was my intention to go in and try on some of these clothes, to see if I would be transformed into somebody appropriately '50', but I couldn't get through the door. What if it worked, what if '50' and me converged as I put on the clothes? And what if it didn't work? By which I mean, what if wearing the clothes made no difference to the image I thought I was seeing in the mirror, because the image I have of myself is entirely subjective? I remember sitting opposite a man at dinner, who was wearing a wig so obvious that it was hard to drag your eyes away from it. What, I wondered, did he see when he looked into his mirror before he left the house? Not what I and the others around the table were seeing, surely? Which thought led inexorably to the question of what I saw when I looked in the mirror before leaving the house, and what the other people around the table, the wigged gent included, were seeing when they looked at me.

Ditto the music I listen to. The books I read. The opinions I hold. My sex life. The variables are too great, the truths are too relative for a simple, satisfactory definition of middle age. Here I am, I might say to the nine-year-old, I have turned 50 and it is like . . . well, it's rather like not knowing what 50 is like when you are nine, but with the added certainty now that time is passing and will pass with increasing speed. And time, as I suspected all those years ago, is strictly limited. Time, of course, is another cultural fiction, but from one end of the planet to the other, for each individual, it comes to an end. And no, I am no better at imagining my own death than I was at nine. A memo then, for myself at the moment of death.

Both Feet Firmly on the Ground

When I tell you that I have been much oppressed by thoughts of gravity these past few days, you will deduce that I lead an almost zenlike existence. And it's true that aside from the odd wrong number, nothing very dramatic, neither heartbreak nor domestic emergency, has happened round here of late. Just as well, there's been no time for any of that sort of thing since I became gripped by thoughts of gravity and its consequences. I'm not talking about high seriousness or solemnity, and a philosophical debate within myself about the shallowness of modern existence and the need for a more profound approach to life. The gravity that has preoccupied my mind every waking moment is the force that keeps us with both feet firmly on the ground, or if not, flat on our face on the pavement.

It started when I woke up on an otherwise perfectly ordinary morning in the sure and certain knowledge that if I were not lying on my bed, I would be sprawled on the floor. Instead of getting up and brushing my teeth like any sensible person who has a pointless morning reverie, I let the thought scamper about a bit. What followed logically was that, since I was a flight up from

21

ground level, the floor on which I would be sprawled if I were not held up by the bed, was itself no more than a device to stop me falling on my downstairs neighbour. And then I was lost in a vision of the world stripped of all meaning save the necessity of holding things up on a planet where everything wants to fall down. Every object I came in contact with transformed into its real self: just another anti-gravity device. The cup keeping my tea in one place, the basin I washed in holding the water that dripped from my face, towel rail, laundry basket, the chair I sat on, the table, the saucepan, spoon, clothes hangers, drawers, buttons, hooks and eyes, stairs, the walls that held the roof up . . .

It was the point at which I saw my own self as a solution to the gravity problem – muscles and bones preventing me from being a formless flop, skin as envelope stopping all the stuff that keeps me going from spilling out – that I decided to go back to bed and start again.

I phoned the most down to earth friend I could think of.

'I've got a problem with gravity,' I moaned. 'It's bearing down on me something awful.'

'Look at it this way,' he said. 'It's a blessing. Without it, all our books would float off the shelves and we'd never keep them in alphabetical order. Oh, I forgot, your books aren't in alphabetical order. But at least they don't keep bumping into you. You've got gravity to thank for that.'

I tried being grateful, but it struck me that books were only weighty bound objects that would hurt if they floated aimlessly about so that the words could be kept all in one place and didn't scatter all over the floor. Imagine the mess the half million or so words of *War and Peace* alone would make on the carpet. Imagine the anti-gravitational suction our vacuum cleaners would need to clear up the letter litter.

'Do you realise,' I said, 'that if we'd evolved on a planet without gravity, not a single thing would be the same. In fact, the only reason why everything is the way it is, is because of gravity. It's outrageous. What about free will? What about design? What's the point of style statements like loft living when all they really do is keep us aloft? Doesn't it make you feel sort of pointless? Accidental?'

But it didn't. It seemed that some people are quite adjusted to gravitational necessity. Probably something to do with toilet training, I shouldn't wonder, but let's not get on to that.

Reading the Labels on the Marmalade Jars

I don't believe in God. Actually, that's putting it too fervently. I don't think it's very likely. I'd be surprised. But then I like surprises, so it's possible I have an ulterior motive. Perhaps, all unknown to myself, I'm secretly on the lookout for the really big surprise. It's best, I find, never to entirely trust oneself when talking on the subject of God. In fact, it's best, I find, never to entirely trust oneself about anything. What I do instead of belief, is read the labels on the marmalade jars.

Real, honest-to-God, zonking faith is, I suspect, a gift, like a great singing voice, or being double-jointed. As it happens, I am double-jointed, so it would be unreasonable of me to expect to be the beneficiary of more than my fair share of grace. The subject of faith comes to mind because recently I had a very dispiriting conversation with someone on the subject of The Purpose of It All. Not that I'm in the habit of such conversations; I generally expect people I know to know that there is no point, and that for better or worse that *is* the point. But I did not know this acquaintance well, and it was late when she murmured that she thought there probably was a purpose in life. I should have taken her statement to mean it was time we both went home to bed, but the chair I sat in was comfortable, and the drink I was drinking was only half drunk. It was a limp sort of statement, more resigned than convinced. What is the purpose? I asked. She said she didn't know, and didn't think about it. Whose purpose might it be? I queried. She didn't know that either, but it was probably God, or at any rate, she didn't mind the word being used. She just thought there must be a reason for it all, and that was that. She wasn't a very happy person, but she said she was sure she would be more unhappy if she thought there wasn't a purpose to existence.

Now, it's not for me to argue about what makes people less unhappy than they might otherwise be. It is true that, unlike (as far as I can tell) woodlice and orang-utans, we all of us have moments when we need to find a reason to keep at it – to get up on rainy mornings, to pay the telephone bill, answer a letter, whatever. This is surely because we have great big brains that have far more capacity than is necessary just to get these jobs done. The *why* is like trapped wind rumbling around in the empty spaces of our thinking apparatus; it's there because there's room for it. I'm pretty sure I and my faintly faithful friend would be less unhappy if we were woodlice or orang-utans. But I don't mean to sound negative. I like the *why*. I worry about our fellow species having to get on without it. It would be like sleeping without dreams. Bad dreams are better than no dreams at all. And what is more, I'm encouraged by the difficulty – by the very unanswerability of the question.

I wasn't being confronted with great faith here, just someone hanging on by their toenails to what they thought of as something rather than nothing. To believe in a purpose without having the faintest idea what it might be, or wishing to pursue the question, seemed no more than a dull attempt at self-comfort, and a waste of all that entertaining spare brain space. I suggested that pointlessness was much more exciting. Indeed, though I'm not one of nature's optimists, the thought that here we all are after millions of years of evolution, sharing the planet with bacteria and strelitzia, woodlice, orang-utans and camels, and what have you, while getting up most mornings, paying our telephone bills, answering letters, even getting on aeroplanes in the hope that the sun will be shining when it lands, makes me laugh out loud and clap my hands with delight at the absurdity and sheer happen-chance of it all.

As far as I can understand it, most of us are grasping at straws, and those who are not grasping have got one clutched in their fist while along with the rest of us they take the tumble down Alice's rabbit hole. The thing about Alice was that she didn't just wish for a soft landing while she fell, she read the labels on the mar-malade jars as well.

Ice Fishing Huts

I've only fished once in my life; off the back of a freighter stilled in the morbid heat of the Gulf of Mexico. The crew invited me to join them throwing weighted and baited lines over the side in a massacre of the small-brained innocents who, learning nothing from seeing their fellows hoiked violently upwards, kept taking the bait and biting down on the hooks. Each line had half a dozen hooks on it, and the fish, seeming suicidal, came up in batches on each line. By the time I got down to the main deck it was alive with writhing, dying creatures, gasping for breath, flip-flopping in a hopeless attempt to find water and life. With the crew watching to see what I was made of, I threw the offered line over the side and waited, hoping that nothing would happen, but it did, and I was instructed to haul in six fine fat fish which were jerking at the nylon thread in my hand. Once I got them on deck I howled my misery at what I'd done. The crew laughed – I was made of what they thought I was probably made of – and my tutor released the only fish I've ever caught, and threw them on the piles of dead and dying.

But I do like the idea of fishing. I've never seen the point of catching a fish, but I do completely see the point of waiting for one that never comes. I'm sure no serious angler would agree with me (I see the ghost of Hemingway battling with a marlin, spitting scorn at my wimpy ways), but it's the sitting still and waiting that attracts me to the notion of fishing. Look at the fishing huts on the ice in Maine, and wonder if that's not a large part of what real fishing is about. Imagine the silence, and the frosty air radiating invisibly up from the ice. You make a habitation, a place to sit, wrapped up against the cold, a bunk to sleep, a lamp to light the pitch black night, a stove to warm your hands and make hot food and drink. Elementary, but every element a noticeable source of comfort, vivid in a way that carpeted, centrally heated, double-glazed suburban living is designed not to be. If you notice the warmth, it's because you are cold, if you notice the comfort it is because you are deprived of it. And if you point the door of your hut made of old beer crates, or packing cases, away from any signs of civilisation, you are as good as alone in a vast field of ice, as good as alone in the world. I can see why you might set up your fishing hut and take off for a few days. I can also see why you might cut a hole in the ice, huddle over it with a rod in your hand and wait. Wait and wait and wait, knowing the four walls, the stove, the lamp, the bunk are there when you want them. But then the fish bite and I get lost just where I suppose the angler feels the whole experience becomes complete. Some creature that has evolved over millions of years to make its living beneath a frozen sky of ice thinks it has found an idiotically easy source of food, that just dangles there waiting to be snapped up. Maybe a whole new world of possibility opens up to it. Maybe it just figures that it's a one-off piece of good fortune. Or perhaps it begins to wonder if there isn't some higher being that has taken a special, benign interest in its welfare. The line jerks and the fish is wrenched out of its world through a hole in the sky to a place of otherness. Too warm, too dry for a life evolved for somewhere

28

else to continue. The angler, beating heart, having reeled in his prey with all the skill I can't imagine, manoeuvres the creature's jaw off the hook, and, let's hope, dispatches the fish with a smart blow to the head. Achievement. Well, never mind. Cut to the smell of fresh, very fresh, fish frying on the stove in the lamp light of the fishing hut, night fallen, absolute silence. No people, no conversation. Time to think, or not think. Getting away from it all. If some smart fishmonger delivered fresh fish to the door, I could quite imagine myself there contented as a human could be. Or I might even settle for pot noodles.

Fashion Statement

In spite of the V&A's Versace festival, and books like *Fashion Statements: Archaeology of Elegance 1980–2000*, I've never been convinced by the idea of fashion as art. I don't see why it has to be; it has so much else to do. When culture and art swan up and down the catwalk bedecked in 'fashion', I find myself scrummaging around in the oversized wardrobe in the spare room at the back of my mind, thinking about my lifelong romance with what I can't help calling 'clothes'. Call them 'clothes', and what some people think of as art and cultural studies become for me private history, memory and a grossly overspent youth and middle-age in search of the perfect garment. I recall a much-published novelist claiming in an interview that she would rather never have written a word than have lost the husband who divorced her a dozen years before. I gasped to read this. Give up writing for love? Really? World peace, maybe, social and educational equality, possibly – though I would demand firm guarantees. Then an image slithered into my head of a cupboard – let's call it a closet – stuffed with slinky Galliano slips of dresses, a handful of witty Chanel suits, a selection of madly deconstructed Margielas and

Demeulemeesters, a St Laurent smoking section, an unworn sprinkling of sparkling Versace, an almost invisible beige shimmer of Armani, and beneath, all in neat array, row upon row of Blahnik, Miu Miu and Jimmy Choo kitten heels. Well, would I have traded work for frocks? Certainly I'd give my right arm for such a wardrobe (I'm left-handed). My soul, without doubt (but then before the tragic days of giving up, I once offered up my soul in return for a late-night cigarette when I'd run out). My integrity you could have for a song, though I value it enough to demand lyrics by Cole Porter or Lorenz Hart. My sanity I gave up long ago when I discussed with a friend whether it was preferable to be mad or fat. But I wouldn't give up writing. At least I don't think so . . .

But it isn't really fashion that has such a hold on me. It is (like the ultimate book in my head, which is storyless, characterless and perfect) an image, without any detail, of the perfect outfit, the one that slips over my frame and drapes itself around my contours in a way that finally defines me – look, this is what I am – just as my flesh defines the boundaries between myself and the world. And it's a private thing essentially, not primarily about being seen in or envied for a fashionable look: indeed, I generally imagine wearing these incomparable outfits in the privacy of my own home. It's stuff to sit on the sofa with that I'm after first of all; then it's OK to go out and flaunt the frocks. Fashion statements and identity statements are much of a muchness as far as I'm concerned. To look like, to feel like and to be like are as close as flesh and bone.

The crucial encounter with fashion occurred when I was 12. Until then I had put up with whatever my mother considered respectable, an accurate mirror of the life she wished to be perceived as having. I balked loudly, it is true, at discomfort, which came mostly in the form of woollen vests that she told me were as soft as butter (meaning expensive and imported from Belgium) but which were actually as scratchy as barbed wire. But by the time I was 12 the family fortunes had taken such a severe down-turn and swerve away from the Belgian imports that Social Services had issued her with a voucher to buy me a pair of shoes to wear at my new secondary school. This was a matter of desperate shame for my mother, returning her to a poverty she had devoted her life to escaping. The idea of handing over – in public – vouchers from the state instead of crisp currency agonised her. Worse, the vouchers were rejected with the disdain she feared at all the shops she usually went to – Daniel Neal did not X-ray any old child's feet. The only place that accepted them was a gloomy little cobbler's shop which, as I remember it, was hidden away under a near-derelict railway arch in the fashion wasteland of King's Cross. The Dickensian and mawkish nature of the occasion as I recall it, the drab light and huddled aspect of the shoe shop, suggest that this may be one of those false memories you hear so much about, conjured up to match the dismal mood of the event. The old man who owned the place, unshaven, bent, gruff and wheezing – the Victorian workhouse vision just won't go back in its box – inspected the voucher, measured my feet, and without a word shuffled to the back of the shop. He returned with a single shoe box.

'See if these fit,' he said to my mother.

Taking off the lid, he brought out a pair of the grimmest black lace-up school shoes I had ever seen in my life. 'Sturdy' doesn't even get close to describing their brute practicality. In today's fashion-diverse world it is hard to imagine the despair I felt at the sight of what he expected me to put on my feet. And then greater despair yet as it occurred to me that I would be expected actually to wear them out in the world. They were so blankly, stylelessly sensible that they might have been orthopaedic appliances (poverty and disability perhaps being seen as equally reprehensible). Great clumping virtuous blocks of stiff leather with bulbous reinforced toecaps, designed (and I use the word loosely as a small bubble of ancient hysteria wells up) never to wear out. The best that could be hoped for was to grow out of them, after which they would still be sound enough to be passed down to generation after generation of the undeserving poor. Probably today they would be at the more moderate end of chunky footwear. I confess there have been times when I've rejoiced in wearing very similar things with an incongruously delicate little number in chiffon – though Doc Martens are ladylike in comparison. But back then – think 1959, the burgeoning of youth culture, rock and roll, multilayered net petticoats, ponytails – I only had to take one look at them, to see myself arriving at my new school with those on my feet, to know and feel, gut and spine, head and heart, the shame of becoming an instant fashion (and therefore everything else) pariah in the cruel girls' world of T-bars, flatties and slip-ons. The shoes would stand for my entire character, my class, my race, my lack of nous, and for ever after my almond-toed peers would deem me a sad case to be avoided and sniggered at as I clunked my solitary way around the playground. But it wasn't just the social disaster of such unfashionability that froze my heart: it was the fear that appearing to be the kind of person who wore such shoes might mean that that was the person I actually was. It wasn't just that my peers would despise me: I would despise myself. I didn't even dare risk seeing my reflection in the mirror in the empty shop.

I said, politely, that I didn't like them, thinking he had mistaken me for someone who might be happy to help him get rid of his unsaleable items and that he must have kept back his stock of fashion footwear. He showed no sign of having heard me. He was not impressed, he wasn't interested in an opinion: he just wanted to know if he needed to bother to get another size. These, it was made clear, were the shoes you got in return for vouchers. Take them or leave them, he told my mother, not so much as glancing at me. Though I sensed that the world was about to end (in the way it often did when things went wrong for my mother) I shook my head firmly. I refused even to try them on. I would simply not have them on my feet. His lip curled at my bad character. My mother's embarrassment redoubled at having to be embarrassed in front of this miserable old man. It was bad enough having to be on the receiving end of charity without having to suffer the charity-giver's contempt. But I shook my head steadily from side to side and kept my toes curled tightly so that even if they used force they would never get those clod-hopping shoes on me. I ought to be grateful that taxpayers were providing me with any shoes at all, the shopkeeper rasped. (Was he really wearing a foodstained, cigarette-burned buff cardigan and checked felt slippers?) It was these, or it was nothing.

'Then it's nothing,' I said, quite prepared for whatever civic punishment befell ungrateful children who didn't know their place (though I looked forward less to the moment when my mother got me home). I would wear my present shoes down to a sliver. If necessary I would go to school barefoot. My mother didn't bother to wait – she shouted at me all the way home. I slunk along beside her in silence. How could I do this to her? she screamed. What did a pair of shoes matter? In fact, they mattered more than her wretchedness, even more than my loved, lost and delinquent father who had put us in this situation. They mattered like life itself. More, perhaps. Now, I am somewhat ashamed of having been obdurate when times were bad, but the truth is that even as I write I flush at the imagined ignominy of wearing those shoes. It was, as it were, my first fashion statement.

Between then and now fashion and my fortunes have been up and down and back again, but at no point have clothes been secondary. In the 1960s, I was in cheap frock heaven, alternating between instant fashion (skirts the width of a belt, crushed velvet bell-bottoms, fishnet tights and purple boots with platform soles from Biba and Granny Take A Trip) and wild antique fantasies

(Victorian lace nighties and velvet frockcoats, original 1940s working-girl bias-cut dresses and moth-eaten movie-star fox-fur jackets) culled for shillings from Portobello Road. Later, it was the denim and boiler-suits of the school-teaching radical 1970s (Camden Market), then the swagger of big-shouldered jackets and snappy high heels, followed by loose, soft, draping viscose (how I thank the gods for letting me be born into the era of viscose) and silk, layer on layer of it (beloved Nicole Farhi), or parodic mannish suits (Emporio).

Buying clothes is an act of bewitchment. As soon as I stand in front of a rail of garments, a trance descends on me. My consciousness rises slightly above my corporeal body so that I seem to be looking down on myself (a near clothes-buying experience) as my hand reaches out and slides the hangers along, one by one (small grating noises, wooden clicks), my fingers twitching the fabric, feeling its texture and weight (no hint of Belgium wool), my eyes drawing a bead on each item, assessing it to see if it belongs in my life. No, no, no: and then – yes! This is the one. I've found it. It has found me. As if I had been drawn into the shop by its presence. As if getting up that morning and leaving the house had been a response to the whispering in my sartorial soul of this garment, reaching out to find me as it waited, created as it was, destined as it was to be mine. I try it on only for the pleasure of seeing myself for the first time exactly as I should look and feel. At last, after all these decades, after all that shopping, I have the garment I was always meant to wear. It's a silk shirt, a linen skirt, a pair of jeans, a sharp suit, a wispy frock, a pair of pink kitten heels, a sweatshirt, a pair of pull-on baggy trousers: but what it really is, is perfect. And (almost) whatever the cost, no matter the state of my bank balance or the condition of my house and car, however many remarkably similar – similar but not *perfect* – things I may have in my cupboard at home, I buy it knowing that now at last I will be content.

And for a while, I am. Yes, of course all the skirts, shoes and dresses in my bulging wardrobe were each the perfect garment when I bought them. And so they remained for days, weeks, occasionally even months, as I existed at last in the world looking exactly like I wanted to look, just right: until I began to feel that scratchy need somewhere in my solar plexus and it seemed to me that I heard a susurration in my inner ear, telling me that something, somewhere was hanging on a rail waiting for me to meet it. The next siren call comes, the last thing bought seems somehow not quite right. And, sleuthing around the shops, I discover once again a garment that in my mind balances perfectly on the narrow boundary between inner and outer definition, which I have been looking for, doubtless, since the day of the implacable black school shoes. That's why fashion as culture, fashion as art, leaves me cold: I'm too preoccupied with clothing myself to pay it proper attention.

DIFFICULT CHAPS

Did Jesus walk on water because he couldn't swim?

*The Children of Noah: Jewish Seafaring in Ancient Times
by Raphael Patai. Princeton 1998*

The title startles. The children of Noah were tower-raisers, nomads, farmers, slaves, desert wanderers, warmongers, city-dwellers, poets and musicians even, but sailors? *Jewish* seafaring? Jewish *seafaring*? Certainly, there were family days out at the sea-side: my father would roll his trousers up to his calves, and my mother discard her shoes to sit on their deckchairs, but neither of them ever ventured seaward beyond the darker, wetter stretch of sand. I was taught to swim (not by my parents, who I never saw buoyant), though, as I understood it, the lessons were so that I could get out of the sea, should I ever be so foolish and unfortunate as to find myself in it. For even non-practising Jews like us, the sea didn't seem kosher. Jewish people I knew were tailors or shopkeepers, their children were supposed to become business-men, doctors, lawyers, academics, no one ever mentioned the possibility of a career as a mariner. It made traditional sense to me: hadn't Moses ordered the Red Sea to part rather than have the Children of Israel get their feet wet?

The late Raphael Patai's book is, it must be said, a slim

volume, and it was over sixty years in the making, whereas his work on the more plausible Jewish alchemists took only ten years to publish. There is no evidence that any of the four great Biblical travellers on water – Noah, Moses, Jonah and Jesus – had what you could call a vocation for the sea.

Boat-building in the Bible, and indeed in the other early flood narratives, is not a skill discovered or intuited by humanity, Patai says. Both the need for boats and the ability to make them are bestowed on mankind from on high. When Atraharsis, in one Akkadian text, is instructed by the god Ea to build a ship, he's at a loss: 'I have never built a ship; draw a design of it on the ground, that, seeing the design, I may build a ship.' Utnapishtim, the Babylonian Noah of the *Epic of Gilgamesh*, also has to receive detailed information from Ea on the construction of his ship. Noah is the only shipbuilder in the Bible, and he, too, gets divine instruction: 'Make thee an ark of gopher wood; with rooms shalt thou make the ark, and shalt pitch it within and without with pitch. And this is how thou shalt make it: the length of the ark three hundred cubits, the breadth of it fifty cubits, and the height of it thirty cubits.' So far as boats are concerned, God, not the Devil, is in the detail.

Neither Noah, nor the ten generations that preceded him back to Adam's time, had any need for boats. Adam is named for the earth from which he was created. His heirs were tillers of soil, and builders of cities. Before Noah, the only time that the sea gets a mention is at the beginning of Genesis, when the spirit of God moved on the face of the waters, which it seems were already there before the start of things. The waters are, Patai explains, according to Talmudic cosmology, *tohu*, of the *tohu bohu* translated in the King James Bible as 'without form and void'; an essential part of the chaos which was all there was before God separated and ordered the world into existence. These were the seas that contained Rahab, Leviathan and other sea monsters which, sings the Psalmist, God defeated before he made the world: 'Thou didst break the sea in pieces by Thy strength, Thou didst shatter the heads of the sea monsters in the waters, Thou did crush the heads of Leviathan, Thou gavest him to be food to the sharks of the sea.' God, it seemed, on some accounts (Psalm 107, the Book of Job, and rabbinical commentaries on Genesis), did not just make the world, he fought with the sea to make it. And having over-mastered the waters, when he wanted to annihilate the world he regretted making, it was the waters he used to destroy it. 'I will cause it to rain upon the earth forty days and forty nights; and every living substance that I have made will I destroy from off the face of the earth.' (The rabbis, wishing to take God's word as gospel, worried about the problem of fish, who clearly would not be erased from the world by a flood. It was solved when one rabbi decided that the waters that rained down were boiling, thus doing for the fish, and allowing God to keep his word to the letter.)

Little wonder that the Jews had no taste for the sea. Noah is silent. Unlike later chosen ones who questioned and debated with God about his plans, even changing his mind, Noah never speaks. He simply 'did according unto all that the Lord had commanded him'. He is a survivor, not a sailor. The waters rise, the world dies and, locked up in the box God designed for him, he endures the wait. But Patai detects at least one element of seamanship in him. He refers to a study by James Hornell entitled *The Role of Birds in Early Navigation* which

adduces reference to the practice of carrying aboard several 'shore-sighting birds' among the ancient Hindu merchants (fifth-century BCE) when sailing on overseas voyages . . . 'used to locate the nearest land when the ship's position became doubtful' . . . The same practice is mentioned in the Buddhist *Kevad dha Sutta* of Digha . . . Five centuries later Pliny mentions the same custom

41

as practised by the seamen of Ceylon when making sea voyages,
as they were unable to steer by the stars.

The raven and the dove give Noah a certain credibility as a sailor,
although Midrashic sources suggest that he spent all his sea-going
time learning what and when to feed the animals in his charge. So
much so, says one, that he never closed his eyes for one minute
during his 150 days afloat. As a sailor, Noah became expert in
animal husbandry. Back on land, Noah showed no further interest
in the sea: he took up farming and planted the world's first vine-
yard. Though in becoming also the world's first drunk, he may
have been exhibiting an elemental trait of the old seadog.

Moses, too, floated to salvation in an ark, though by now, it
seems, boat-building skills had been acquired and there was no
need for direct guidance from God. When the mother of Moses
'could no longer hide him, she took for him an ark of bulrushes,
and daubed it with slime and with pitch, and put the child
therein; and she laid it in the flags by the river brink'. This is
more river than seafaring, but it's an oddly watery start for a
prophet whose life was dominated by mountain and desert.
Neither Noah nor Moses journey on the water for the purpose of
trade or discovery. The Bible refers on both occasions to the ark
as *tevah*, that is, a chest or box, and not a ship (*oniyah*).

Though Patai doesn't mention him, Jacob is another who, like
my parents, exhibits a reluctance when faced with water. At
Jabbok, needing to ford the Jordan, he sent his wives and worldly
goods across, but remained behind for the night during which he
encountered the wrestling angel who would change his name to
Israel. For all that scholars might suggest his motive was anxiety
about facing his brother, Esau, whose birthright and blessing he
had stolen, it seems to me possible that he was in a watery funk.
Only an extremely unpleasant night sent him wading across the
river the next morning.

Jonah, too, becomes a seafarer through a greater fear of something else. Rather than proclaim against the city of Nineveh, as God wishes, he takes flight and buys a passage on a ship about to sail across the Mediterranean from Joppa (Jaffa) to Tarshish, which is thought to be on the Iberian Peninsula. The crew of this ship are not Jewish, and when the Hebrew God foments a storm, they show both proper sea-going superstition and seamanship by crying 'every man unto his god, and they cast forth the wares that were in the ship into the sea, to lighten it unto them'. Jonah, strangely, sleeps through the whole thing, perhaps because he is such a landlubber that he doesn't know it's time to panic, or because he's such a landlubber that he's been rendered barely conscious by seasickness.

Jesus also sleeps through a storm aboard a boat in the Sea of Gennesareth. The disciples cry: 'Master, carest thou not that we perish?' And he awoke and rebuked the wind, and said unto the sea, 'Peace, be still!' Of course, Jesus is more concerned here with being the Son of God than a Jew in his casual mastery over the sea. Possibly overcoming a dislike of water was part of the new teaching. When he walked on the water, it was with the overt purpose of testing Peter's faith, but it suggests to me a lack of swimming skills on both their parts.

However, if none of these Biblical characters convinces me of a longstanding Jewish attraction to going down to the sea in ships, the fact remains that ancient Palestine had ports on its long Mediterranean coastline, and that there was certainly much toing and froing, warring and trading in the area. Of Solomon, we are told in 1 Kings 10.22, 'For the king had at sea a navy of Tarshish with the navy of Hiram: once in three years came the navy of Tarshish, bringing gold, and silver ivory, and apes, and peacocks.' It's not at all clear whether the ships were built by Solomon's men, but in Judah, King Jehoshaphat 'made Tarshish ships to go to Ophir for gold', although Jewish shipbuilding skills are thrown into doubt when we find out that these ships 'were broken at Ezion-Gever' either by a storm or because they were inexpertly built. Whether it was at this moment that Jehoshaphat jumped we are not told.

According to the Mormons, however, Jewish seafaring was an ancient tradition. America, claimed Joseph Smith, was populated by a remnant of seafaring Jews. The Book of Mormon tells of a group of Jews living in the early sixth century BCE under King Zedekiah in Jerusalem, who, in an attempt to escape from an unfriendly government, sailed, via the Straits of Gibraltar, across the Atlantic Ocean, to arrive somewhere on the American continent 344 days after starting out. So perhaps seafaring is a lost Jewish art, after all.

Patai offers plentiful evidence in the form of religious laws for life at sea, Midrashic commentary on the Hebrew Bible, and folklore to suggest that the Jews, reluctantly or otherwise, were indeed a sea-going lot. But this doesn't necessarily mean they liked it. The commentating rabbis were ambivalent about sailors, though they weren't enthusiastic about other professions either: 'Let a man not teach his son to become a donkey driver, a camel driver, a potter, sailor, shepherd, or shopkeeper, for their trade is the trade of robbers,' the Babylonian Talmud warns. Patai paraphrases the great Rashi, on the other hand, saying 'that sailors live in constant danger, and therefore their hearts are inclined toward their Father in Heaven; they travel to places of much danger and are always trembling at the perils that beset them.' The distaste for the sea continues. Were it not for divine dispensation, says a Midrash on the Book of Leviticus, 'every man who goes down to the sea would die at once'.

Sea journeys had become an unfortunate necessity and laws were established for sea-going Jews. The Sabbath had to be kept at sea, during which time no riding or sitting in any vehicle is permitted, so the laws state that journeys had to start no later than

Wednesday and that a Jewish traveller had to come to an agreement with the skipper that he would break the voyage for the
Sabbath. This was highly unlikely, but it allowed the Jew to
blame the Gentile for breaking his word. Not that all skippers
were Gentile. Patai gives an account of the fourth-century Jewish
shipmaster, Amarantus Navicularius, with whom Bishop Sinesius
sailed from Alexandria to Corynna. In spite of his Latinised
name, Captain Amarantus was not so assimilated into
Alexandrian culture that he failed to observe orthodox Jewish
law. The Jewish owned and manned ship was recalled by the
Bishop:

> All the sailors of the ship, their number being 12, and together
> with the captain 13, were Jews, the children of that accursed
> nation which thinks it is doing a good deed by causing death to
> the Greeks . . . They were all deformed in one or another part of
> their bodies. As long as we were not in danger they amused them-
> selves by calling one another not by their proper names but by
> their bodily defects: Lame, Ruptured, Left-handed, Squint, and
> so forth . . . We were about fifty passengers on board; among us
> a third part were women, mostly beautiful and charming. But,
> nevertheless, you should not envy me. Even Priapus himself would
> have behaved piously in a ship steered by Amarantus, who did not
> allow us even one short hour of pleasure in which to be free of
> mortal fear.

The problem was a storm that blew up as the Jewish Sabbath
arrived with Friday's sunset:

> When Amarantus perceived that the sun had gone down, he
> dropped the steering rudder from his hands. The passengers
> thought that he had done thus because of despair. When it
> became known to them what the real reason was . . . and all their

requests that he should return to the rudder were in vain – because as we entreated him to save the ship from danger he only continued to read his book – they tried to threaten him. One brave soldier . . . drew his sword and threatened to cut off the man's head unless he instantly took the rudder again into his hands. But the captain, like a true Maccabean, could not be moved to transgress the commandments of his religion. Later, however, at midnight, he returned to the rudder voluntarily, saying, 'Now our law permits it to me, because there is a danger of life.'

The Talmud states that when life is at risk, Sabbath rules are suspended, but what pleasure Amarantus clearly has at the Bishop's expense in keeping to the letter of the law. Here, at last, is an honest to God Jewish seafarer.

A Life, Surely?

The Ossie Clark Diaries, edited by Henrietta Rous.
Bloomsbury 1998

Ossie Clark, for those who never hankered after his confections in the late Sixties and early Seventies, was a dress designer. His designs are in museums of fashion quite as legitimately as a gold necklace from ancient Egypt is displayed in the British Museum, or the uniform of the Light Brigade is illustrated in the Imperial War Museum. Each item tells us something about its time and place, certainly not everything, but something. Nevertheless, they become a good deal more vivid and more informative when we are given a living context for the artefacts. The most exquisitely chipped stone arrowhead is better appreciated if we know something of the life of its maker.

The always perceptive reader of the *London Review of Books* will have detected desperation in the preceding attempt to justify this review of a spoilt, petulant anti-semite whose main claims to fame were, in his own words, 'to dress frilly people in colours that confuse the eye', and appearing as a peevish young icon slouched on a chair with a moody, come-hither expression, a pure white cat on his lap and his bare feet submerged in the pile of a white rug in *Mr and Mrs Clark and Percy*, the portrait by David Hockney that aspired to Gainsborough as a take on the aristocracy of London, *c.* 1971, but owed more to *Harpers & Queen*. The fashion bubble of Sixties London was not quite the fourth dynasty or the historical watershed of the Crimean War. What *was* of interest at that time cannot be deduced from Ossie's frocks any more than the Eighties can be captured by the design and effect of the first dress Ossie Clark made for the editor and annotator of his diaries, Lady Henrietta Rous.

> Ossie made a skirt, knee-length, with 84 panels, like a wonderful balletic creation, with a purple fitted corseted top and romantic puffed sleeves. The colours were yellow, turquoise, red, green, pink and mauve . . . This dress was later photographed in Los Angeles and I wore it in Monte Carlo to Craigie Aitchison's exhibition . . . I immediately acquired a new admirer: Prince Rainier's chamberlain, no less. He rang the gallery and asked, 'Qui est cette fille délicieuse?' and described the dress.

Alors.

Gradually, however, I found that, for myself at least, there was some point in puzzling over the diaries of Ossie Clark. When I run out of very big things to worry about – should there be fiscal harmonisation in Europe; are we just a cocktail of amino-acids shaken but not stirred; how much longer before I die – I fall to brooding about that devastating term of abuse of our times, the Peter Pan crow of complacency: *Get a life*. I am impressed and rather envious of those who use the phrase: that they can be so certain that they know what a life is, and so convinced that they have one. From the note of disdain with which the phrase is spoken, it seems that having a life is a matter for self-congratulation, and therefore the result of an individual's character rather than merely the fact of existence and the effect of a series of random circumstances. Some lives are 'life' and some are not, but the precise nature of 'a life' is never defined. I suspect that the existence described by Ossie Clark during the Sixties and early Seventies might qualify. I'm not, however, at all clear about it. The Ossie who partied every night, snorted coke with Mick, Marianne and Brian Jones, made frocks for Faye Dunaway, Elizabeth Taylor, Sharon Tate, Brigitte Bardot and Liza Minnelli, slept with Celia Birtwell, David Hockney, Patrick Prockter, Wayne Sleep and assorted tall, thin models: was he the one who had a life? But the later fallen, paranoid speed-freak Ossie, who fished in the wishing-well in Holland Park for the price of a packet of ten cigarettes, and cruised Hampstead Heath in the early hours for anonymous sex without bothering to mention that he had crabs, who stole fivers from the handbags of his few remaining friends and reckoned they deserved it: did he no longer have a life? That might be one way to understand it. But though the fall of Ossie Clark from a state of fashionable grace might look like the transition from having a life to losing it, it's a trajectory I am not entirely convinced by. It might be quite the other way around. It depends on who is doing the telling and who is being told.

Ossie Clark expressed the wish that Lady Henrietta Rous should edit his diaries for publication. Lady Henrietta, after being educated at Cheltenham Ladies' College and Camberwell School of Arts and Crafts, worked, we are told, as a bookseller, florist and decorative painter before becoming a journalist and writing for *Harpers & Queen* and the *Evening Standard* diary. In 1979 and 1983 she stood as a Parliamentary candidate for the Wessex Regional Party. She met Ossie Clark in 1982 after he was acrimoniously divorced from the fabric designer Celia Birtwell, and when he was masochistically devoted to the love of his life, the inconstant Nick. Lady Henrietta was 'besotted', and 'devoted the whole summer to him. We went to parties together.'

49

Their affair was brief, just six months long, before Ossie 'french-kissed a girlfriend of mine. I slapped both their faces. Ossie whacked mine back on both sides, quite hard. It was salutary.' After not speaking to him for a further six months, they were reconciled in 'a close, bonded friendship and mutual care, concern and compassion for 12 years'. All of this, of course, constitutes life, his, hers and theirs, but it doesn't sound much like the life you would want to get if you didn't have one.

In Ossie's heyday, Lady H. tells us, 'wearing Ossie meant being part of it all'. So back then, at least in retrospect, it was easy enough to judge if you had a life or not. But when fashions change, how does anyone, including the maker of the frocks that once constituted being part of it all, know if they have a life or only seem to have one? Ossie Clark began in a working-class family in Warrington in 1942. He had a natural talent for cutting and making clothes which was developed first at home by his mother, and then at Manchester Art College (where he met Celia Birtwell, with whom he had two children), and the Royal College of Art in London (where he fell in with David Hockney). His success was immediate and Ossie rose like froth to superstar dressmaker status in the Sixties London stylocracy. Ossie's set, Lady H. explains,

> included some of the most fascinating people of the era. Cecil Beaton entertained Ossie and Mick Jagger at his house . . . Jagger invited Ossie to stay at Villefranche in the south of France. Ossie famously visited Tony Richardson's La Garde Fresnais, where he behaved outrageously and threw a gaggle of ducks into the heated swimming-pool. In 1969 he and Celia holidayed in Marbella with John Aspinall's half-sister, Jennifer . . . In London he spent every night in clubs like the Aretusa, the Speakeasy, Tramps and Yours or Mine . . . He holidayed in Marrakech with Paul Getty's wife, Talitha, Christopher Gibb (close friend and

mentor of Mick Jagger and the society antiquaire) . . . He frater-
nised with the Andy Warhol group and experimented with drugs,
drag queens, alcohol.

Surely, this is what is meant by 'having a life'? And yet, Lady H.
detects a hint of trouble even at such a pinnacle of living. The
drugs, drag queens and alcohol 'and his temperament sometimes
got the better of him. In New York he preferred to lie in bed in a
duplex decked in Lichtensteins than see an important buyer.'
Certainly this was worrying for business, but with all that entertainment, visiting, clubbing, holidaying and fraternising with the
famous and their friends and relations, who can really blame the
man for wanting a bit of a lie-in?

Ossie's diaries record all these events and the names attached
to them religiously, in bright colours and swirling paragraphs, but
with no detail at all. On 14 April 1975 it was: 'dinner at the
house of gallery-owner Claude Bernard with George Lawson
(drunk) and Mick Jagger – excellent food but boring really'. In
vain you look for an account of the conversation that made the
evening so tedious, or even a soupçon of insight into what made
the food so good. Nothing. Not here, not anywhere. Evenings out
are judged boring or interesting, but seem to have no actual content. There are no conversations, only events and names, even the
dresses he designs and cuts so exquisitely are barely described.
Even so, all this glamorous toing and froing must constitute the
sort of life that those who don't have one should get. In 1973,
when teachers' salaries had just received a hefty hike to a decent
£1000 a year, he was designing for Radley, with Alice Pollock,
and earning a salary of £23,000 a year from the business. A life,
surely? And when, in the middle of this year, he complains that
he is £10,000 overdrawn at the bank, this is only further confirmation of a life being lived to the full.

But the business, his control over his drug use and his marriage all fell apart more or less simultaneously. The glamour slipped away so breathtakingly fast, leaving behind just speed, Valium, alcohol and depression, that it might cause those of us who suspect we may be without a life to wonder if we want one after all. Celia Birtwell divorced him for incontinence with both sex (both sexes) and drugs, and when he beat her up she took out an injunction against him. He mourned the loss of access to his sons and the effects of the uppers and downers he juggled meant that he failed repeatedly to get out of bed and make clothes. Soon his house was repossessed for non-payment of his mortgage and he began living in a succession of rooms and flats belonging to his friends, each of whom turfed him out when he failed to pay them any rent or trashed the place. He was made bankrupt, and spent his last years anxiously dependent on the arrival of his DHSS giro for his food, drink and drugs.

The diary entries chart his plummeting lifestyle with an awe-inspiring lack of insight. After the marriage split, Ossie Clark frequently returns to the house in Linden Gardens where Celia and the children, Albert and George, live.

> I got drunk . . . went back to Linden Gardens where I gave way to my temper and smashed a window after I had fallen asleep on Albert's bed. I can see now I was too heavy, perhaps . . . they [Adrian George, the painter, and David Hockney] have poisoned Celia completely against me to such an extent that she really believes I will beat her to death. Well, I refused to move, indirectly threatening to destroy the flat, saying I didn't realise (which is true) that matters had gone so far that I might lose her, and I would do anything . . .

The following day Celia tries to get the children, toddlers still, out of the house after Ossie has kept her up arguing until six in the morning. 'I snatched her handbag and almost broke down in tears saying to Albert, who was hysterical, that Mummy was trying to take him away from me.' Two days later he is back. 'I confiscated her keys and was too heavy again, but it worked – I'm afraid I can't trust her.' Three weeks later, he collects Albert from school and is breathalysed for drunk driving. Celia is not pleased and takes legal action to limit his access to the children. 'So I split to Linden Gardens and was so furious I beat her and kicked her and her nose was a bloody mess – then I forced her to speak to her lawyer lady and it was she who sent the police round.' (The gentility of that 'it was she' would be a masterstroke in a piece of fiction.)

When he does take the children out, the diary entries record: 'To Portobello on angel dust after being up all night . . . the children were a joy to be with . . . More angel dust, cocaine and lots of old friends – accidentally burnt George's eye. The children really enjoyed themselves – played the drums.' 'I drank a Guinness and the children ate an ice-cream each and unfortunately Jimmy, Ronnie, Mo and Mick turned up – bit rowdy. Poor Albert banged his head.' 'On the way back stopped for a drink – the children very excited. George fell over – bloody lip.' 'I had a conversation with Albert and asked him, if it came to it, who he would choose and without hesitation he said: "I'd choose you." How I love him.' On a trip to Hong Kong, he moans,

There's nothing to go back for except that big empty house and maybe a real suicide. I don't really want to die – but I can't see any point in living without her and just seeing my beautiful Albert and George occasionally. Listening to the radio, almost every song reflecting my feelings for Celia, wondering, dare I phone her up? Or could I write her a letter to express my feelings in a way she would understand? But then you're not Marcel Proust, Os, so take your Valium and go to sleep.

An intermittent boyfriend, Peter, walked out on Clark for good one night, but stopped at Ossie's request to explain why:

> He said I looked battered. It was all so untidy and depressing, cig-arette butts in the sink. I seem to represent a side of him he prefers to forget – it was my charm and big dick which brought him, his words . . . It took me quite aback – 'I know I asked you what's wrong but I didn't expect the answer to be so heavy.' 'It's all so tacky,' he said . . . 'But we fuck so well,' I protested. 'Makes no difference. I'm not seeing you again' . . . Eccentric is what I am. Sex-mad eccentric? Or worse, as Peter thinks, tacky, battered and charming.

But he was not too charming. 'Got collared by Peter Stringfellow – do I want to help in "Fashion Aid" . . . a charity to help the starving Ethiopians? . . . I told [him] I don't really give a fuck about the starving in Ethiopia – I thought it part of the world's natural safety mechanism.' He finds a swim with Nick in Highgate Pond refreshing, 'Nobody there except a few hideously hairy and very grotesque Jews and their equally overweight sons. [Nick] dropped me off at Bella Freud's. Her toiles are looking OK, just about.' And he allows himself to be interviewed for a retrospective article in *Elle* magazine by a male journalist and 'a typical Jewess with bad skin and I suspect halitosis (though I never got close enough) . . . They asked specifically about 1967 – I told them I thought the period the last great flowering of the individual.'

Clark's decline, according to the fashion guru, Suzy Menkes, is 'such a sad story, but the temperaments of artists mean that often they do suffer'. David Hockney, rather less romantically, dis-missed Ossie's insistence that he was to be excused his business and social failures because he was an artist: he couldn't be, Hockney said, because all the artists he'd ever known worked very hard. But temperament, if not necessarily artistic, does seem to be at the root of Clark's meteoric decline. Though he whines, steals and scrounges, there is not a moment when he expresses real surprise at his changed fortunes. 'Spoke to Janet Street-Porter. She will pay my phone bill. "One tries so desperately HARD." "What's happened to you? – I've heard you've fallen." "Yes, I fell long ago."' The satisfaction is palpable. The man is so in love with the maudlin, with his own misery and degradation that his fleeting, flashy success begins to look like a cunning way of achieving and enhancing his later, more enduring humiliation. The relish with which he describes his squalor, the pleasure he takes in describing unprotected sex with strangers on the Heath while recording the deaths of his friends from Aids, the lip-smacking accounts of gathering stubs from the pavement of Holland Park Avenue to satisfy his last lover Diego's demands for a cigarette, make it apparent that Ossie Clark's real life began with his failure, not his success. Standing conspicuously in the Tate Gallery in front of Hockney's painting, he records with grim satisfaction that nobody recognises him. It is as if this is the real peak of his achievement.

Whether the first or the second part of Ossie Clark's existence was the valued 'life', it was a life from which he could draw no conclusions, develop no insights into himself or the rest of the world. The emptiness of mind spanned good times and bad. His circumstances changed, but whether barefooted because he liked the feel of the luxury pile rug under his feet or because he couldn't afford shoes, Ossie plodded on, seeming to know exactly where he was going without ever stopping to wonder why.

Clark's nemesis was the homeless and psychotic Diego, described by Lady Henrietta as being 'considered good-looking by some; to others he had the look of the devil', and having 'repulsive manners'. Ossie explained to her what he saw in Diego:

'I like the peasant quality – Caravaggio, Henri.' Diego finally performed what you can't help thinking was required of him and murdered the 54-year-old Ossie Clark, in a fit of madness, mistaking one or other of them for Satan.

The People's Tycoon

Branson by Tom Bower. Fourth Estate 2000

I find myself nostalgic for the time, long ago, when one thing the very rich and very famous could be relied on to do was shut up. Paul Getty, Mrs Kennedy-Onassis, Princess Grace of Monaco wrapped their money around themselves in the form of impenetrable walls and/or designer sunglasses and kept silent while the world wondered and chattered. And you would imagine that if money could do anything for you it would be to insulate you from having to care what other people thought. The people don't have to vote for you, they don't have to love you. But even princesses and tycoons these days have to seem to be democratic and lovable. They have to sell their brand by selling themselves. Sometimes their brand is themselves. There are power lists and personalities of the year, decade and century, and however filthy with wealth you are, you have to worry about *the people*, you have to care what they think of you. We've had our people's princess, desperate to become the queen of people's hearts, and we still have the people's tycoon noisily committed to running the people's lottery, apparently free of charge. The pitch is to demand to be seen as ordinary folk, essentially just like you and me, only richer and more glamorous, of course, because it does the populous a power of good to see images of what might have been their own selves if only, kitted out in fine frocks and indulging in dangerous sports no one else can afford. And in spite of their morale boosting high life, they want it known, they nonetheless devote themselves to the well-being of others, and the greater benefit of the nation. They nurture, they improve, they innovate, they care. They are also, these modern icons, consummate moaners. They complain loudly and publicly about being misunderstood, underappreciated, and afflicted on all sides by the negative forces of repression, tradition and evil. They suggest that, being on the side of the people, any attack on them is tantamount to an attack on the ordinary folk they would like us to believe they represent. They are, as it were, latter day saints, deflecting and taking on themselves the slights and assaults of the elitist convention-bound enemy, becoming martyrs and shields of the people. But my god how they whine, how they snivel, how they demand our attention and sympathy.

The Princess of Wales timed her exit impeccably, still riding on a wave of sentiment that may have had little more energy left in it. It is tempting to think that Richard Branson at least unconsciously also understood that public adulation is likely to tire and turn into its own opposite. Blonde, blue-eyed, apparently artless, like the Princess, he took what seemed to be life-threatening risks by boat and balloon, and nearly came a cropper once or twice, so that he too might have gone while the going was still good. As luck (or his carefully chosen fellow adventurers) would have it, however, he has survived, and it may be that he is about to outlive his popular acclaim. It seemed appropriate that Branson's grinning face, on the cover of the Virgin Publications' ghosted autobiography, was seen in virtually every episode of Big Brother, and while the graspingly hopeful housemates came and went, the Branson book stayed, to be taken up by the decreasing remainder as a favourite read. Surely it must have been the devious, miscalculating and ultimately naïve Nick who brought it into the house? Nick got sussed by the public and eventually his fellow inmates. Is the same thing going to happen to Richard Branson? He who lives by public relations will die by public relations.

There have, of course, always been those who have had their doubts about Richard Branson's self-proclaimed status as a millionaire with a heart of gold, and who have declined on principle to fly Virgin planes, drink Virgin Cola or wine, invest in Virgin life insurance, wear a Virgin wedding dress, ride a Virgin train or speak on a Virgin mobile. Among these hold-outs, I wouldn't be surprised, might have been Tom Bower, who tells us that he was reluctant to write the Branson biography until he found himself in receipt of a writ for defamation of character after an article Bower wrote in the *Evening Standard*. One way or another Virgin gets into your life, though Virgin Writs is not, so far as I know, registered at Company House. The writ arrived after Branson failed to get Bower to agree to submit his as yet unwritten manuscript to him before publication, and it was against Bower personally rather than the *Evening Standard*. A ploy, Bower believes, to discredit him personally and therefore the book he was considering writing. The case comes to court next year.

Bower has some fine and important books to his credit. He takes a responsible and well-researched interest in the hidden dealings of the rich, corrupt and powerful. Tiny Rowlands, Fayed and Robert Maxwell have all received the treatment and been carefully scrutinised. His account of the affairs of Maxwell delved into the murky depths, but he also kept a wary eye on the dubious ethics of the business world around the man, and produced an interestingly complex account of Maxwell's psychology. The investigation of Branson's business activities is thorough and compelling, but what is missing, for the satisfaction of the reader and perhaps the writer too, is the slightest indication of complexity or depth of character in its protagonist. Either Bower has missed it, or Branson is in fact so shallow that the book can't help but suffer from a lack of humanity in its tale of a rich man who is of no personal interest whatsoever. It is not that one hasn't suspected that the self-aggrandising prankster who races to court at every opportunity and continually complains of being done down is lacking substance, but it is something of a disappointment to find that there is nothing more there than one thought.

There is no room for doubting that Bower doesn't like his subject – not unreasonably if the subject is suing him. The smiling golden boy on the cover of Branson's autobiography is replaced at the front of Bower's account by a cold-eyed and menacing prince of darkness. The dislike is much more visible in this book than in others Bower has written. Branson is berated for lacking conscience when at 23 he became a millionaire, although 'wealth troubled many in that socialist era'. There were clearly also many it did not trouble. Youthful millionaires who started with a more than decent financial base are not often afflicted by bad conscience, one imagines. Those that are prone to it, probably didn't do what had to be done in order to accumulate wealth. It seems almost unreasonable to berate Branson in particular for having the qualities that failed to prevent him from becoming and remaining personally wealthy. He is accused in the early pages of an untroubled conscience, a 'lust for fame and fortune', an early preoccupation with earning money, a disdain for authority and intellectuals, an oily ability to treat and charm susceptible journalists, a canny use of offshore trusts, a ruthlessness that allowed him to dump those who were no longer of use to him: all or some of these must be attributes of anyone who makes a great deal of money. Sometimes Bower comes across as quite disingenuous in his apparent belief that it is possible to make and keep large sums of money while maintaining the personality of a Poor Clare. It is, after all, precisely that fond and fruitless wish in all of us that Branson plays on as he attempts to maintain the fiction that he is Britain's favourite do-gooding, fun-loving, once hippie, now laddish millionaire.

He is, of course, a millionaire. The unexpected vast sales of Mike Oldfield's dreary and portentous *Tubular Bells* saw to that in 1973. The money was salted away in offshore family trusts which has ensured Branson's personal wealth no matter what dire difficulty his companies might be in. Even at the time only the very gullible imagined he would be using the money to improve the lot of the poor. Richard Branson in the earliest days was always a guy on the make, a capitalist with a talent for PR and camouflage. Before the record shops, Branson started *Student* magazine. There is a photograph in Branson's autobiography of the front line of the 1968 Grosvenor Square demonstration: Branson is marching beside Tariq Ali and others. According to Bower, Branson simply attached himself to the student leaders, who were quite oblivious of him, but the press accepted his claims to be in the forefront of the revolution and *Vogue* featured him as a representative of Britain's student rebellion, when he actually represented that other side of the Sixties, the rise of the go-getting individualist.

Branson is, if you like, an emotional con artist. But I find myself ambivalent about Tom Bower's expressions of outrage, just as when I watch or hear one of those programmes that pursue the cheats and frauds who prey on gullible consumers. I feel a kind of guilty sympathy with the hounded wrong-doer. What do you expect? They were only doing their job, making money by making promises. Why are you asking them why they did it? Why are you asking if they are ashamed of their deceptions? Why not ask why people believed them? Why not ask why they were so stupid as to deceive people illegally when it is so easy to do it in a completely legal fashion and receive acclaim for it?

If you think that capitalism and global brand merchandising have a great deal to answer for in relation to world poverty, and you have a distaste for the vulgarity of publicity stunts involving naked women and pointless feats of derring-do, then you will not much appreciate Richard Branson. You will feel that a life could be put to better uses, that money could be better spent, that there is something terribly wrong with a society in which 47% of the public wanted Richard Branson to become Mayor of London and voted him Britain's favourite boss, best role model for parents and teenagers and most popular tycoon. But Branson does provide an insight into the workings of late twentieth century capitalism and its social forms. He has made himself rich by making himself famous and made himself famous by making himself rich. He has manipulated public opinion because the manipulation of public opinion has never been easier, as people accept publicity as an alternative to thought and willingly buy into fashionable stereotypes. He presented himself as buccaneer and victim, a virgin forever being interfered with by corrupt and powerful old men, a dewy David battling the thug Goliath, a youthful hero eternally at the jealous mercy of age and power. And people, *the* people apparently, have loved it. They love him being rich, having his own island in the sun, shaming the suits at board meetings, tieless in jumpers knitted by his auntie, getting drunk and randy, blowing millions on hot air adventures in the sky. He is, in his business dealings as well as his public persona, a triumph of lack of style over substance. He feeds the friendly hacks, flies them to his island in his aeroplane, lets them mingle with the famous and fatuous, and they dutifully turn out the Richard Branson the public wants. Just a bloke who does with his money what any ordinary bloke, nice as you like, would do if he had any to spare.

When Bower digs beneath the lack of substance to see how Branson actually operates, he makes it sound like a state of perpetual panic. In 1999, apart from his airline and rail franchises, all 150 or so of Branson's major companies were trading at a loss. For decades, his trick has been to keep things afloat by shifting money around between profitable and failing parts of the business to persuade the city to keep faith with him. The family offshore trusts are used to inject a look of profitability at crucial moments. Part of his apparent charm and popular appeal is his public admission of ignorance. Bower tells how in 1999 he gave the Millennium Lecture at Oxford University and told the admiring students that only those rejecting university would become millionaires. Industry was dead, only brands would be of value in the future. It is not necessary to know about what you are marketing. He knew nothing about music and the airlines business. 'Get the right people around you and just incentivise them.' Bower gloomily sums up the speech and the beliefs of 'Britain's greatest entrepreneur': 'Ignore education, ignore expertise and ignore technology. In a citadel of academic excellence, Branson had preached anti-knowledge. The new generation, he urged, should believe that sustainable businesses could be created without "a great business plan or strategy. Just instinct."' Probably the students in the citadel of excellence loved it.

But actually, Branson's instincts seem rather frail, or at any rate to be much more related to sheer survival than innovation. Virgin airlines, cola, finance, internet access, mobile phones, gas and electricity provision, all come after these commodities have been well established by others. He is always a step behind, complaining loudly how unjust it is that by being ahead of him others are stopping him from being in front. Even though he started later, it's plain not fair that anyone should be in front. And, proving that shouting loudly is a very effective form of argument, people in authority are inclined to agree with him, or at least not to want to become unpopular by disagreeing with him. He revels in being the little man held back by the big bully, though you come to suspect after reading Bower's book that little bullies are just as obnoxious. He decides to market Virgin Cola, and complains that Coca Cola is taking unfair advantage of being the market leader, by, as it were, being the market leader. Actually, he seems to be complaining about anyone fighting back (or just carrying on as normal) if he has entered into the ring. The long court and publicity battles with BA were much the same. Branson accused them of 'Dirty tricks' when it appears BA did little more than any business would do to maintain its edge. He railed about their powerful monopoly as if it were preventing Virgin Atlantic from flourishing, when BA had little more than 30% of the market and Virgin Atlantic consisted of no more than a handful of planes, fewer than other independent airlines. A price war among suppliers, we were always being told by Thatcher, is how the free market is supposed to ensure the benefit of consumers. But Thatcher-loving Branson, the Tory's favourite capitalist (also, of course, New Labour's favourite capitalist), moaned about BA cutting prices and it simply not being fair to him. He went to court, sometimes winning and sometimes losing, but always gaining the publicity edge as the people's champion in the sweater being bullied by the beastly faceless ones in suits. Quite why Virgin Atlantic had a God-given right to survive (it was never the cheapest way to fly to the States and it always had the least leg room) is not clear. The answer seems to be that Richard Branson is a very nice man and jolly well deserves to be a success in all things.

Bower dismisses the idea that it is fun being a Virgin employee. It seems that they are very likely to be badly paid, overworked and then given the boot when they are no longer useful. More than all that, they are frequently obliged, according to one ex-employee, to witness the boss 'exposing himself all over the place' at parties. Bower goes into some detail about Branson's personal relations with women and his penchant for cross-dressing, but it fails to make the man more interesting and it's irrelevant to his argument. Much more pertinent is the regularity with which people he worked with were sacked and financial partners out-manoeuvred by fancy legal footwork. Bower describes Branson's tears when he told his staff of the sale of Virgin Music, to be followed by a flat refusal to share with those who lost their jobs any of the £560 million he personally made from the sale. But that's business for you.

The dream of running the lottery is Branson's latest grand passion. Once again he took his competition to court, claiming that Guy Snowden of GTech had attempted to bribe him to drop his bid for the franchise. The case was based on a note (the original of which was never found) Branson said he made of the bribe when Snowden had been invited to lunch. Quite why Snowden waited to be invited by Branson to lunch before offering the bribe was never explained, but Branson won the case and made GTech's ambitions look very ugly compared to his own non-profitmaking People's Lottery. When in 1994 Camelot won the lottery franchise, Branson screamed, 'I've been robbed,' and burst into tears. He threatened to take the then regulator, Peter Davis, to court for negligence and maladministration as he had once appealed to the High Court when a decision for a television franchise went against him. Bower describes how the regulator, fearing a judicial review, explained why the People's Lottery had lost: 'Camelot planned four times more retail outlets to sell tickets than Virgin; Branson's projections of the money to be raised for good causes ranked only as average among the eight applicants; and the amount Branson anticipated generating for the whole lottery fund was the sixth lowest. On other assessments, Branson's bid ranked bottom . . . Oflot's calculations showed that Branson proposed to take out more in service charges than Camelot and contribute less to the fund for good causes. His hugely vaunted promise of a non-profitmaking lottery was suspect because the 'profits' appeared to be hidden among 'administrative costs'. During the five years since that bid, things have not gone entirely well for Branson, in spite of receiving a knighthood from that other prime ministerial admirer of entrepreneurial high profile, Tony Blair. The stakes were very high for his new bid for the lottery, according to Bower. 'His failure to fulfil his predicted successes in many different Virgin enterprises, his recurring financial losses and the inscrutability of his offshore trusts were persistent sources of unease. To remove the doubts, Branson established an unnamed holding company without shareholders and seven non-executive directors to supervise the People's Lottery, his new private company.' Camelot's bid was rejected by Dame Helena Shovelton because of doubts about the probity of GTech. But Branson's bid was not accepted either. Although, as Bower puts it, 'the billions of pounds of lottery money flowing perfectly legitimately through a private company with a single shareholder would place Branson in an unprecedented position of power and influence', Shovelton had problems with his bid. 'In particular . . . the Commission had identified how the financial claims of lottery players might not be protected if Branson's lottery became insolvent, lost its licence or failed to raise as much money as he predicted. In Shovelton's opinion, Branson's proposals on those crucial financial issues were "so conditional and so uncertain" that the Commission harboured, "significant concerns about the financial viability of the People's Lottery if the ticket sales were much lower than expected".' Branson was sent away to sort out some more substantial backing, Camelot won a judicial review suggesting that they had been treated unfairly by not receiving similar treatment and Shovelton has resigned. It seems that the final decision will be make or break for Branson's ambitions and credibility.

Branson claims that only brands count, and up to now he seems to have been proved right. People seem to think that all things Virgin have their best interests at heart. They were amazed to discover that having been told by Branson in his ads that Virgin PEPs would be the cheapest in Britain, they were actually subject to a 4% commission which made them the third most expensive. They were astonished to find that instead of Virgin Trains being 'fun', and despite the promises to 'increase quality and bring down prices', they were routinely running late, were overcrowded, and costing up to 30% more in fares. There was a time when we knew that people who made a great deal of money were not likely to have other people's best interests as their prime motive. In spite of decades of universal education we seem to have gone soft in the head. Nothing Branson has done since his teenage years, when he avoided paying purchase tax on record sales, has been illegal. Much of it has not been pleasant, humane, straightforward, but that is allowed in the accumulation and protection of personal wealth. Perhaps we choose to admire Richard Branson because we cherish the hope that one day we might find ourselves fabulously wealthy, and we'd like to think of ourselves in that golden future as nice as well as stinking rich. Richard Branson sits in the soggier parts of our minds and represents the possibility of our dreams coming true and not having to despise ourselves. What is Tom Bower doing to our fondest hopes by suggesting that Branson might not gleam through and through? If we can't believe in Branson, the people's millionaire, what can we believe in?

The Daddy of All Patriarchs

Abraham on Trial – The Social Legacy of Biblical Myth
by Carol Delaney. Princeton University Press 1998

To accuse the book of Genesis of being patriarchal is like complaining that cats throw up fur balls, or dogs sniff each other's
bottoms. It's not pleasant, but that's cats and dogs for you. But
you can choose not to have a cat or dog, whereas, says Carol
Delaney, Genesis we're lumbered with, deep in our psyche and
social structure. She says we need 'a new moral vision, a new
myth to live by'. This is to accept that we are helpless victims
rather than interpreters of myth, and that our consciousness is
solely conditioned by it. It is a bleak view of humanity's capacity
for analytical thought, and an even bleaker view of the consequences of feminist criticism of patriarchal stories. However,
Delaney concludes modestly, 'I cannot provide such a myth – no
one person can do that', and so her book is not taken up with
offering new gender-free myths to live by, but with a surprised
and outraged analysis of the patriarchal assumptions in the story
of Abraham's near sacrifice of Isaac. Her surprise is somewhat
surprising. When Delaney declares that she has discovered 'sexist
presumptions' in Luther's understanding of the scriptures,

adding, 'Nor does he ask what right Abraham had to involve other people in such a unilateral decision', and announces that she believes that the story of the binding of Isaac 'represents the construction, establishment, and naturalisation of sex role *differences* [her italics] . . .', you can only shake your head and murmur, 'Well, yes, and the Pope's a Catholic . . . '

If God is the Daddy of them all, Abraham is the patriarch of patriarchs, the acknowledged founding father of Judaism, Christianity and Islam. After God tried and gave up on the children of Adam and Eve, drowning the lot of them, and then scattered the offspring of Noah, he narrowed his sights to Abraham, a more manageable single individual of whom he would make a nation. It could be argued that Sarah was a necessary part of the package. She was already married to Abraham, and is claimed by all three religions as their matriarch. But there's little point in pussy-footing about: the Hebrew scriptures – prepare yourselves – do not promote feminism. You can change Yahweh into a mid-gendered *s/he*, you can point to the odd strong woman – the men-murdering Judith and Jael, you can admire the wiliness of Rachel in devising the plan for stealing the blessing and birthright for her favourite younger son, but sit down and read the actual text and you soon enough discover that Yahweh can only be male, while the women are merely furthering the ambitions of sons and husbands. Even Eve's original and splendid disobedience comes to be regarded not only by the rabbis as useful in providing ammunition against the dangers of all future women, but also by the Christian Fathers as the *felix culpa* that made necessary the passive and virtuous Virgin whose uterus nurtured the sacrificial remedy to Eve's solecism. The relationship between the scriptures and male domination has been noted before, and it is clear that neither God nor his chosen ones were signatories to the international convention of human rights. That's a shame. It has made, as Delaney rightly suggests, a difference to how we have gone about living on the planet. But it is not a sufficient explanation for gender discrepancy.

Delaney's key proposition is that the obsessive interest in seed, paternity and patriliny in Genesis stems from a theory of procreation that is biologically in error and therefore constructs an over-inflated meaning for *fatherhood*. As an associate professor of Anthropology she explains that the meanings of kinship terms do not necessarily reflect the 'natural facts', but – once paternity is understood to exist – promote a procreational theory that constructs the male role as creative and the female role as nurturing. (Delaney berates biblical scholars for missing the crucial fact of mistaken theories of procreation in Genesis. Robert Alter is praised for telling it like it is and insisting on using the word 'seed' in his translation of Genesis, where others fudge the problem by using 'posterity', 'descendants' or 'progeny'. But the praise is immediately revoked: 'Writing in the late twentieth century, he cannot be excused for neglecting that women, too, have 'seed'; but because he did, he also lost the opportunity to challenge the theology that is so interdependent with it.' Alter, as a literary biblical critic, probably did not consider it his task to challenge theology, but Delaney clearly thinks if it wasn't it ought to have been.) The male 'seed' is the animating, soul-instigating substance of life; the womb is merely the soil in which it grows. This common, ancient theory of monogenesis is the basis for monotheism, which proposes the sequence of a single male creator god bestowing the promise of generations on his male creation in return for complete obedience. Men's life-giving ability allied them structurally with God the Father, giving both the power of life and death over their creations. This is something of a chicken and egg argument, since in order successfully to promote such a theory men already had to have gained the ascendancy and taken charge of constructing and disseminating the theories that justified the status quo. There is, as far as I know, very little evidence for true matriarchal societies in ancient history, though matriliny, where the line is controlled by the brothers of women rather than their husbands, was (and is) not uncommon. Tales of matriarchies of dominating women were more likely to be stories men told each other to scare themselves witless and to confirm the wisdom of their own already established power. Somehow, I suspect, even if the biological realities of the equal contribution of male and female to reproduction had floated down on a fluffy pink cloud of revelation, the history of gender relations would not have been very much different. If there was ever a time when no one had any idea how babies were made, then perhaps men and women got along more or less as equals, everyone providing the services that they performed best; though the fact that it was always women who had the babies would surely have made some difference. But once the idea of paternity had been grasped, men found themselves in a position of fatal weakness. Paternity was unprovable, whereas maternity was a certainty. Women were then to be distrusted and feared, and the construction of social and religious justification for their control by and circulation among men, a matter of urgency. It wasn't the lack of Crick and Watson and knowledge of what we hold to be the facts of reproduction (presumably just another theory of procreation) that held back the equality of women for six thousand years, so much as male womb envy. If it's a wise child that knows her father, it's a woman-controlling father who knows his child.

We can as easily read underlying male anxiety into the biblical account of both God and his chosen ones, as we can detect the universal conspiracy against women. Male chauvinist fundamentalists can see their story in the Bible, but so can the infuriated feminist see hers in the male writing and reading of it. It is a fact, though Delaney doesn't mention it, that Jewishness is passed on to children by women. A child is recognised as fully Jewish only if her mother is Jewish, and not Jewish at all if her father is but her mother is not. A practical recognition, perhaps, of the social and biological realities that so unnerved the men.

The first creation in Genesis 1:27 is a unity:

So God created man in his own image, in the image of God created he him; male and female created he them. And God blessed them, and God said unto them, Be fruitful, and multiply . . .

The confusion of pronouns must reflect the nervousness of the King James' translation committee. More recent translations by Alter (he of the lost opportunity) and Everett Fox, both intent on retrieving original meanings, replace *man* with the more accurate *human* and *humankind*. But it's only a brief escape from gender division. The second creation account of Genesis derives woman more famously from the man who was created in God's image. But the confusion of the Authorised Version reflects the reality at the root of patriarchal control of society; the politics of power are inherent in the original gender division, and the desire to control the future is a direct consequence of human consciousness.

The early books of the Bible don't offer any personal future beyond death. Nowhere in the five books of Moses is any notion of an afterlife to be found; the individual is snuffed out, returned to the dust that Adam was made from. Neither God nor man suggests even the possibility that any form of existence continues after the death of the body. But death is very real and present. Only children – begetting – can offer a type of life after death. And so the obsession with seed and generation in Genesis is not surprising. Mankind bargains with God for the only posterity on offer. The only hold God has over man is the promise or denial of that posterity, since death will come to all sooner or later. The future in the form of future generations is the central concern of both man, woman and God, all of whom exist, as they must, within their own understanding of how such generations

72

are achieved. No one in Genesis asks to live for ever, but everyone is concerned with having children who will survive them.

'*Far be it from You to do such a thing, to bring death upon the innocent as well as the guilty, so that the innocent and guilty fare alike. Far be it from You! Shall not the Judge of all the earth deal justly?*'

Understandably, the church in the name of family and social conformity wishes to appropriate one reading of Abraham, but there are other readings to be made. If we throw out the story as politically inappropriate (along with *Hamlet* and *Lear* . . . well, most of Shakespeare . . . well, most of literature and all classical myth) we lose the chance to read it again differently, more carefully, less reverentially.

Among those who might have made more radical meanings of the story of Abraham and Isaac, is Freud, who instead, and inaccurately, chooses Moses as his archetypal patriarch, in order to avoid, Delaney says, the upsetting of his dubious theories of fathers and sons. Freud is rebuked for failing to use the binding of Isaac to criticise his own theory of Oedipal guilt. What is left out of his analysis of the myth, and of the cause of the problem as he outlines it in *Totem and Taboo* (the father's hoarding of the females, his murder by the sons, their guilt and sublimation of their guilt in father worship), is the guilt of the father. Laius wanted his son dead, laming and exposing him. Oedipus did not will his father's death, but killed him by accident. The sons were provoked by the greed of the father of the primeval horde. Abraham is the real myth he should have used, Delaney insists (even though it's the one she wants to get rid of), since it describes the murderous intentions of the father towards the child victim – a far more pertinent cause of family dysfunction, she suggests, in her chapter on the prevalence of child abuse, than the story of Oedipus and the primeval boys. The sacrifice of the Isaac is the precursor of the sacrifice of Christ by his father.

Isaac was silent, but Christ was said by John to cry, 'Father, father, why have you forsaken me?' 'Through the ages,' says Delaney, 'theologians and, more recently, psychoanalysts have tried to drown out that cry as over and over children are sacrificed to the will of the father(s).'

The nexus of monotheistic religion, power and male authority in the foundational story of Abraham and Isaac give us the outline of the 'myth that has shaped our lives and the social legacy we have inherited'. The Akedah speaks to us of the 'willingness of the father to sacrifice his child, and the child's obedience and submission to the father'. Authoritarianism is rooted in paternity, and this underlying assumption in monotheistic religions, Delaney considers, helps to justify the marginalisation of women, parental abuse of children and the right of the State to send its children off to war.

But what happens when an actual, contemporary man takes his child, his favoured one, whom he loves, and kills her because he has heard the voice of God instructing him to do so, is that our present society puts him on trial, questions everyone involved very carefully, and finds that he is guilty of murder, but insane, and therefore in need of close medical care rather than prison. It is hardly the outcome you would expect from a society in thrall to the biblical norm, but it is nonetheless neither a surprising nor an unjust verdict. The case is her key metaphor. Cristos Valenti, a recovering alcoholic, previously a hard-working devoted family man, began to hear the voice of God, and when in 1990 it told him to kill his youngest daughter, he did so and then told his eldest daughter to call the police: 'I have given her to God.' Her chapter on Valenti is entitled *Abraham as Alibi? A Trial in California*, yet Valenti did not offer the binding of Isaac as a mitigating religious precedent. The modern day court seemed well able to distinguish myth from practical sickness and human tragedy, and yet Delaney finds grave error in it. 'The verdict of "not guilty by reason of insanity" may be a way of showing mercy, but in this case, anyway, and however much below the surface, it was also a way of affirming paternal power . . ., a man's right to determine the fate of his child unilaterally, that is without consulting the mother. He was never asked: by what right did you take the child without discussing it with her mother? And the question never came up in court. It was a crime of omission on two counts.'

Valenti, like Abraham, did not seek permission from the child's mother, or query his own entitlement when ordered by God to take the life of the child. But then, if you believed you were truly hearing the voice of God, I suppose you wouldn't stop to debate it with anyone. If Valenti had been capable of questioning the nature of his voice, he might have been capable of questioning the demands it made. And in that case, he probably wouldn't have heard the voice in the first place. Where justice isn't available, mercy has to do, as Abraham, in his relations with his demanding God, knew only too well.

The Lights in the Land of Plenty

Beautiful Losers/The Favourite Game
by Leonard Cohen. Penguin 2002

Some people wondered, when I moved to Cambridge from North London, if I wouldn't miss being at the hub of literary and political conversation. Think of all the dinner parties I would miss where my next door neighbour whispered in my ear the latest gossip from Millbank or Faber and Faber. In fact, it had been some time since I managed to get past my front door to attend such dinner parties – the latest gossip having come to seem strangely similar to the oldest gossip. And surely one of the privileges of living in Cambridge is that you are always within reach of intellectual excellence. Indeed, intellectual excellence will pass you the salt, if you ask nicely (though sometimes it speeds things up if you make the request in Latin). So when after dinner as a guest at High Table I sat surrounded by dons classical, literary and historical in the Senior Common Room I was not surprised to hear Don One, opposite me, ask the assembled illustriousness if anyone was able to come up with a line written in the 20th century that could better anything written by Ovid. I was about to lob Joseph Heller into the ensuing, thoughtful silence – *Cunnilingus, like herding sheep, is a dark and solitary business, but someone has to do it* – when I was saved from being consigned to the academic wheelie bin (degreeless lady novelist, no better than she ought to be) by Don Two to my left who with glazed eyes began reciting:

And if you hear vague traces of skippin' reels of rhyme
To your tambourine in time, it's just a ragged clown behind,
I wouldn't pay it any mind, it's just a shadow you're seein' that
he's chasing.

It was only a matter of moments before having briefly paused to consider the deeper meaning of Joni Mitchell's *Little Green* we were all singing at the tops of our voices:

Sunshine came softly through my window today
Could have tripped out easy but I've changed my ways . . .

Now that's what I call an intellectually satisfying evening: from Ovid to Bob Dylan to Donovan in three minutes flat. It gave me the courage to check on something I had suspected for some time: that there are few groups of people over the age of 50 who, if asked when well fed and slightly drunk, will not admit, after a brief and cowardly hesitation, to spending more than a passing moment of their youth listening to the songs of Leonard Cohen. Listening and singing along.

Certainly I did. Confessional writing is fashionable these days, but while I'm happy to discuss my drink and drugs problems, it comes hard to acknowledge those solitary hours, stoned and mournful, which I spent duetting with the troubadour of onanistic gloom. He seemed to delineate my existence with uncanny precision:

And then sweeping up the jokers that he left behind
You find he did not leave you very much
Not even laughter . . .

He was just some Joseph looking for a manger . . .

I told you when I came I was a stranger . . .

I'm just a station on your way,
I know I'm not your lover . . .

But who were all these card-sharps, Josephs, strangers and stations in my life that I sighed and sang along about them? I was only twenty or twenty-one at the time. Looking back I can hardly pinpoint a one, but then, they seemed to have been legion. No doubt most of the strangers who stopped by flipping their packs of cards also saw themselves reflected in Cohen's cod-courtly melancholia. Who wouldn't be a Joseph looking for a manger rather than some insensitive bastard following his cock? Then, anyway. These days the myth is reversed. The insignia on the young man's shield now is a crushed beer can and a pierced nipple rampant. I'm not sure the present vulgarity isn't more honest and that it doesn't at least provide a sturdier platform to grow up from. All those young men back then, their brains riddling with their own poetic necessities, how were they going to grow up in the world? Only some of them could become part-time Buddhist priests in LA (smoking and coffee permitted) and continue making a living with mournful dirges like the new Leonard Cohen album. Actually, only Leonard Cohen was going to do that. For the rest, those that could not continue to live their lives in a cloud of unknowing, how did they come to terms with their earthbound reality? At the very least a lot of disappointment, I suspect.

And as for the women, as for us Suzannes and Mariannes manqué . . .

And the sun pours down like honey
On our lady of the harbour

And she shows you where to look
Among the garbage and the flowers . . .
While Suzanne holds the mirror . . .

Now so long Marianne, it's time that we began
to laugh and cry and cry and laugh about it all again . . .
. . . you make me forget so very much.
I forget to pray for the angels
and then the angels forget to pray for us.

It was their unreachable wispiness that I craved. Their frocks, you knew, came from Granny Take A Trip or the classy section of Portobello Road's second-hand clothes stalls (far too expensive – Suzanne and Marianne surely had private incomes). As they moved, these vaporous creatures, a perpetual light breeze flurried their chiffons and lace, rippling their flowing tulip sleeves, billowing their transparent harem pants, and streaming their gossamer blonde hair which seemed always to be drifting in water. I was never able to get to such airiness. Well, wetness, in truth, but it was hard to tell the difference in those days. I longed to attain their other-worldliness. I perceived myself as heavier than air – nothing to do with actual weight, but perhaps to do with height and a certain assumption about having every right to make your wafty way about the world, and, of course, about being fair-haired. It wasn't until I read the Thomas Mann short story, *Tonio Kröger*, that I found my place in the scheme of things precisely described. The dark-haired one, always falling in the dance. Another myth, of course, but useful and better suited to my needs. Perhaps Cohen saw himself in the same way in relation to those exquisitely gentile women. Cohen went undercover, layering his laddishness in a sticky-sweet Pre-Raphaelite medieval coating.

Like a worm on a hook,
Like a knight in some old fashioned book
I have saved all my ribbons for thee . . .

Marianne holds on to him 'like a crucifix' and he stands lean-ing from his window with 'one hand on my suicide, one hand on the rose'. His body is a reverse transubstantiation: his flesh turn-ing, for the women who worship it, into the bread and wine of life. A rather Jewish misreading of Jesus and his disciples. One of the cheeriest TV moments of the 1960s was during *Late Night Line Up* (a live arts review) when Cohen read one of his poems. He was, before he made his first album, already published as a poet and novelist. At first the camera was on the poet, but quickly the canny director realised there was something better to watch and panned to the presenter, the prim and lovely Joan Bakewell, and kept the focus firmly on her face as it dawned on her what Cohen was reading about.

When you kneel below me
and in both your hands
hold my manhood like a sceptre,

When you wrap your tongue
about the amber jewel
and urge my blessing,

I understand those Roman girls
who danced around a shaft of stone
and kissed it till the stone was warm.

Kneel, love, a thousand feet below me,
so far I can barely see your mouth and hands
perform the ceremony . . .

In the songs, Leonard (may I call him Leonard? I feel I know him so well) is not only god-like, but mystically dedicated.

I heard of a saint who loved you
So I studied all night in his school . . .

You know who I am,
You've stared at the sun,
Well I am the one who loves
Changing from nothing to one.

Our parents had *Smoke Gets In Your Eyes*, and *Let's Face the Music and Dance*: just as full of heroic, or self-regarding, sentiment, but precise and literate at least. And to their credit neither Jerome Kern nor Irving Berlin were under the impression that they were latter-day Davids or Jesuses rewriting the psalms by the light of their phalluses. Then again, whose fault is it (Cohen's or mine) that I didn't spend 1968 humming *These Foolish Things* rather than *Suzanne*? Mine as much as his. No doubt Cohen was encouraged in his narcissism by his hum-along fans. The two reissued novels *Beautiful Losers* and *The Favourite Game*, acclaimed at the time, read now as if the tricky intricacies of sex and family had just been invented, so breathlessly excited are they by their own notion of darkness. But then many of us were under the impression that no one had ever fucked before or at least hadn't figured out that sex was *complicated*. The novels, like the records, are period pieces.

Cohen was more morose than melancholic, more miserable than meaningful. You sort of moped along with Leonard Cohen. The songs were dreary hymns, not a patch on a rousing chorus of *To Be a Pilgrim* or *Rock of Ages*. They were dirges on a par with *We Shall Overcu-u-um*; anthems of glumness groaned out in a monotonous bass that had no right to be called singing at all. But it was the tuneless drone that made them work. Like Tom Waits, Dylan, Nico, Fred Astaire or Marlene Dietrich, Leonard Cohen couldn't sing, but he did have a voice. There was just enough suggestion of self-parody to make you think the man might, after all, be a comedian and that you were getting the joke. Well, maybe.

So what of these days? Cohen is now 67: he was already over thirty when his first record came out, and over thirty was beyond any age I thought I was ever likely to be. After a gap of ten years he has released a new album called, with ominous accuracy, *Ten New Songs*. With the aid of an elementary drum machine, some leaden guitar playing, and a woman who can sing harmonising in the background, Cohen breathes and growls his way through the songs. I have always had a bit of a soft spot for Buddhism. If you have to believe in something, nothing seems to make the most sense. I grant it's a bit hands-off, a little absent from the struggle of the daily grind, but, as I understood it, Buddhists meditate, practise watchfulness, pray, chant. I imagined, however, that they might be relied on not to put out records. I thought that the really good thing about Buddhists was that they understood that some things are better not put into words, indeed that words make even the tritest insights yet more banal. *Ten New Songs* begins with the revelation that Cohen knows 'what is wrong and what is right, and I'd die for the truth in my secret life'. As indeed we all would, if only someone put a very urgent case to us. Repeatedly, he imparts the wisdom he has gained through the years. Summed up, this amounts to the information that everyone lives and everyone dies and love comes and goes and hey ho there you go. Though without the lightness of touch of, say, Eeyore or Marvin the Robot. Politics is left for the last song, a corker of warm floppy feeling, with the chorus: 'May the lights in the land of plenty/Shine on the truth some day'. And it's not that I don't want them to, I'm sure it would be very nice if they did – or at least brighter – but that I don't ever want to hear anyone singing about it. And no one who is grown up, let alone getting down-right old, should be writing a song about sitting in his room watching the dust motes dancing in a shaft of sunlight and being beamed up into the formless infinite love of the nameless. I'm sorry but there's what is wrong and there's what is right . . .

VISCERAL STUFF

Get It Out of Your System

The Anatomy of Disgust by William Ian Miller. Harvard 1997

It would be nice, wouldn't it, a sort of comfort in a morally confusing world, to find some sweeping generalisation we could all agree to, regardless of history, culture or class? Only a brave and doubtless partially informed person would claim definitively to have found anything which all humanity has in common beyond microbiology. Try a life without love being meaningless, the need for the individual to have control of the means of production, or the ubiquitous appeal of the smell of frying onions, and there will always be someone ready to show that these truths are not universal. It's just possible, however, that William Miller has cracked the problem with his simple but glorious statement: 'One simply did not drink pus, even back then.' If we want to find a common response on which all people at all times and all places can agree, then the pus-drinking activity of St Catherine of Siena, *c.* 1370, is surely where to look. The usual mêlée of cultural and emotional variation falls away in the face of it. Relativism withers at its mention. Not even those whose pus St Catherine drank managed any degree of equanimity. As her hagiographer, Raymundus de Vineis, tells it, only Catherine was prepared to attend one of her fellow nuns whose suppurating breast cancer smelt so bad that no one else could abide being in the same room. So far, so decent. When, however, Catherine came to dress the wound, the stench caused her to vomit. In order to punish her wilful body, and get a saint-like hold on herself, Catherine decanted the pus into a cup and drank it. The patient was less than grateful; she came to loathe Catherine, taking the rather modern view that whenever the 'holy maid was anywhere out of her sight . . . she was about some foul act of fleshly pleasure'. She was not so far wrong. Christ appeared to Catherine in a dream, and as a reward for subduing her nature, drew her mouth to the wound in his side and let her drink to her heart's content. We may or may not, down the generations and across belief systems, consider this behaviour holy, but would anyone deny that it is disgusting? Mind you, relativism dies hard: there are South American peoples who regularly feast on manioc root softened with the saliva of the women of the tribe, and groups who make soup out of the ashes of their dead, so let us say that in a variable world it is impossible for us in this time and place to imagine anyone not finding pus-drinking disgusting.

In so far as disgust belongs in the realm of the body, it would not be unreasonable to suppose that Christianity has a lot to answer for in its construction in the West, with the ambivalence of the Church in matters of the flesh and the curious implications of the adoption in 1215 of the Real Presence in the Eucharist. Hatred of the body as the material prison of the spirit combined uneasily with the dogma of transubstantiation. Although 'disgust' was not to enter the English lexicon until the early 17th century, Wycliffe was able to make clear his emotional response to the idea of eating the actual body of Christ at Mass: 'If thou' were to 'see in liknesse of fleisch and blood that blessed sacrament, thou schuldest lothen and abhorren it to resseyve it into they mouth.' But Miller suggests that Christianity's troubled attitude to flesh and blood is only part of the story of disgust.

The deliberate echo of Robert Burton in his title signals his wish to produce a meditation on the natural history of disgust and his belief that it is as much hard-wired as socially induced. His claim is that 'for all its visceralness' disgust 'is one of our more aggressive culture-creating passions'; that 'matter matters and . . . only polemical foolishness will allow us to ignore the fact that some of our emotions generate culture as well as being generated by it.'

At an individual, organic level, disgust seems easy enough to describe. Our own physical body is the gateway of disgust. What is inside us, while it is inside us, is all right, but whatever emerges from the inside of the body to the outside world, with the exception only of tears, is unclean. Clearly, this is true of what emerges from other bodies and threatens to enter our own, but it also holds for our own bodily products. Miller offers a thought experiment proposed by the psychologist Gordon Allport. Think of swallowing the saliva that is in your mouth, or do so. Now imagine spitting out some saliva into a glass and drinking it. The individual can – has to – live with being what both Heraclitus and contemporary abuse refer to as a sack of shit, but once the shit is out of the bag, it is impure and never to be reincorporated. Unless, of course, you are a child. The failure of small children to feel contaminated by their bodily wastes, and their casual capacity to reincorporate all manner of them, argues strongly for the cultural creation of disgust. We have to learn to be disgusted, and it takes an uncommonly long time. It is the central task of early parenthood to teach toddlers not to touch, smell, taste and thoroughly enjoy their excretions. 'Dirty' is the word we commonly use to them, but the face we make is the 'disgust face' – wrinkled nose and curled lower lip – that Darwin described in *The Expression of the Emotions in Man and Animals*. Even knowing this, it is hard to marry the evidently socially conditioned nature of disgust with the instinctive feeling of disgust as we experience it, though there is perhaps a clue in the other great exception to disgust rules – being in love.

Perhaps, cunning symbolisers that we are, we expend vast efforts on teaching disgust rules to children, in order to provide a set of regulations to be transgressed. Sex demands that we suspend our feelings of revulsion about the incorporation of foreign substances into our bodies. Indeed, it rather depends on our rejoicing in doing so. It is a two-way thing according to Miller: 'To the thrill of transgressing another's boundary is added the thrill of granting the permission to be so transgressed upon. Somewhat strangely, it is the granting of permission that may be more transgressive than the transgression it authorises, for it is the permission that suspends the disgust rule, not the boundary-crossing that is thereby allowed.' Not so strange if the boundaries have been rigorously enforced precisely in order that they might be flouted. Ambiguity is not the preserve of the Church, it only aped what humans do best of all, and have the most fun with. Sex, Woody Allen said in happier times, is only dirty if you do it right.

Conversely, disgust gets you off the hook of love if you nurture it as Swift did, both tormenting and releasing himself with the thought: 'Nor wonder how I lost my Wits;/Oh! Cælia, Cælia, Cælia shits.' There is a price to pay for this game, and it's a large one, especially for women – gender parity no more applies here than it does in most other places. Miller makes Lear stand for men's fear and abomination of the vagina:

> Beneath is all the fiend's.
> There's hell, there's darkness, there is the
> sulphurous pit, burning, scalding, stench,
> consumption; fie, fie, fie! pah! pah!

But Miller suspects that vaginas evoke disgust not just because '"Love has pitched its mansion in the place of excrement" or that they are surrounded by pubic hair, or that they secrete viscous substances, or that they are victim of centuries of misogyny'.

Their real crime is that they are receptacles for semen, 'that most polluting of substances'. It's true that both the retaining and the expelling of semen have been deemed destructive of male mental and physical health, and Miller's belief is that what most disgusts men about ejaculation and causes them to regard women's acceptance of it with contempt is an over-arching dismay at fecundity. We recoil instinctively at evidence of 'generation itself, surfeit, excess of ripeness'. It's life, death and the whole cyclical thing we can't stand. Semen, menstrual blood, excrement are a holy trinity of disgust. They are life itself: birth, death, decay and the next cycle of production. We are appalled by life's fertility, and anything that reminds us of it, especially anything that provokes thoughts of excess, will be found vile. What is most disturbing about lower forms of life is their teeming, swarming, seething, rotting, regenerating nature. So we are disgusted by the nature in human nature. Vegetable excess reminds us that we are part of the organic game. This, I suppose, is not good news for the ecology movement; the more it reminds us that we are an integral part of Mother Earth's interwoven life plot, the more our stomachs are likely to churn. Our treatment of the planet, cutting down prolific forests, replacing them with sterile concrete roads, might be more indicative of what we really feel than the current greenish rhetoric. Our present eco-hero, Swampy, would be well advised to change his nom de guerre, if Miller is correct.

Sexual disgust is related to this. We are disgusted by overindulgence; surfeit of something desired is likely to result not only in boredom but in distaste:

> There lives within the very flame of love
> A kind of wick or snuff that will abate it,
> And nothing is at a like goodness still,
> For goodness, growing to a pleurisy,
> Dies in his own too-much.

Orgasm, the legitimate end of the sexual enterprise, is by definition excessive. Enough is too much, and the surfeited man falls
asleep, not with exhaustion, but in the face of despair, according
to Miller. (Women, inured by childcare and the workaday business of menstruation, knit post-coitally, though this is a little
known fact to the sleepier half of the world. It would seem from
Miller's tale that women are altogether less fussed by fecundity
and too-muchness.)

We are, of course, deep in Freudian territory here. For him,
disgust was part of reaction formation: the trio of disgust, shame
and morality worked to prevent the activation of unconscious
desires. Disgust may make the fair foul, but it also makes the foul
fair in providing a barrier that we will inevitably find alluring. 'So
much pleasure is tied up in the violation of rules we are committed to, the very commitment providing the basis for the pleasure
in violation.' As to the disgust of surfeit, Freud wonders why
wine 'always affords the drinker the same toxic satisfaction' when
men are rarely satisfied with the same sexual partner for long.
Mothers are his answer; or rather the fact that the compulsive
seducer is always failing to find his mother in his mistress. But
Miller demurs. Orgasm is the thing: 'If wine produced orgasm or
if orgasm had the gentle sloping moderate pleasures of wine . . .
then Adam would be as content with Eve day in and day out as
Freud was with his Bordeaux.' Miller doesn't say what vintage he
considers the female orgasm to be, but it seems to have kept her
standing by her flighty man, so maybe we should bottle it and
resolve the biological double standard for good.

There might be a historical slant to this. Disgust appears to
require a relatively modern degree of privacy in order to exist. It
looks, superficially, as if increasing civilisation is a prerequisite for
revulsion at unacceptable public behaviour. Yet Miller cites an
11th-century reference to yielding 'to the call of nature' to suggest
that this euphemism was already available, and that where

euphemism exists disgust is not far below. In a 16th-century hand-book on manners it is strongly suggested that dinner guests should not 'foul the staircases, corridors, or closets with urine or other filth' and that 'it does not befit a modest, honourable man to pre-pare to relieve nature in the presence of other people . . . Similarly, he will not wash his hands on returning to decent society from pri-vate places, as the reason for washing will arouse disagreeable thoughts in people.' Both private places and embarrassment at bodily activity were well established centuries ago, even if the hygiene rules have changed. This is true even in heroic cultures. The Icelandic *Laxdoela Saga* describes the escalation of a feud in which the hero Kjartan surrounded the farmhouse of the people of Laugar, 'blocked all the doors and refused anyone exit and they had to relieve themselves inside for three days'. A shared sense of disgust had to exist for such a strategy to work. Indeed, the people of Laugar 'thought it to be a much worse dishonour, greater even than if Kjartan had killed one or two of them instead'.

Things take a murkier turn when Miller moves from flesh and nature to the more abstract aspects of disgust. Once we leave the world of vomit, excreta, semen and pus, and find ourselves using the word 'disgust' as a moral condemnation, the argument gets fuzzy. Are we, as Miller states, disgusted by hypocrisy, and if we say we are, do we mean it in quite the same way as we do when we observe someone spitting in the street? Does the 'disgust' that he claims as 'central to moral discourse and the construction of moral sensibility' stem directly from visceral revulsion, or are we playing with the idea for hyperbole and emphasis? Miller is quite specific. Contempt is not disgust, he claims. Contempt implies indifference and is therefore well suited for democracy with its implication that we should live and let live. It belongs to the world of social hierarchy. Our social inferiors elicit our contempt, and they in turn feel contempt for us. Thus, everything stays in balance. According to Miller, however, disgust is a separate condition that occurs when we observe necessary evils such as hypocrisy, betrayal, fawning and cruelty. We are reminded that fair is foul: we know the politician and the lawyer must lie, but it turns our stomachs to see the moral order contaminated. Adam Smith observes of the unsocial passions – anger, resentment, hatred – that even when 'justly provoked there is still something about them which disgusts us'. And for Hume, Miller says, 'nothing quite disgusts . . . like the fool.' This does not feel right. The activities of St Catherine make me feel sick; thinking about being sick makes me feel sick, but cant does not turn my stomach more than metaphorically – it makes me feel angry and ashamed. The shame (at the reminder of common humanity or animality) is the link, I suppose, that Miller uses to connect the visceral with the moral, but it doesn't convince.

Miller proceeds with the argument by referring to George Orwell's difficulties with disgust. To feel disgust is to feel threatened with contamination, as Orwell suggests in *The Road to Wigan Pier*. Whereas contempt remains complacent, disgust is intolerable and therefore itself threatening to the concept of democracy. He was disgusted at the lack of hygiene in his lodgings above the Brookers' tripe shop, at their slurping of soup, and he knew that no rational socialism was ever going to change his learned visceral responses. So well were they learned that, as a scholarship boy at a private prep school, he could smell that he smelt: 'I had no money. I was weak, I was ugly, I was unpopular, I had a chronic cough, I was cowardly, I smelt . . . I believed, for example, that I "smelt" but this was based simply on general probability. It was notorious that disagreeable people smelt, and therefore presumably I did so too.' But Orwell's fastidiousness is always physical rather than moral. He knew perfectly well why the lower classes smelt, the practical and psychological reasons – poverty makes cleanliness more difficult; his own middle-class upbringing was inescapable – but smell they did.

To say one is disgusted by hypocrisy, obsequiousness or stupidity is surely to use the diction of physical revulsion as analogy. Moral outrage may be accompanied by dismay at being reminded of our capacity for low behaviour, just as physical disgust may contain our distress at being implicated in nature's frenzy, but the idea of being sickened by moral failure is borrowed from rather than fully integrated with the notion of contamination. I suspect that in the moral sphere *disgust* is one of the names we give *contempt*. Miller develops his anatomy of disgust without enough regard for the elasticity of language and the satisfaction we get in stretching it around analogous corners. It isn't that we don't mean what we say, but that we mean so much more than the words we use.

Oh, Andrea Dworkin

Misogyny: The Male Malady by David Gilmore.
Pennsylvania 2001

It's a male thing, misogyny. No matter where you look, then or now, here, there and everywhere, up ethnographic hill, down historical dale, men disparage women. In his trawl of anthropological data, historical records, literature and letters, art and music, David Gilmore finds that men have always and everywhere expressed fear, disgust and hatred of women. From the peaceful and gentle !Kung San Bushmen to the urbane and civilised Montaigne, from folk legend to Freudian complex, from Medusa to the Blue Angel, men blame women for their discomforts and disappointments. Yet while Gilmore's round-up suggests to him that anti-female feeling is universal among men, he believes its obverse is so rare that no term for it trips comfortably off the tongue. He half-heartedly suggests 'misandry' or 'viriphobia' as names that might be applied to the female version of misogyny, but since the only practitioner he can come up with is Andrea Dworkin, it's hardly worth the coinage. In the 1950s and 1960s there used to be a term for it, though lately it has fallen into disuse. In those days it cropped up regularly in conversations that went roughly like this:

MAN: Do you want to come to bed with me?
WOMAN: No.
MAN: What are you, a man-hater?
WOMAN (*making her getaway*): It's less general than that.

In those pre-feminist days, everyone knew what man-haters were: they were lesbians (or lesbians were man-haters), ugly (and therefore lesbians), or they were women who wanted equal pay or work parity (and probably lesbians), but mostly they were women who didn't want to sleep with you. However, Gilmore is right; man-haters were identified as such by men – I can't remember any woman calling herself one – and the designation was just another aspect of a deep institutional dislike and fear of women that does seem to have been expressed by many men in all times and all places.

Gilmore is an American anthropologist whose ethnographic work has been on the culture of machismo and shame in contemporary Spain, and whose previous books have been on the cultural meanings of masculinity. Maleness is his bag. He claims, rather startlingly, that misogyny is a neglected topic, and sets out to remedy the rarity of 'comparative and synoptic studies of continuities within cultural variation'. Though I would have thought that the prevalence of male prejudice against women has been extensively noted, Gilmore nonetheless compiles instances from standard ethnographic, historical, biographical and literary sources to demonstrate the global nature of misogyny. He produces a digest of universal male disgust. While he acknowledges that its expression can be varied, Gilmore is in search of an explanation for its ubiquity. After all, women do not have the same visceral loathing of maleness – excluding, he parenthesises, 'the modern-day feminists like the redoubtable Dworkin' (what a useful woman she is). What exists among 'many more sensible women' is a dislike of obnoxious and abusive men and 'specifically "masculine" qualities like machismo, bravado, or the puerile braggadocio that sometimes appears in the locker room'. Women (apart from Ms Dworkin, of whom I am growing fonder by the minute) are, it seems, more reasonable, more adult and less obsessive because they are less psychologically damaged than men who, we are going to be brought round to believing, are suffering from what amounts to a 'gendered psychosis'. So we don't have to worry about women, except – you've guessed it – Dworkin and those 'radical feminists' and 'social constructionists' who take the 'reductionistic and sexist view' that male endocrinology is destiny.

Instead, we can concentrate our thoughts and concerns on the real victims of the malady of misogyny: the psychogenically challenged male who needs all the understanding we can give him. Apparently men's psyches are 'troubled', they are in 'masculine turmoil' as a result of universal experiences in 'the male developmental cycle'. Lord, how easily the image of the oppressed is appropriated. If women think they've had a hard time as a result of being loathed and bullied by men, it's nothing compared to the hardship suffered by men that has resulted in their feeling the loathing. If you are beginning to get an uncomfortable sense of milky mothers and moist mermaids looming on the horizon you are right, because men's fear of helplessness, suffocation and submergence, in the inescapably female and deliquescent form ot uterus, breast and vagina, is judged to be at the root of it all. Women drip with danger for men, who, as we know, first can't live without us and then can't live with us. You can love your mother for a while, but then she betrays you with your father and you have to marry other men's sisters: enemies, outsiders, who as like as not are plotting against you with their sexuality and secretions while trying to abort your sons on whom the patriliny depends. Of course, it's not women's fault that it's all their fault – Gilmore has all the rhetoric of a modern man and throws his

hands up sadly at the unfortunate social and biological arrangements that make it this way – but men suffer from having been
given birth to by women from whom they have to separate in
order to become men; they suffer from having to desire people of
the same gender as their mother (my, this is very awkward,
Jocasta), and they suffer because they cannot perform the miracle
of reproducing the species directly from their own bodies. Men
suffer. No, they do. It's awful.

Gilmore's evidence for the commonalities of misogyny is
based initially on anthropological research, and there is a difficulty here. His pick and mix approach takes some classic, not to
say hoary, old ethnographies at their face value – a bit of a problem, since almost every generation of anthropologists has
condemned previous researchers for faulty studies, imperialistic
or colonialist arrogance, or plain doctoring of the material. The
idea of the participant observer has little credibility in academic
circles, and the standing of much ethnographic research is these
days roughly on a par with reality TV. Some of the studies
Gilmore quotes were done in the 1950s, when fieldwork attitudes
were very different, and he quotes the not highly reliable J.G.
Frazer and Margaret Mead alongside other, less discredited
anthropologists. There are several references to the Yanomamo, a
Venezuelan tribe who have become, thanks to Napoleon
Chagnon's decades of research, a byword for violence and misogyny. These men, Gilmore says, 'are notorious wife-beaters,
infamous for their brutality'. But Chagnon's work has come
under scrutiny recently and doubts have been raised about the
validity of his findings in Patrick Tierney's *Darkness in El
Dorado*. A report on the argument in the *New York Times* suggests that anthropology has become the academic equivalent of
The Jerry Springer Show. In any case, objectivity and ideological
agendas aside, anthropologists are notoriously the butt of hoaxes
and practical jokes or are kindly given what they seem to want by

those in the simpler societies being studied who are not quite as simple as they seem.

All Gilmore's anthropological borrowings from studies made in Amazonia, the New Guinea Highlands, Africa and India attest to male terror of female physicality. Men huddle together, cowering in fear of women's secretions, which are unclean, polluting and contagious, and likely to cause disease, decay, even death if not strictly controlled. Gilmore's florid attempt to describe the phenomenon betrays a certain relish at having to say the unsayable:

> Misogynistic fear centres on the flesh that makes woman man's opposite and renders her unknowable to him. Misogynists tremble before the bodily labyrinth: veins, intestines, sexual organs. With her lunar cycles and genital effluvia, woman destroys the idealist's illusions of a pristine universe. But physical repugnance is only part of the picture. For many misogynists revulsion grows into an indictment not of feminine flesh but of her spirit, her intellect, her character and will.

It is, of course, a love/hate thing. Along with the abuse and fear of women, men, in these ethnographies, are forever cross-dressing, standing in streams cutting the underside of their penises in mock menstruation, and howling in agony while their women are in labour. And it's because they can't help wanting women so much that men hate them. Men, not being animals, have constantly to restrain themselves, especially since the human female gave up oestrus. Men want women, but they've got better things to do than think about sex all the time. 'This inner struggle is probably sharper, more physiologically driven, in the male than in the female because of the peremptory power of the testosterone-driven male libido. The result is not only unremitting tension, frustration, and the inevitable aggression against the object of desire, but also moral self-doubt and, in the case of puritans, self-hatred.' (And women?

Well, 'women suffer in their own way from sexual conflicts, but the result is not anti-male hysteria.') In Melanesia and parts of Brazil, women are not permitted ever to be physically higher than men, for fear of deadly dripping, but, as Gilmore points out, the sexual fantasy of women astride men is nearly universal. The ambivalence between sexual fantasy and social phobia is key: desire equals danger, an imagined loss of control of the libido threatens the social order, an irresistible physical need undermines an independent spirit. These fears operated just as effectively for the ancient Greeks, the early Christians, the medieval intelligentsia or the Elizabethans as they do for contemporary tribal societies. Gilmore gives us the well-aired rants against women from Hesiod and Homer, St Paul, Bernard of Cluny, Shakespeare and Swift to prove that his case goes beyond the merely anthropological. We hear, once again, Lear railing against 'the sulphurous pit', Milton moaning about 'this fair defect of Nature', Swift sniffing about 'all her stink' and Yeats complaining that 'Love has pitched his mansion in the place of excrement' – though I'm not clear why this last should be interpreted as a distaste exclusively for women. Gilmore makes his point by leaving no misogynistic cliché unturned. Splitting spirit and flesh, will and desire, intellect and imagination is a game as old as Methuselah, and the division of humanity into two genders is as handy a way of representing it as any. But these views of misogyny all presuppose that women, who do not seem to have this same ambivalent reaction to men, either do not suffer from compelling sexual desire or have no interest in sustaining the civil rather than the sensual life. Women, at least in Gilmore's book, are curiously passive creatures who take whatever is dished out to them – or did until the unsensible likes of Andrea Dworkin came along.

Men, however, suffer not just from distress at the strength of their own passions but from an endemic dread of regressing into infantile vulnerability. The danger of the sexual woman is that she is the same creature whose body bore and nurtured the male child, who having dragged himself away from her apron strings must now re-encounter her. His fear of being engulfed or consumed is a terror of returning to helpless dependence, a fear, when it comes right down to it, of oblivion and death. We are just a hop and a skip here from Freud's Oedipus, and only a triple jump from Klein's object relations theory. Either way, psychoanalytic theory indicates to Gilmore that men need to wrench themselves from the power of maternally and sexually nourishing women in order to run the world. Moreover, men are very, very cross with women because, running the world as they do, men have so arranged it that they are in fact dependent on women for their physical and domestic comfort. What could be more irritating than, fearing dependence above all, finding that in order to have time to lead the properly male life, dependent is exactly what they are? The simple solution to all this, which is that men give up the project of run-ning the world and settle down to childcare and making supper, is not an option apparently, because maleness is a near impossible dream, and a man's got to dream what a man's got to dream.

Gilmore suggests that the enterprise of maleness is so difficult that it must be protected against encroaching underlying femaleness. Maleness is a developmental afterthought, he points out. We all begin in utero as female and only some foetuses develop into males. By analogy, social maleness is a cultivation that needs protecting from rampantly natural femaleness. Maleness can be seen, says Gilmore, as 'a fragile pose, an insecure façade, something made up, frangible, that men create beyond nature'. Here men, valiant but feeble, are fending off entropy itself. Standing against extinction in the form of their own innate inner femaleness. Whatever way you look at it, men are poor but brave old things.

In search of his own unifying theory, Gilmore gives credence to many of the obvious and available psychoanalytic and sociobiological explanations for women-hatred. He is less inclined, however, to trust feminist and Marxist views on misogyny, which tend to place the blame more squarely on men's desire for political control and domination. Too crude, too reductionist, he says. Though as a straightforward solution to the coincidental problem of the universality of misogyny and of male hegemony, I'd say they are hard to beat. To my shame, I have to admit to a growing inclination to agree with John Major's once dismaying view that we should understand less and condemn more – at least in the face of Gilmore's gathering of pop-psychoanalytic excuses for the sorry state of gender relations the world over.

In the end the patchwork of woman-hating instances of which most of the book consists brings Gilmore round to his conclusion, which hardly seems to merit the painful reading we have been required to do: 'many theories are needed to explain this malady in all its diversity and richness. Misogyny is complex and has many, often unrelated causes.' He is not hopeful of a final cure, but thinks the problem might be mitigated by desegregation in schools, the sharing of bathrooms, paternal childcare and consciousness-raising for men in the form of 'ambivalence toleration' or 'conflictedness training'. He considers his proposals for the amelioration of misogyny to be 'wishful thinking' but since men 'are and always will be divided in their feelings about sex and about women . . . only self-knowledge and tolerance can help men appreciate the degree of their conflict.' What is going to help women put up with these sorry sharers of the planet, he doesn't say. He continues: 'Only self-knowledge can free men from fear of women, and self-knowledge in this case means the acceptance of the divided self within and an imperfect universe without.' The imperfect universe being one that has women in it, I presume. Finally, 'only through an acceptance of wholeness can men appreciate the loveliness, gentleness and beauty of women.' Oh, Andrea Dworkin, where are you when we really need you?

Feel the Burn

Pain: The Science of Suffering by Patrick Wall.
Weidenfeld 1999

You may have missed out on love, transcendental oneness with the Universe, the adrenaline rush of the warrior, but you've had a headache or a bad back. Pain is the one engulfing, undeniable, incommunicable experience we've all had. And yet for all its ubiquity, pain is a solitary encounter, a lonely way of discovering the certainty that you exist. I hurt therefore I am is rapidly followed by I hurt therefore I am alone. Two people in pain are not nearly as likely to commit themselves to each other for life, or found a religious community, or become comrades in battle as they are to curl up silently in separate corners of the room to suffer alone what can't be shared. Nasty business. One of the nastiest we can think of. Fear of death in a secular society is largely fear of pain. It's not hard to imagine longing for death as a release from pain, but very difficult to believe one would wish to trade the blankness of death for living agony. Even self-confessed masochists are clear that the pain they want is the pain of their choosing, at the time of their choosing and with the sadist of their choosing, not an attack of toothache or appendicitis.

Yet masochism in some more general form must be implicated in the mysterious fact that the technology of pain relief has been so neglected by our pathologically innovative, life-improving species, which has always and everywhere suffered from it. We have developed as far as the pre-washed lettuce and the Flip-Down Magnifying Eye Make-Up Glasses (Innovations, £9.99), but can do nothing for your current migraine attack. Lurking somewhere is the belief that pain is good for you, and/or deserved, because pain as punishment and salvation is our cultural sine qua non. 'Because you have done this . . . I will greatly increase your pangs in childbearing; in pain you shall bring forth children,' our first story tells us. And we are only to be redeemed through the agony of Christ's crucifixion: a sharp blow to the back of the head or a firing squad just wouldn't have done. Hold still, darling, while I pour iodine onto your cut, yes I know it stings, but that's because it's doing you good. Stop complaining, of course the poultice is unbearably hot: it won't work otherwise. No pain, no gain. Feel the burn.

Actually, I'd rather not, and the blessed Patrick Wall, neuroscientist and pain doctor, wishes it to be known that pain is almost entirely useless and good for nothing but getting rid of. He cites cancer pain, with the impatience of one who is suffering it himself, as the apogee of pointlessness. Cancer only hurts once the tumour has grown large enough to become an obstruction or irritant. Before that, when something might be done about it, cancer grows in painless silence. Wall has no time for those who justify pain as a warning system.

Just about every high-school biology text contains a diagram where a finger touches a saucepan and is rapidly withdrawn. It is used to 'explain' pain as the method of avoiding injury run by a reflex mechanism consisting of sensory afferents which make motor nerves withdraw the hand. I despise that diagram for its triviality. I would estimate that we spend a few seconds in an entire lifetime successfully withdrawing from a threatening stimulus. Unfortunately, we are destined to spend days and months in pain during our lifetime, none of which is explained by that silly diagram.

Children born with the rare condition of congenital analgesia have no sensation of pain but rapidly develop strategies to avoid danger and rely on other symptoms to know that they're ill: appendicitis is diagnosed by fever, inflammation and gut motility; danger is apprehended and learned through the alarm and teaching of others. It is a matter of tactics, which are themselves integral to the experience of pain, Wall suggests. The deep, spreading, sickening pain that follows the first intense stab of twisting an ankle serves to make the sufferer guard the wound against movement or pressure that would prevent repair. If they are bombarded with injury messages, the spinal-cord cells become hypersensitive and stimulate both biological repair systems and appropriate behaviour. Like children having their wounds kissed better, we can be distracted from the worst of pains, since attention is a major and early factor in its development. Pain even dismisses itself when there are more urgent priorities. The need to get away from danger, or towards safety, can put pain into abeyance: many soldiers wounded in battle do not feel pain until behind the lines. This isn't heroism, which would require the pain to be felt and ignored, nor is it shock, at least not in the layperson's sense, since that tells us nothing about the process. Wall describes with some relish the unpromising, unfancied racehorse, Henbit, accelerating away from the pack to win the Epsom Derby in 1980, not just in spite of, but because of breaking his leg in a stumble during the early part of the race. The horse only began to limp in the paddock. The fracture healed perfectly, but Henbit never outclassed himself again and was put out to stud. 'Smart horse,' says Wall.

How much pain people (and horses) feel depends on factors beyond mechanical damage, including their own and other people's expectations. In an emergency room study of people who arrived in pain, Wall's colleague Ron Melzack discovered that the complaints were assessed by the professionals as if there were objective and appropriate levels of pain. The emergency room staff thought that 40 per cent were making 'a terrible fuss', nearly 40 per cent were 'denying' pain, and 20 per cent gave an 'appropriate' answer. Clearly, Henbit was in denial. On the other hand, an Israeli Defence Force lieutenant who had one leg blown off during the Yom Kippur war by an exploding shell showed what might be thought of as appropriate signs of deep distress and tears, but when asked about the pain, replied: 'The pain is nothing, but who is going to marry me now?'

Wall wants nothing to do with the distinction between bodily pain and anguish of mind. He puts the blame firmly on Descartes for our tendency to separate physical and mental pain. At a recent lecture, he showed the dreaded dualist's picture of the pain pathway – an illustration from *L'Homme* – in which a stimulus of fire yanks on the pain cord that ends in the common sense centre in the pineal gland. 'How silly it is and always was,' he snapped, and surely the shade of Descartes shrank in shame. In his book, Wall gives the shortest of shrifts to the theory that divides the sensory system from the mental processing of received messages: 'That route has been taken for two thousand years, from Aristotle to John Searle and Daniel Dennett. Pain has been used repeatedly as the simplest possible example of a physical stimulus which inevitably results in a mental response. We will not retrace this route, dropping the names of Bacon, Hume, Berkeley, Kant and Wittgenstein . . . Nor will we join my fellow emeritus academics in their obsession to greet our oncoming senility with a discussion of consciousness.' Asked at the lecture if he would like to comment on the role of consciousness in pain, he replied with a brisk 'no'.

His reasons for such a curt dismissal are not merely ideological: they stem from a plainly humanitarian wish to rescue people in chronic pain from being labelled malingerers and neurotics just because their doctors cannot trace the pain directly to damaged tissue. Medical training still requires pain to be a symptom of a clear pathological process which it is the doctor's job to cure. Dealing with symptoms has traditionally been passed down the hierarchy to nurses and physiotherapists, just as, historically, caring for the dying has not been seen as the concern of the doctor, who once he or she has established that no cure is possible perceives the patient as a failure. Wall's forty years as a neuroscientist have left him with the conviction that a 'hard-wired, line-dedicated, specialised pain system did not exist. Rather, there is a subtle multiplexed reactive system that informs us simultaneously about events in the tissues and in the thinking parts of the brain.' What is obvious to him is that 'the separation of sensation from perception was quite artificial, and that sensory and cognitive mechanisms operated as a whole.'

This hardly simplifies things, especially when the tricky business of the placebo effect is considered. No one likes the placebo effect. Drug companies have to prove their active chemicals are more efficient than a sugar pill that alleviates symptoms. Doctors fear they might turn out to be no more than the quacks they have been taught to despise. And patients, told that a blank tablet made their pain disappear, are not delighted to discover that they are suggestible, or even that their pain may have been as phantasmal as the cure. 'I have responded to placebo trials myself,' Wall writes, 'and I am always mortified and ashamed of myself.' But suggestibility and fantasy may have nothing to do with it. Using an ultrasound machine to massage the faces of people who had just undergone wisdom-tooth extraction gave as many patients relief from their pain when the machine was turned off as when it was on. What's more, it reduced the symptomatic swelling of the jaw and improved the ability of patients to open their mouths, thereby matching in effectiveness a substantial dose of anti-inflammatory steroid. Well, wouldn't you feel a fool?

Not if cultural and learned expectation were taken to be part of the account of pain. Young children do not respond to placebos as adults do, not having learned about the therapeutic effect of pills. Pharmaceutical companies have been quick to understand the power of expectation. A coloured tablet with corners is better than a round white tablet. The colour red is associated with power; green and blue with calm. Capsules containing coloured beads are better than any tablet, while an intramuscular injection is understood to be a much more serious therapy. At the top of the list is an intravenous injection – even of saline. That'll sort it. According to Wall, one professor of medicine taught his students to give patients a tablet held in forceps while explaining that it was too powerful to be touched by fingers. Placebos work because we know that medicine works. Perhaps because we know a pill is likely to do us good, the natural endorphins kick in. When patients are given a narcotic antagonist, experimenters can no longer reduce their tooth-extraction pain with a placebo. But placebos do not work when given to a patient in secrecy. There must be some evidence of intended treatment. A patient is inclined to expect a beneficial effect with any kind of therapy. 'The placebo is not a stimulus but an action which experience has taught may be followed by relief.' A degree of optimism is needed, however. Tests by clinical psychologists to prove that placebo responders were hysterics, neurotics, unusually suggestible or introspective, showed none of these traits to be diagnostic of a good response. Depressives, however, are poor responders, because, after all, low expectation is in the nature of depression. 'Avoid pessimists if you are looking for placebo reactors,' Wall warns.

Isn't there something worrying here? The placebo effect is

getting to be quite old news. Surely, the more word gets out that snake oil works as well as serotonin re-uptake inhibitors the less effective the effect will be? If the doctor might as well hand you a pill made of talc instead of some chemical worth more than its weight in gold, why wouldn't she? And once you've had that thought, what's to stop an outbreak of reverse placebo action, and the general inhibition of a positive response even to active medicines? There is such a thing as a nocebo effect: it's what you get when you look at the leaflet that comes with your pills telling you of possible side-effects. In any case, the nocebo effect works the same way as a shaman's death curse. Perhaps it's best not to think too much about it. Would we, knowing what we know about the placebo effect, be astonished to learn that Prozac or Viagra or some new miracle migraine relief were in fact placebo experiments on a worldwide scale? Don't say you haven't been warned.

AWKWARD DAMES

Someone Else's Work

The Girl from the Fiction Department – A Portrait of Sonia Orwell by Hilary Spurling. Hamish Hamilton 2002

There must be people who, during their lifetime, get their minds right enough not to feel bitterness as the end looms and they realise that nothing much else is going to happen to them apart from death. I understand from reading and anecdote that some people do die with a smile and the words, 'It's been a good life' on their lips. But not many, surely? It seems to me almost unreasonable, indecent even, not to feel some degree of regret as life winds down towards the end. And life, of course, has generally only just got properly started before it begins to show signs of not going on forever. So when I read in David Plante's *Difficult Women* that Sonia Orwell in her final years complained to him, 'I've fucked up my life. I'm angry because I've fucked up my life', it doesn't seem to me necessarily to imply a particularly tragic or wasted life. At least not necessarily more tragic or wasted than most. Unless you take the Chinese view, an interesting life is the best we can hope for in an existence which ends, for all of us, prematurely with illness or ageing and death.

There can be no doubt that Sonia Orwell had an interesting

life; vivid and complicated in her early years, drunkenly angry and anxious towards the end, but with friends who cared enough about her to put up with her and even, decades later, to write a biography designed, as Hilary Spurling's explicitly is, to stem 'the tide of venom that pursued her into and beyond the grave'. The venom was largely a result of the way, as George Orwell's widow, she managed the literary estate. She was deemed to be tyrannical, grasping and only interested in the income the estate generated. She was remembered – by men in particular – as having slept around copiously in her youth – though when you think of who was available in the 50s of London and Paris to sleep with you can only wonder that she made time to do any work as an editor at *Horizon*. And, of course, as an older woman, she was feared for her vicious tongue. Hilary Spurling begs to differ, or at least explain.

The trouble with attempting to redress a blackened reputation is that in the process of countering the allegations you are always in danger of directing the reader's attention to the original criticism. In order to refute the general condemnation of her friend, Spurling acknowledges the difficult older woman David Plante knew: 'Fear, suspicion and hostility lay increasingly close to the surface. Insecurity or drink released an aggression that made her many enemies.' A nephew compared being on the receiving end of one of her public tirades to a drive-by shooting. But even then, says Spurling, 'beneath the trappings of the hardened old warhorse you could still see traces of the impetuous young thoroughbred, who had enchanted [Michel] Leiris and others a quarter of a century before.' Well, yes. Most of us were easier to take when young, especially if we were beautiful, energetic, bright and eagerly ambitious, as Sonia Orwell clearly was. We should, however, be grateful for the transformation; young thoroughbreds, if they don't become old warhorses like the Widow Orwell, are inclined to prance unprettily about, all unaware of the effects of time, and set one's teeth on edge.

But we are in the realm of contemporary biography, and Spurling, with several lives to her credit, will not settle for a memoir of Sonia Orwell that merely has her decline into harsh disappointment through the effects of loss of youth. The heroine must be driven in some way towards the sad end made importantly tragic by a seed of self-destruction planted when she was very young. And indeed, Sonia Orwell was well equipped with potential demons in her youth. Her childhood was a colonial mess. Born in Calcutta, she had a father who died, perhaps by suicide, when she was a few months old, and a mother who remarried a year later to a man who was at least a drunk, if not a psychopath. When she was six, she was sent, as if to complete the gothic theme, to the same awful convent school that Antonia White attended and wrote about in *Frost in May*. Vicious nuns, a minimal education for middle-class marriage and – something, at least – a powerful enemy to kick against. As an adult she would spit on the street if she saw nuns. Earlier, she had a more sophisticated mode of expression. 'I'm so bored I wish I'd been birth-controlled so as not to exist,' she announced in the hearing of a nun at a school hockey match. For this one moment of perfectly aimed revenge, she is, in my view, to be forgiven everything. The drive-by shooting began much earlier than her nephew thought. The tough old warhorse began battling young and was, it seemed, pretty well equipped for the fight. This may well be what people so resented about her. She doesn't look much like a victim at any point in her life, even when things aren't going so well. There is something very slightly diminishing about placing her in the role of a woman at the mercy of her circumstances and wronged. Spurling describes an accident that happened to Sonia Orwell when she was seventeen and living with a family in Switzerland. Spurling offers it as a defining, life-long trauma. While sailing with three other young people the boat overturned in a sudden squall. Sonia headed for the shore but returned to the boat when she realised that the others were not following. They couldn't swim. Two of them went down and she tried to save the last boy who struggled against her in his panic and tried to pull her down with him. 'Unable to save him,' says Spurling, 'pushing him away, fighting in his clutches for her life, she tore free as he went down for the last time.' According to her biographer, 'Sonia never forgot the terrible embrace of a convulsive male body stronger than her own, and its even more terrible consequences.' Clearly, a dreadful experience. But Michael Sheldon, George Orwell's biographer and in Spurling's view one of those responsible for disparaging Sonia, has a slightly different take on the event. Interviewing her sister and half-brother, he claims that fearing for her life in the struggle with the boy she was trying to save, 'She grabbed him by the hair and pushed his head under water. She was able to hold him down for several seconds, and then she let go, thinking he would stop trying to fight her and would come to the surface. But he did not come up.' This is the story she told her mother and sister when she returned to England and Sheldon says, 'She later told the story to her half-brother, Michael, to whom she was very close, and she left no doubt in his mind that she considered herself responsible for the one boy's death. "I held him under," she said . . . A few of Sonia's close friends knew about the incident in Switzerland, but they were generally led to believe that the tragedy for her was simply that she was the lone survivor. She seems to have left out the details about her struggle with the drowning boy.'

Perhaps Hilary Spurling was one of those friends who got the more helplessly guilty version and, writing the memoir, simply related what she was told. It's a terrible enough tale. But the stronger story, that she fought against the boy's life for her own so that she felt responsible for his death, does not do her a greater disservice. The will to live of most 17 year olds is and should be very strong. It does however rather change the tone of the memory of that embrace of the 'convulsive male body, stronger than her own, and its even more terrible consequences'. She was dealing with something more than pure survivor guilt and she is not then or at any point as far as I can see a simple victim. Only in a very bi-polar world would that make her a simple villain.

Of course, the childhood Catholicism scored its troubling mark, as Spurling repeatedly insists. Her theory is that Sonia Orwell was permanently consumed with the crushing guilt which the Church is so adept at instilling: the kind of free-form guilt that just washes around waiting for any opportunity to overflow. The life is portrayed as driven essentially by revolt against her convent days, tempered by this guilt about which she could do nothing. Sex was one obvious way to kick against her upbringing, and she is known to have kicked vigorously. Spurling also suggests that her love, her worship even, of writing and painting was another form of rebellion against the conformity demanded by her schooling. Rebellion they might be, but sex and art are also sources of pleasure. There are worse ways of fighting back. But Spurling suggests that sex was not so much pleasure as weapon for Sonia. 'She would love many men, and sleep with many more but, for her, true love in its most intense and deepest form was not primarily sexual. On the two or three occasions when she broke this rule, the results were catastrophic.'

She left suburbia and found herself a world of arty glamour in Fitzrovia. She was the Euston Road Venus to William Coldstream, Victor Pasmore, Lucien Freud and other lovers who painted and adored her youth, her over-compensating fierceness of opinion, her looks and some mysterious sadness that she carried inside. She was an insecure, uneducated girl who glorified men who painted pictures and wrote books, who thought there was nothing better that could be done by a person, and who wanted to be part of their life. It wasn't hard for her. Older, very clever men were devoted to her. Cyril Connolly brought her into *Horizon* where she learnt fast, and eventually, to the chagrin of some who were not used to receiving editorial decisions from twenty-five-year-old women, more or less ran it, while its editors went off in search of love and sun. She went to France and was fêted by the likes of Michel Leiris, Lacan and Merleau-Ponty – who became the lost love of her life when she couldn't accept the French distinction between love (his wife) and *un amour* (herself). Merleau-Ponty, before he tired of her needy demands that he leave his wife, was 'transfixed . . . by the sorrow underlying her surface gaiety'. He delighted also in her practical take on the intellectual life, such as her description of spending time with Roland Barthes and Dionys Mascolo from Gallimard:

> They talked about civil war as one talks about a visit to the dentist. When they came to discussing how to make efficient bombs out of bottles with petrol, I could have knocked their heads together with rage, and I only refrained from screaming when they said any form of personal pleasure was a waste of time, because they were so busy getting tight and so pleased with the clothes they had bought on the black market that it became rather touching.

An old story of all mouth and no trousers, I think.

It must have been a heavenly time, and if the great love didn't work out and later life couldn't live up to it, it was surely an enviable youth. The sorrow, of course, was there, but it was a necessary attribute for a girl who wanted to be loved by wiser, older men. They are suckers for sadness.

She turned Orwell down at his first proposal, as did the several other women he asked to marry him at the same time. She slept with him, but only once, then Orwell went off to Jura to write *Nineteen Eighty-Four*, with Sonia as the model for the innately freedom-loving, contrary Julia: '. . . the girl from the fiction department . . . was very young, he thought, she still expected something from life . . . She would not accept it as a law of nature that the individual is always defeated . . .' Orwell asked Sonia again, not long after the split with Merleau-Ponty and this time she accepted. He was dying by then and his reputation was rising so, according to Michael Sheldon, Sonia accepted him with a view to becoming a rich, literary widow. Her friends say that Orwell wrote to her to say that he believed that marrying her would prolong his life, so, she told Spurling, 'you see, I had no choice.' He made her his executor and asked her to refuse all requests for a biography. Clearly, she had proved herself enough in the world of books for Orwell to trust her to be his literary widow. If it was not a love match, it apparently cheered Orwell up in his last three months, according to Anthony Powell, though it greatly annoyed Stephen Spender who resented being told by a snip of a girl to limit his political conversation with G.O. to twenty minutes.

Her next marriage was in 1958 to Michael Pitt-Rivers, who had been jailed four years earlier in the scandalous homosexuality trial that led the Wolfenden Committee to recommend legalisation. The marriage did not work out. Sonia was not a woman who married for love. Spurling doesn't dispute this, but says that she came to love both husbands and lost one while failing to convert the other. According to Natasha Spender, 'When [George] died, it was cataclysmic. She had persuaded herself she loved him intellectually, for his writing, but she found she *really* loved him.' As Sonia said to David Plante when he laughed about someone's dalliance, 'No one seems to understand what happens in human relationships, and the sadness of it all. It isn't anything to joke about. It really isn't.'

Both Plante and Spurling talk of her generosity, her capacity to turn up with small, delightful gifts to hearten the cheerless. She took on the even more difficult Jean Rhys in her old age and put up with no end of fuss and fume from her, recognising perhaps another talented beauty grown old and enraged. Plante found her refusal to talk about his deeper self painful. 'I wonder,' he asks her at lunch when she is complaining that one of her shelves is wonky, 'if I feel more isolated here in Europe than in America.' Her reply is deliciously Mad-Hatterish: 'You might as well ask if you'd feel isolated on Mars. The question doesn't have much consequence. No, no. Don't think about it. Now, I've got to get that shelf up properly, as I have some French house guests coming.' Self-absorbed, he calls her. A pairing made in heaven, I'd say.

The major complaints about Sonia Orwell come from those who wanted access to George's papers, especially potential biographers. She was fierce in her control of the estate, or doggedly loyal to her husband's wishes. To Spurling, her attempt to retain control of Orwell's estate and her failure to do so after a court case against the accountant who ran it, was the root cause of her death – a difficult one this, since she died of a brain tumour. At any rate, at the end of the 1970s she suddenly gave up the house in which she had held a literary salon and went to France, living in a bed-sitting room and shunning her friends. Reading was her only consolation. 'But when I put them down or when I wake up, it's all there again . . . this terrible endless tunnel into which I've drifted which, naturally, I feel is somehow all my fault but from which I'll never emerge again, but worse [I feel] that I've damaged George.' Michael Sheldon, on the other hand, sees her as battling to retain *her* rights and income.

Sonia Orwell was a good editor with a fine nose for talent, but she did not produce anything of her own. Instead, her life is an insight into the lives and times of others. According to Michael Sheldon, 'Orwell's widow, Sonia, who had married him only three months before his death and who was fifteen years his junior, had her opinions, one of which was, "He believed there is nothing

about a writer's life that is relevant to a judgement of his work."'
It seems her opinion was correct. Orwell himself wrote in an
essay on Salvador Dali, 'One ought to be able to hold in one's
head simultaneously the two facts that Dali is a good draughts-
man and a disgusting human being. The one does not invalidate
or, in a sense, affect the other.'

It's a kindness to want to rectify the denigration of friends
who cannot defend themselves. This memoir is plainly that, and
good-hearted. As to the truth, who knows? Perhaps, it is the best
kind of biography. Orwell might have thought so. Sonia never
wrote anything of her own, so nothing can be illuminated or
misconstrued except the subject herself. But to admire the capacity for art in others must surely make one wish to produce it
oneself. It may be that this was the final source of her sadness
when life was coming to a close and someone else's work was all
there was to fight for.

Perfectly Human

Lillie Langtry: Manners, Masks and Morals by Laura Beatty.
Chatto 1999

Véra (Mrs Vladimir Nabokov): Portrait of a Marriage
by Stacy Schiff. Random House 1999

Whatever the truth of the appealing though dubious proposition that by forty everyone has the face they deserve, it looks as if getting the biographer you deserve post-mortem is pretty much pot luck. Here are two beautiful, displaced, canny women with a powerful sense of their own purpose. For Stacy Schiff, the Véra Nabokov she introduces is 'the figure in the carpet . . . Hers was a life lived in the margins, but then as Nabokov teaches us – sometimes the commentary *is* the story.' Laura Beatty, however (including the word 'Morals' in the title for more than mere alliterative satisfaction), prefaces her tale of Lillie Langtry with the following deadly judgment: 'Motivation is the key to character, and Lillie's reasons for doing the things she did, range through panic and muddle to greed and plain wrong-thinking. She was after all seduced, and it will not be possible to exonerate her from the ultimate charges of corruption and betrayal of self . . . The genius is the only type of human whose agenda is pure enough for his [sic] motives to be incontrovertible. Lillie was not a genius.'

One of these women devoted her accidental gift of beauty to carving out a vivid, hectic and erratic life of her own, the other used her accidental gift of intelligence to support and protect the genius of the man in her life. Both women died quite sad and lonely, but then, dying sad and lonely is for humans close to tautologous; it proves, as Schiff understands and Beatty certainly doesn't, nothing much about the moral quality of a life.

It never becomes clear how, exactly, Lillie Langtry betrayed herself, or what the pure self she betrayed consisted of. In fact, self seems in Beatty's understanding to be coterminous with soul, an even more slippery notion, but one which enables what Nabokov called the biograffitist to thunder on both counts with all the moral fervour at her disposal that Lillie had 'sold her soul' and in the very first line that 'this is the story of a woman who sold her human nature for a legend.' The legend, essentially, is the one in Beatty's fevered mind of a Faustian compact, a Dorian Gray-like perversion of human destiny. But Lillie was just trying to make the best of things under the circumstances: a perfectly human way to proceed, I should have thought. As for her soul – who's to say?

Lillie had the good fortune not just to be born physically attractive ('What woman would not be beautiful if she had the chance?' she demands), but to have a philandering, radical Nonconformist Dean of Jersey as a father, who would have scorned the cant in the pages of his daughter's biography. Lillie herself showed a proper disrespect for moral outrage in the inscription she had written on the minstrels' gallery of the house the Prince of Wales had designed for her: 'They say – What say they? Let them say.' She was allowed to ramble carelessly through her childhood around the countryside with her six brothers, and then in 1874, at the age of 19, made the understandable error – wishing for something more than rural domesticity – of marrying the wrong man. Ned Langtry, then in his thirties, was neither as rich nor as fascinating as she had imagined, and the longed-for broadening of her provincial life turned out to be a charmless house on the fringes of Southampton, the social isolation of being a wife, and a near-fatal bout of typhoid. The doctor, egged on by his patient, prescribed London for the convalescent, and the convalescent prescribed for herself the great daily parade of seeing and being seen in Rotten Row, while Ned stayed home to begin his career of drink and debt.

She was seen.

> At first it seemed a very young and slender girl, dowdily dressed in black and wearing a small, close fitting black bonnet: she might have been a milliner's assistant . . . or a poorly paid governess hurrying to her pupils. As I drew near the pavement the girl looked up and I all but sat flat down in the road. For the first and only time in my life I beheld perfect beauty. The face was that of the lost Venus of Praxiteles, and of all the copies handed down to us must have been incomparably the best, yet Nature had not been satisfied and had thrown in two or three subtle improvements.

Doubtless the model-agency scout who spotted Kate Moss on a plane would have thought much the same as the painter Graham Robertson when he noticed Langtry walking past Apsley House. Lillie began her career as muse, model and archetype to the likes of Millais, Whistler, Burne-Jones, Watts and Poynter within the month. Society was just as quick to take her up. *Vanity Fair* gushed in 1877: 'All male London is going wild about the Beautiful Lady who has come to us from the Channel Islands . . . She has a husband to make her happy, but still awaits a poet to make her known.' Her husband most certainly did not make her happy, but Oscar Wilde volunteered for the poet's position and spent a night composing a poem to her on the steps of her house – 'To Helen, formerly of Troy, now of London' – and tutored her in Latin and Greek (essential languages for a goddess).

But it looks very much as if the plain black dress – and Langtry's grasp of the nature of style – was the key to her social triumph. When she arrived in London she was in mourning for her favourite brother, and due to poverty, that black dress was the only one she had. London society, coutured to within an inch of its life and bored to distraction, was enchanted by such stark simplicity, unable to imagine the condition of having no alternative. The Prince of Wales and all her other lovers adored it. Lillie's genius was in retaining the dress for as long as she could, collar turned in or out according to the time of day, until it was deliberately borrowed and trashed by her friend Lady Cornwallis West, when she had another black dress made. Her first downfall was a failure of style, not soul. She put herself into irreparable debt and lost her uniqueness when she finally ordered a full and fashionable wardrobe of frocks to die for.

What lies at the heart of Laura Beatty's condemnation, however, is the notion that she exchanged true love for a career. Beatty's contribution to Langtry's biography is the discovery of letters to her lover Arthur Jones. Most of what we know of the woman is gossip-column scandal and her own heavily massaged memoirs. She destroyed her own papers, and told her story as she wished it to be heard. Arthur Jones may or may not have been the father of her secret child; it was just as likely that Jeanne was the daughter of the Prince of Wales or Louis Battenberg. But he accepted the role, from something of a distance, and while she hid in Jersey she wrote the letters that suggest to Beatty that he was the real love of her life.

You *won't* go back my darling till you know what I am going to do. *Please* promise not to. If you love me you can't be so unkind as to leave me . . . You are very unkind not to write to me . . . The sea is dreadfully rough. Do come Artie for Heaven's sake if you care for me . . . You must try to get back to help me more . . . won't you darling. I always have you at all events darling haven't I? To care for me whatever happens.

Given the circumstances (the Prince of Wales supplied money and kept the bamboozled husband out of the way, but he was not going to admit paternity; Battenberg was sent overseas for a year by his alarmed family), it could as well have been that she was desperate to keep him standing by her and the baby. In the end, however, she knew from her experience of going home to find the bailiffs sitting in the hallway and Ned dead drunk upstairs, that someone had to earn a living, and if it was to be her it would be at the expense of romantic love. Jones was no better a bet than her other lovers – she had execrable taste in men or had the misfortune to be the taste of execrable men – gambling and drinking and making vague promises of his presence while she begged him to visit her in her seclusion and depression and take charge of her life.

So Jones faded out and Lillie pulled herself together. This, Beatty claims, was her 'terrible exchange: money and fame for the security of self'. It was, you might think, no more than survival, what anyone must do when there is no one and nothing to fall back on. When her social and artistic triumph waned, she took acting lessons from Ellen Terry, knowing herself to be no natural on stage, but marketing her beauty and notoriety as she had to. She took off for and stormed America and its cattle and railroad millionaires and when that palled, she returned home, adjusted to reality yet again and played the music halls. Finally, in her fifties, exchanging a fading mask of beauty for a mask of masculinity, she took up a life of racing. Since the Jockey Club only admitted men, she became Mr Jersey in order to race her stable of horses. Beatty, positively smacking her lips, sees some form of nemesis in this: 'Photographs at this time' – 1910 – 'show her mouth set, at her most masculine, in an attempt to drown out the voices of her lost past. She towers, inappropriately in white lace, over slight young men at Goodwood, or stamps down the London pavements military style, lantern-jawed, heavily upholstered, arms swinging, toes turned out. Gone are the soft smile, the curves and the sleepily sensuous eyes. Now she is angry and huge and male.' Not only beauty, but independence and achievement, too, are indeed in the eye of the beholder.

Doubtless, Laura Beatty would have approved of Véra Nabokov, who grew more beautiful with age and remained a wisp of a thing. Proof perhaps that devotion of the heart is good for the complexion. There was nothing monstrous about Véra, except perhaps her capacity to divest herself of herself. 'She had both the good and the ill fortune to recognise another's gift; her devotion to it allowed her to exempt herself from her own life while founding a very solid existence on that very selflessness.' Or if she is a monster, she is a Nabokovian monster, and is well served by Stacy Schiff who understands mirrors, magicians and doppelgangers well enough to appreciate the double creation that was V.N. and V.N., and who has the wit and style to eschew moral judgment for something more perceptive. 'Véra saw her husband always before her; he saw her image of him. This optics-defying arrangement sustained them at a time and in a place when little else did; it was the first in what was to be a repertoire of deceptive techniques, for which the couple had only begun their magic act.'

Véra wore an actual mask at their first rendezvous – a promise to the man she had clearly studied of what was to come. Thereafter for more than fifty years she earned money, typed, edited, corrected, corresponded for, drove, agented, protected, cleared snow from the car, and whole-heartedly agreed about everything with the man of whom she made her life. She was, according to friends, 'the international champion in the Wife-of-Writer Competition', 'the Saint Sebastian of wives'. The marriage and Vladimir's artistic greatness, as they both perceived it, was the only real country to which either of them belonged once each had been geographically exiled. Their son, Dmitri, was given residential rights, though he must have felt an exile of another kind. They never settled anywhere (their final 30 years in a hotel in Montreux was to both of them provisional) except with each other. Véra was the keeper of the flame, the muse who was 'the shadowy figure in the foreground' of Vladimir's life and work. When a friend suggested she needed a rest she responded: 'V. is the one who works very hard (I do write an enormous number of letters, also an occasional contract, and I read proofs and translations, but this is nothing compared to his work).' Vladimir was her sense of self, and if that sticks in the onlooker's craw, her power was more than felt by those who tried to get in touch with the great man, professionals, fans, friends or even family. She conducted his life with the world at large; sometimes she signed his name to letters she wrote, at others it was V. Nabokov, Mrs Vladimir Nabokov, Véra Nabokov and for special occasions, J.G. Smith. Those in the know addressed themselves to the complete set; 'Dear V. and V.'.

Véra's individuality was most publicly evident in her Jewishness. Unlike her husband, she was a double exile: a refugee from the Bolsheviks and from Russian anti-semitism. She lost no opportunity to remind the Gentile world that she was Jewish. In pre-war Berlin she was advised to apply for a stenographer's job in the office of a German minister organising an international congress. 'I said "they won't engage me, don't forget I'm Jewish."' When she applied and got the job, she recalled querying the decision: '"but are you sure you want me? I'm Jewish" . . . "Oh," he said, "but it does not make *any* difference. We pay no attention to such things. Who told you we did?"' In 1958 she wrote to the *New York Post*: 'In your article you describe me as an émigré of the *Russian* aristocratic class. I am very proud of my ancestry which actually is Jewish.' When she was asked if she was Russian she replied: 'Yes, Russian and Jewish.' She was appalled when her sister Lena, living in Sweden, renounced her Judaism, or as one family member happily put it, had 'gone the whole hog into Catholicism'. When, in 1959, not having seen Lena for years, she considered making a visit, Véra wrote first: 'I have one question to ask you. Does Michaël' – Lena's son – 'know that you are Jewish, and that consequently he is half-Jewish himself? . . . I must admit that if M. does not know who he is there would be no sense in my coming to see you, since for me no relationship would be possible unless based on complete truth and sincerity . . . Please answer this question frankly. It is a very important one for me.' Lena wrote back fiercely that Michaël knew very well who his ancestors were, but that Véra had escaped much of the difficulty when she left Europe in 1940. 'You were not involved in the war. You didn't see people die, or be tortured. You don't understand what it is to barely escape a violent death. I did that twice. You don't know what it is to, alone, build a life for two.' The sisters remained estranged.

The editing of past events that Laura Beatty so disapproves of in Lillie Langtry, is taken to its highest form by Véra Nabokov. 'She engaged in a veritable cult of denials. She swore up and down that she had never said a single word Boyd quoted her as saying; she abjured all marginal notes, even those in her firm hand; she went so far as to deny to a reporter that she was proud of Dmitri.' The perfect marriage was not without its troubles. Fourteen years into it, Nabokov fell passionately in love with Irina Guadanini in Paris and wrote extensively to tell her so. Véra, living with his confession and the reality of his affair, dealt with it by never mentioning Irina. 'I know what she is thinking,' Nabokov wrote to Irina. 'She is convincing herself and me (without words) that you are a hallucination.' The affair came to an end when Vladimir, deciding as any sensible genius would to go for reliability, announced to Irina that 'he could not slam the door on the rest of his life'. Véra attempted to deny the whole event to Boyd until he told her that Guadanini, more concerned about her own life than Véra could imagine, had kept the letters in spite of Vladimir's own attempt to expunge reality by asking for them back and claiming that they contained 'mostly fictions'. At Wellesley, Vladimir mooned over several of his students, 'kissing and fondling' one young woman who testified: 'He did like young girls. Not just *little* girls.' She claimed he told her: 'I like small-breasted women.' In the margins of Andrew Field's biography, where this is cited, Véra – displaying the makings of a sense of humour – denies the truth of the quote: 'No, never! Impossible for a Russian.'

What counted for Véra was the fiction, the suppression of fact was merely in the cause of that overarching good. In this sense, Véra was not so much the sorcerer's apprentice as the magician herself. Vladimir had little patience with his own reality, explaining, as Schiff says, that 'the living, breathing breakfasting Nabokov was but the poor relation of the writer, only too happy to refer to himself as "the person I usually impersonate in Montreux".' 'It is a false idea to imagine a real Nabokov,' their friend Jason Epstein concluded. The reality of the life was for the two of them alone, only the writing and the selling of the books mattered, and Véra attended to that with the tenacity of a literary rottweiler. 'It was her fervent and unreasonable conviction that books should be accurately translated, properly printed, appropriately jacketed, aggressively marketed, energetically advertised . . . she seemed to believe that [royalty statements] should be intelligible and arrive punctually.' This was Véra's life, and Schiff contends plausibly that it was only different in detail from that of any other good wife: 'It has been noted that women are accustomed to tending to chores that are repetitive in nature, tasks that are undone as soon as they are accomplished. The pursuit of the accurate royalty statement, of the carefully proofread manuscript, were not the Sisyphean labours those who first observed this phenomenon had in mind. But they constituted the dusting and vacuuming of Véra Nabokov's life.' Véra is the devoted wife that all writers, regardless of gender, long for and for whom the most passionate believer in the right of individuals to pursue their own destiny might well give up his or her principles. Who knows what lurked underneath her passion for her husband's art, what might have been? She was a kind of art form herself. Seconds after Vladimir Nabokov died, 'a Lausanne nurse precipitated herself bodily upon Véra with condolences. Véra pushed her away with an acid, "S'il vous plaît, Madame."' And yet, after her son drove her back from the hospital that day, Véra sat in silence in his car for a few minutes and 'then uttered the one desperate line Dmitri ever heard escape her lips: "Let's rent an airplane and crash."'

A Slut's Slut

Dangerous Muse: A Life of Caroline Blackwood by Nancy
Schoenberger. Weidenfeld & Nicolson 2002

At the age of 86 and with a broken hip, the Marchesa Casa
Maury was interviewed by Caroline Blackwood for her book about
the last dreadful days – months, years rather – of the Duchess of
Windsor. The Marchesa had been the Duke's mistress for fifteen
years when Wallis Simpson arrived on the scene. Blackwood
explained to the old lady how the Duchess was being sequestered
in Paris by her lawyer maître Suzanne Blum who was obsessed
with her, and that she was officiously being kept alive, although
rumoured to be comatose, to have turned black and to have shriv-
elled to the size of a doll. The ancient Marchesa began shaking
with laughter and continued until tears ran down her cheeks. She
managed to pull herself together, but as Blackwood was leaving,
started to laugh again as she tried to apologise for her behaviour. 'I
really shouldn't find it so funny. It's awful of me to laugh about it.
Do you promise you didn't invent it all? There's something so
comic about the situation. It's the idea of that horrible old lady
being locked up by another horrible old lady . . .'

Blackwood prefaces the book with a reader's note that is

perhaps something more than just an attempt at a legal disclaimer: '*The Last of the Duchess* is not intended to be read as a straight biographical work. It is an entertainment, an examination of the fatal effects of myth, a dark fairytale.' All the old ladies were long dead by the time the book saw the light of day, and Caroline Blackwood, though not so very old a lady at 63, was physically wrecked by booze and in fact had only a year to live, so who knows if one horrible old lady really shrieked with laughter about the fate of all the other horrible old ladies? What is certain is that malevolence is in the air, a view of life as black as the Duchess of Windsor's old hide, a scent of sulphurous gloating wit stemming from a very particular vision of the way of the world.

Most of Blackwood's fictions or near-fictions are dark fairytales. There are wicked stepmothers, doomed children, malicious harridans, knights in shining wheelchairs and none of them are fully alive enough to drown out the cackling of their creator: Lady Caroline the baleful. Isherwood met her in Hollywood in the mid-1950s. 'Caroline was dull, too; because she is only capable of thinking negatively. Confronted by a phenomenon, she asks herself: what is wrong with it?' The former wife of Grey Gowrie was a friend. 'If you sat in a car with her, and you were driving, and she was a passenger, at every crossroad she saw someone being run over and being mangled. Almost every minute of her life she saw an appalling disaster happening right in front of her eyes . . . that's the life of somebody who's involved with alcohol.' Or perhaps why someone gets involved with alcohol in the first place.

All this makes her, of course, prime biographical material. Elemental (not to say elementary) fictions written by a Guinness heiress with a title from the Anglo-Irish aristocracy, give her biographer no end of clues to a wayward, drink-sodden, chaos creating life. And the disordered, self-and-other-destructive life offers all manner of interpretations of the fiction. Nancy Schoenberger is not interested in literary criticism; Blackwood's books (along with the poetry of Robert Lowell and the painting of Lucian Freud) are discussed entirely with reference to the life. To do this is some-what to demean a writer, I would have thought, but perhaps it is true that Caroline Blackwood's life-in-its-time is of more interest finally than her work. These days biography sells like hot cakes, and perhaps we are moving to a point where fiction is being seen to be no more than a useful biographical resource.

Blackwood's Lady-Carolineness, her unhappy childhood, busy sex life, connections to major figures in art and literature, and gaudy drinking does make her a toothsome biographical subject. As indeed she must have realised. Schoenberger was suggested by a neighbour to Blackwood, by then living in Long Island, when she said she was looking for a biographer. They spoke on the phone, but Blackwood went into hospital for a cancer operation the day Schoenberger arrived in Sag Harbour, and died in New York two weeks later, so that they never met. As a result, apart from assis-tance from Blackwood's sister Perdita, Schoenberger found herself writing an 'opposed biography', as the adult children eventually refused to co-operate. All grist to the mill. 'Once I got to know Caroline better, I understood why.' The witchiness of Caroline Blackwood is dangled at the reader before the book starts, in the acknowledgements. The biographer began to feel haunted by her subject (don't they all?) and when Schoenberger had a car accident after having returned from seeing Blackwood's daughter, Eugenia reacts with 'I bet you were thinking about my mother when you hit that car.' Making a surprise visit to Lady Maureen Dufferin, Caroline's mother, she bends to pick up a scrap of paper from the front step. It reads, 'Just remember I am a witch.' Ooh er.

John Houston referred to the three Guinness girls, one of whom, Maureen, was Blackwood's mother, as 'lovely witches'. To say that someone was brought up as a wealthy, landed aristocrat (moneyed, narcissistic mother, aristocratic fey father) is almost tantamount to saying that they had a deprived childhood. To have a rich, deprived childhood is probably no better than having an impoverished one; at any rate it's arguable. The Blackwood children (Caroline, Perdita and Sheridan) were half-starved, beaten and neglected by a series of vicious nannies. Still, there was scope for narrative and adventure. They had each other, and like babes in the wood, they were given titbits to eat by their Irish tenants who felt sorry for them. Like children in an Arthur Ransome or C. S. Lewis novel, they rambled unnoticed around the great house and were given to disappearing on their bicycles up the dual carriageway to the nearby town.

It is well known in the world of fairytale and post-Freudian analysis that it is not a good thing for a child to have a wicked witch, especially a lovely wicked witch, as a mother. It is also probably not a good thing, in the world of getting on with your life, if you happen to have such a parent, to be too eager to perceive yourself as doomed by story and psychoanalytic theory. Both Blackwood and her biographer see her as doomed by her beginnings. Becoming what she did it was clear, if somewhat teleological, that she could not have been anything else. Having a self-regarding, unaffectionate mother makes it perfectly understandable that Blackwood would, in an attempt to escape her third husband, Robert Lowell, in a manic phase, leave her eldest daughter, Natalya, aged fifteen, alone in their London flat without any money. It is taken as inevitable that patterns are inevitably repeated. Blackwood becomes a lifelong drunk given to hysterical and unsuccessful relationships, and it is no surprise that Natalya dies of a heroin overdose at the age of 17. Blackwood is acknowledged even by her friends as having some responsibility for this, not least because two years before she had published *The Stepdaughter* which has in it a savage portrait of a fat, unhappy, dim-witted and doomed adolescent who everyone

saw as the less-than-loved Natalya. Ivana, aged six, suffered third
degree burns when she tripped over the lead of a kettle of boiling
water and friends thought the chaotic house and Blackwood's
drunken neglect had something to do with the accident.
Schoenberger tries to smooth out the general judgement.
'Caroline would always acknowledge how important her children
were to her, but her ability to look after them was becoming
increasingly impaired.' The blame is muted, because, in retrospect, what else could possibly have happened? If you were not
loved and taken care of then you can't be expected to love and
care for other people, other than destructively. This is now so
irrefutable a truism that it is the unquestioned basis for most
biography. Strange that the very generation who decided that
they would not be dominated by biology should have so completely accepted their psychoanalytically prophesied destiny.

In fact, not very much is made of Blackwood's conformity
with her times, when it was frightfully fashionable for the upper
classes to mingle with louche artistic types – and, of course, vice
versa. She met Lucian Freud in the early 1950s at a party given
by Lady Rothermere. He was the beautiful untidy young man
standing at the back next to Francis Bacon and booing loudly
while everyone else clapped Princess Margaret's execrable ren-
dering of a Cole Porter medley. Here, nicely arrayed, are the
components of the Bohemian life of that period. Scruffy, wild
and very good-looking artists (geniuses only – and no harm if
they come with very famous grandfathers) drank and pranked
as licensed fools among the aristocracy who included them on
their party lists and popped into the Gargoyle and Colony
clubs with them in search of a little edge. Few of the Soho mob
could have been more satisfactory than Freud, dismissive and yet
a devout social climber attendant on his upper-class sponsors.
He munched a bouquet of purple orchids, but, in spite of her
voice, 'accompanied Princess Margaret to night-clubs wearing

saffron socks' (Freud, I think), and put up with the ingrained anti-semitism of his chosen milieu. Evelyn Waugh called him that 'terrible Yid . . . a jewish [*sic*] hanger-on . . . called "Freud" . . . He has very long black side-whiskers and a thin nose'. Well obviously, wealthy (her unloving mother had settled the astonishingly large sum of £17,030 a year on each of her children in 1949) and angry Caroline was going to marry the man. And of course the man was going to divorce his wife and marry Lady Caroline. Soho life was very seductive for a poor little rich girl who was also very beautiful. Her lovers included all the right intellectuals, and there were degree courses to be had in drinking yourself stupid at the Soho academies in Dean Street and Old Compton Street. To be accepted by Muriel at the Colony Club and Gaston at the French Pub had a kudos that made up for the twilit and self-conscious life of a Soho drunk. Self-image was as important then as it is now. In Rome she found the men who hung about her unacceptable, except for one who stroked her bare arms and said, 'Morbida' which means 'soft'. Her ex-lover, screenwriter Ivan Moffat, explains: 'She couldn't speak Italian, really. So she thought, "Ah, here's a man who knows what he's talking about", so she invited him up . . . it wasn't until the next day that she came to know what he meant.' Moffat tells this, as Blackwood must have told him, as a joke. 'A very disillusioning story – but funny! It told me a lot about Caroline Blackwood.' Schoenberger intones, more solemnly, that it 'revealed to him an essential aspect of her nature'. She was also conscious of her origins and never let go of being *Lady* Caroline. According to Ian Hamilton, 'she had a kind of aristocratic sense of entitlement and was capable of great vindictiveness when she *didn't* get what she wanted.'

Not only was she beautiful, smart and a Lady, but she could fund the arts – or at any rate her chosen artists. She bought houses in London and the country for her brilliant but broke husbands. Between inspiring and housing Lucian Freud (Caroline is Girl on a Bed) and Robert Lowell (Caroline is The Dolphin) she married Israel Citkowitz, a composer considered by Aaron Copland to be a genius, with whom she had two of her three children (though Ivana it turned out was, as her name might have suggested to anyone paying attention, Ivan Moffat's daughter). Citkowitz had already given up composing, being too clever or lazy or something, and became Blackwood's house-husband, doing the childcare, cleaning up, shopping and cooking. This was fortunate because Blackwood was epically undomesticated and usually too drunk to notice that the cigarette butts she threw on the floor were still alight. Citkowitz continued in this role after Blackwood married Lowell, living on the middle floor of the London house, taking care of the children who resided on the ground floor, along with a series of passing nannies and au pairs. Caroline and Robert had the top flat in which to be mad, bad and dangerous to know to their hearts' discontent.

Like a proper upper-class girl, Blackwood was a slut's slut. She is variously described by those who knew her as filthy, unwashed, careless with her hygiene, stinking, and it took no more than a few days for her to reduce a room to a fearsome slum. Lowell's friends describe a visit to their New York apartment: 'The squalor was unbelievable. There were bloody sanitary napkins on the floor; cigarette butts, bottles of liquor, and empty pill boxes were scattered around the room. It looked like the room of an addict.' Towards the end of her life Blackwood visited Stephen Aronson in a borrowed house in Long Island. Aronson placed buckets of water all along the corridor leading to her room for fear of a fire hazard from her cigarette ends. After she left the maid arrived to clean up and went into the room Blackwood had occupied. '. . . she backed right out and said, "Mr Aronson, don't go in there." . . . she reported that it was chaos, with empty pill bottles and vodka bottles strewn all over the floor, and "an acrid, all-too-identifiable odour."' Aronson learned later from a friend in the industry that Caroline 'was on a list that hoteliers keep of undesirable guests'. How else is a rich, upper-class rebel to behave? Perdita took to breeding horses and running a charitable riding school for disabled children; Sheridan inherited the grand house, married amiably and died of Aids. Someone had to be Caroline.

However, what makes Blackwood more than just good biography bait is that there isn't only the grand guignol life, there is the work. She was a serious alcoholic but she took Bacon as her model when it came to productivity. She might down a couple of bottles of vodka a day, but once the marriage to Lowell was over, she wrote doggedly most mornings and produced a decent body of work in a short period, fiction and non-fiction. She was not content, as Schoenberger says, to be a beautiful muse. Really, the time for muses was past. By the 1950s even beautiful women either drank themselves to death or finally got round to doing some work. And the work is at the very least interesting, even if not, as the press handout bizarrely suggests, comparable to that of Edna O'Brien, Iris Murdoch, Muriel Spark and Samuel Beckett (though I wish just for the sake of the gaiety of the nation that someone's work was comparable with all those writers).

The writing strains towards being very good, but is sabotaged by fear. Blackwood's friends are agreed that she saw only the bleakest, most negative aspects of the world and the people in it, and it is surely from that place in her that she writes. According to Barbara Skelton, Caroline 'on hearing of someone's ghastly misfortune . . . would double up laughing'. Both as a woman of her time and the woman that she was, she maintains the coldest eye she can manage, shying away from sentimentality as if it were death itself. Death, indeed, seems to be preferable. The cruelty of the stepmother in her first novel is virtually unrelieved, apart from a moment of faint decency that is immediately rendered irrelevant by the disappearance and probable death of the stepdaughter. The characters in the very similar stories *Good Night Sweet Ladies* share cosmic self-centredness and, while they might discomfort others, have no larger view than their own troubles. The reader is not offered anyone or anything to like in Blackwood's fictions, the bleakness of the vision is everything, even in the spuriously upbeat ending of *Corrigan* where the con artist turns out to have made a sad old woman very happy in her last months by permitting her to live an illusion. But although the place she writes from is an authentic writer's place, the fiction is not greatly helped by the entirely unilateral vision: a tunnel rather than the truthful vision it is supposed to be. The novels, though strange and intriguing, are slight, because for all their capacity to look into the void, they shed no light on it. They describe pathologies of varying degrees, give no quarter, lack any generosity; finally you say *so what?* They are indeed dark fairytales, and they have the rigidity of fairytales. Sentimentality is a very bad thing in the writer, but simply to deny its existence and its expression in the writing is to avoid one of the central textures of human life. The fear of sentimentality in the end condemns the work to smallness. Sentimentality comes to equate with all feeling and emotion, and the lack of sentimentality adds up to little more than a superficial wit and cleverness. The books show a sliver of the world, but offer no more truth about it and the nature of human beings than the coyest of romantic fiction. Even the laughing old Marchesa stopped for a moment between cackles: "'Love affairs . . . They don't really matter in the end. They seem so important at the time. But in the end they don't matter . . . I wonder what does matter in the end." She seemed bewildered. "Family, I suppose . . . I had all my grandchildren around here the other day." Her face lit up. "It was amazing to find oneself head of such a large, lovely clan."' Perhaps if Caroline Blackwood could have hit on something that mattered, her work might have loomed larger than her biography.

Turn the Light Off, Please

A Slight and Delicate Creature: The Memoirs of Margaret
Cook. Weidenfeld & Nicolson 1999

The problem with Nancy Mitford, according to one of her sisters (The communist? Possibly. The Duchess? Probably. The troublesome, giggly one who fancied Hitler? Not likely), is that she never came first with anyone. It's doubtful if coming first is actually part of the human birthright, but it does seem to feel as if it is, both to those who do come first with someone, and those who don't. Coming first is coterminous with being loved, which is a definition of having a place to stand in the world, but to a weary eye it seems a pretty unlikely proposition. Coming second is a more reasonable ambition, because surely only your own self can be relied upon to put you first. This is a discovery everyone makes sooner or later: if sooner you may end up a little bitter and twisted, but you will avoid great disappointment; if later you will almost certainly take to your word processor and key in the story of your life. Historians in the future, historians in the present worry, will be overwhelmed by the avalanche of primary sources lying around on floppy discs. History itself will be choked to death by information overload. Everyone has a story to tell and eventually in a bid to come first with themselves and posterity, everyone will have committed their story in its unedited detail to paper. Among these mounds of autobiography will be Margaret Cook's effort at self-valuation. It may be all the historian needs to find, for it is a classic of the genre. Dr Cook's memoir has, unlike most of these productions, been professionally published, but that is the consolation prize she received for having had the misfortune or bad judgement to be married for thirty years to the current foreign secretary.

Robin Cook most certainly comes second in his ex-wife's memoirs. It is wishful thinking on the part of excitement seekers to call the book an act of revenge; the main thing is the transformation of Margaret Cook from a woman barely noticed during a long marriage and summarily dismissed at the end of it ('What would you do if I . . . committed suicide?' 'I should, of course, be sorry . . .'), into a person with a life and achievements of her own. Carried through to its logical conclusion, with no mention of Robin Cook at all, the book could in fact have been a masterpiece of revenge literature, but that project was scotched by the publishers and serialisers who, true to human form, did not put Margaret Cook and her best interests first, offering money and fame only on condition that she dished some dirt on her more famous husband. Dr Cook, revealed as nothing if not a realist in her memoirs, obliged, but halfheartedly, and thereby sullied the perfect retribution of her self-regarding husband by failing to ignore him altogether, and disappointed the hopes of the salacious (that is, me and probably you) by insisting on presenting herself as the more interesting of the two of them.

There is no point in reading Dr Cook's book for insight into the politics and personalities with whom Robin Cook was involved during Margaret's time. She met Gordon Brown just after her marriage, but she has 'little remaining impression of

Gordon, whom I have met only once or twice since then, and he seems, like many famous people who start their careers almost as child prodigies, to have suffered burn-out of his private personality. This may be an erroneous impression, fostered by years of Robin's unconcealed antipathy.' Cook's other antipathies are noted, against Bob Cryer, John Prescott and Roy Hattersley ('Try as I may, I cannot remember what the agony was all about . . .'). His failed ambitions are mulled over. After John Smith's death he considered his possibilities and decided he did not have enough support. 'I did not believe, frankly, that he was the right person for the job. There was a lot of very foolish talk in the press about his lack of good looks, but this would not have mattered if he had shown greater capacity for relating to people.' The leader in waiting is a mystery to her. 'I had never met Tony, and knew next to nothing about him; indeed, it was my perception that he'd popped up from nowhere with little to recommend him other than a pretty face.' But everything, the devolution and unilateral disarmament debates, the formation of New Labour, the Falklands and the Gulf War, the winning back of power by Labour, are all subsumed to her own family and career story, mere signs of the passing of time.

The fact that she cannot write has been mentioned a good deal in reviews, but it is the way in which she does write that is more interesting. The much put-upon future historian wading through the 50 million or so autobiographies will discover that there is a notion that *writing* is a requirement of the genre. Almost certainly, Dr Cook, who is a haematologist, writes up her patient notes in a plain and decent English, but sitting down to write a book, she knows she must have a style, and the style of choice, as if there were no choice, is the kind of genteel archaic over which, I am sure, she has taken infinite trouble. Heat is 'unwonted', people do not get out of cars and walk but are 'decanted' into lounges, letters are 'missives', previous is 'erstwhile', 'forthwith' is ubiquitous, and no one is ever to be described as merely *saying* anything:

> 'Did you cancel the papers?' I ventured.
> He exploded, 'No, of course not, how – '
> I interjected calmly, 'Okay, I'll do it.'

When the gentility collides with the wish to seem informed, informing and interesting, there is genuine delight for the reader: 'I was also visited by wonderful dreams about flying which I later learned are said to be an indication of sexual desire. Whether or not this is true, the dreams were deliciously exciting, though having to stay airborne required much concentration . . . I'm regretful that I no longer have these dreams. Vague erotic fantasies, undirected to any particular person, and centred on excretory function formed another intensely private experience.'

Along with her inner erotic life, we are given complete details of her struggles to study for and pass ten 'O' levels (correction: 'I had become very specialist now, studying only physics, chemistry and biology in preparation for A and S levels: and some maths in order to do additional maths O level (my eleventh) that year'), 'A' levels, piano grades, medical exams, postgraduate qualifications and subsequent promotion efforts. Other achievements are recalled such as the dirndl skirt in check gingham she sewed in 1953 and the subsequent red checked gingham rabbit she made (having finished her skirt before anyone else) which won first prize in the local arts and crafts show (children's class).

This may be more than you wish to know about the young Margaret Cook, but perhaps the nature of autobiography is precisely that it is all more than you wish to know about another person with whom you are not presently infatuated. For reasons that doubtless have more to do with my childhood than professional integrity, I feel obliged to read every word of any book I review, but though I doggedly and probably neurotically followed Dr Cook through all her youthful adventures, I confess to skipping pages and pages devoted to the various horses she owned and her sensitive anguish at their individual experiences of croup or colic or whatever it is that horses are inclined to suffer from. We all have our limits.

I did however take full note, and pass on to you, her tremendous early success with men. Chapter 10 is entitled, as it has to be, And So To Bed. When she begins an affair with her drama teacher, she gives boyfriend Edward his 'marching orders'. It was brutal and without warning but although she felt bad about it, 'one cannot dissemble under these circumstances'. At Edinburgh University 'I had dates with eighteen different fellows in my first term alone.' She was, you see, popular; she had a choice, lots of choices; she did not have to marry the sombre and arrogant young red-haired man who was secretary of the debating society when she became its publicity convenor. As the reader's heart leaps with relief as at last Robin saunters into view, she reiterates, 'I continued to have a succession of boyfriends; as soon as one liaison ended someone else was waiting in the wings.' The wise reader draws a deep breath and understands that she must wait patiently just a little longer before Margaret feels quite validated enough to get cracking on the subject of her future husband.

It all began during a clinch in a taxi after what must have been an unusually erotically charged debate on the motion that 'The world owes less to Marx and Lenin than to Marks and Spencer.' We are told of the clinch, of the re-routing of the taxi to his place, of the ease of conversation and finally matters come to a head.

'When you touch a person it can completely change your perception of him. Messages are imparted and received well below cerebral level. My sensorium went into overdrive that night, accepting and welcoming my alter ego.'

Translated into the first sexual encounter between young

Margaret and the even younger Robin (he was 18 months her junior, but he had read most of Dickens by the time he was ten, she explains) this too might be more than you wish to know, or dare to visualise, but as if aware of her readers' potential discomfort she excuses us: 'But now I shall ask my reader to withdraw discreetly from the room, and turn the light off, please.' This reader very nearly broke her mind's ankle over the coffee things left thoughtlessly on the floor, so rapidly was she absenting herself from what Margaret describes as the Cooks' sacrosanct moment. The bit where the fairy tales end came fairly rapidly. After a few days spent mostly in bed, apparently admiring her French tan, he announced that he was falling in love with her. Immediately following this he wanted her to have his baby, and then, just two weeks into the romance (possibly with an eye to the inadvisability of having a love child blight any future political career) he asked her to marry him. She said she'd think about it. He looked crestfallen. She said yes. And they did not live happily ever after.

Let's get the aesthetics out of the way. Dr Cook has enough good taste not to dwell on the looks of her husband, but not so much as to ignore the subject completely. She believes she must have been responding to a question of his about his appearance when she told him, 'You're not classically handsome, but by no means ugly.' Though appearance was not uppermost in her mind when it came to men, she 'did not like obese men and preferred to look upon an elegant and graceful form; which, it must be said, Robin did not have. But he had interesting green eyes and a fair complexion.' She is, in fact, a mistress of diminishment, a skilled practitioner in the art of damning with faint praise. She worried about the way her 'rather colourful love life contrasted with his . . . he had had so little opportunity to sow his wild oats, and I felt there was a distinct risk that he would seek to do it later, particularly as he, competitive in this as in virtually everything, also felt at a disadvantage.' Although he 'lacked the qualities required to make friends easily . . . some people like to associate with him because his intelligence and dominance had a certain magnetism; this was one feature that attracted me.'

As the years roll on, Margaret Cook puts up with her husband's tantrums, his remoteness, his absences, mostly in the name of the sacredness of the family. When he first admits to an affair in 1987, he asks for five others to be taken into consideration (whether he is cleansing his soul or boasting is not clear), but Margaret is most outraged that he chooses to tell her at the moment when she was 'breaking my heart' over her horse which earlier that day broke its leg and had to be put down. This has a ring of truth about it. Margaret's heart is for her horses, Robin's for his political career. Least taxing for both of them, you suspect, are emotional entanglements. His long affair with his secretary, Gaynor, was tolerated by Margaret, who moved him out of her bed (largely on health grounds) but maintained public and familial relations with him. Apart from those remembered febrile first two weeks, passion is not the subject of the Cooks' marriage. She feels hard done by not so much for being rejected by her loved one, as in the method and the timing of her ousting. She had had only a single visit to Chevening as the wife of the Foreign Secretary before the marriage came to an end. She felt this badly. 'It might be deemed appropriate, or even artistic, to protest that I wish I had never visited Chevening, since I was only to enjoy it for one solitary weekend.' She concedes, 'I am not ashamed to admit that of course I regretted the loss of those privileges that came to me as wife of the Foreign Secretary, though they were way down the scale of afflictions.'

The marriage is brought to an end by New Labour, rather than by husband or wife. With the threat of exposure by the *News of the World*, mobile phones go berserk as the Cooks arrive at Heathrow for a three week riding holiday in Montana (*and* she'd bought him lovely new green suede chaps for the occasion). Alistair Campbell and Tony Blair instruct Cook to end his marriage there and then. The consensus is that he must not do a Parkinson and dump the mistress in an incredible attempt to prove loyalty to the old wife, but that New Labour style dictates New Marriage with the dumping of the wife and the marrying of the mistress. In the current corridors of power, heterosexual love conquers all, or at least averts a needless resignation. According to Margaret, they were merely trying to save the Foreign Secretary's bacon. She remembered what he said when he first confessed the affair with Gaynor: 'It's been going on for two years now. It's very foolish and I've wanted to end it many times, but she just won't let me.' When the affair continued, she saw that Gaynor 'could make life very unpleasant if he treated her badly. Possibly there had been threats.'

The former Mrs Cook received a letter of condolence from Tony Blair for her distress in being caught up in a media storm, but he did not mention his sorrow at the break-up of her marriage. Her response was a furious letter back to Blair, who was in Tuscany, and this elicited an anxious phone call from Peter Mandelson trying to smooth things out. The main plan seemed to be to stop Margaret talking to the press. The spin doctors might as well have tried to stop the earth from turning on its axis. Margaret had begun to sense her power. Robin was being difficult about giving her the house in the divorce settlement. It occurred to her that there were 'one or two things' she wanted to say publicly. She granted an interview to the *Sunday Times* about the hours required of a senior doctor and how they might have contributed to the split in her marriage. She intended, she says, only to bring up the matter of medical policy. Cook conceded his share of the house.

She had got a taste for self-expression, however, and wrote a letter to the *Scotsman* about the intense time-pressures on politicians, which 'drive a person from his natural pace', and 'coupled with the addiction to praise and acclaim, do induce a form of madness'. Robin suddenly visited Margaret and wondered if she had finished writing to the press and she confirmed that she had no more plans to do so. But power, as she perceived, is addictive. 'Conscious of the considerable personal satisfaction I gained from positive reactions to my brief forays into the press, I sat down and penned a letter to the *Times*,' this time on the subject of avoiding the suffering of children at the break-up of a marriage, and how theirs had not suffered, even though Robin now had less input into their upbringing. It was, she deemed, hardly controversial and yet, once the other papers had picked the letter up and turned it into headlines, Robin was on the phone to announce that he had put a gagging clause into the terms of the divorce. The subsequent conversation she had with Linda McDougall in which she spoke freely and poured out her woes, was, she was sure, supposed to be off the record. But the writing came thick and fast, nevertheless: a piece for the *Sunday Times* on the commercial interests of pharmaceutical companies and a novel about her early medical experiences. Unfortunately 'the article didn't immediately appear, and my novel didn't seem to find much favour'. Further interviews, however, rendered Robin apoplectic. 'Do you want to destroy me?' he cried over the phone. 'When he calmed down a bit, he said that he would have to talk of his forthcoming marriage in glowing terms to the press. I said, say what you wish of Gaynor. But just make sure you cast no unpleasant asides on me. He said with feeling, "I would be happy if I never had to see or hear or think about you, ever again!"' An agreement was signed in which she promised to remain silent, but she so much enjoyed writing that she did a couple of diary pieces for the Scottish *Sunday Times* and at last, feeling that Robin had survived the worst, she felt free to do what she most wanted 'beyond anything else' and write her autobiography. 'I am sorry if it will cause discomfort to certain people, some of whom I would prefer to spare. But for once I have done a thing entirely for myself.' A woman I know once poured the contents of a large tin of Tate & Lyle's Golden Syrup, at night when they were out, on the threshold of her ex-husband and his new wife's brand new house with its brand new carpets. This must be a high point in the history of revenge, and she found it, she says, deeply gratifying. But Margaret Cook has gone further, beyond the passing pleasures of revenge, to the real recuperation of finding that if no one else will, she can put herself first, and she has done so, and will quite likely go on doing so, at great and self-satisfying length.

HEART'S DESIRE

One

Consistency is a quality I neither possess nor particularly admire, but I'm a little abashed to say the least at the unexpected turn my life has recently taken. I'm perfectly sure that I was commissioned to write a summer diary (everyone's away, let's keep it low key) around the studied uneventfulness I'm always declaring my life to be: a page of nothing happens in meticulous detail. Yet here I am embarked on an ill-considered project of selling the flat I've inhabited and worked in for fifteen years, leaving London where I've always lived, and buying a house in the provinces, all, my dears, in wild pursuit of my heart's desire. In the first place, I don't do wild, and in the second I don't have a heart. These, I would have said, were givens. I can still be heard to mutter testily that they remain so, as I instruct estate agents and fail to receive with good grace the amused congratulations of my friends, but I'm uncomfortably aware I'm only trying to salvage a little self-respect. The Poet and I have been love's middle-aged dream for eighteen months now, and the sixty miles between Cambridge and London has become an insufferable distance. The more so since Camden's resident parking policies mean that I am only allowed to have a lover who stays for no longer than four hours at a time. There are all day parking permits, but residents are enti- tled to purchase no more than ten of these a year. This interesting piece of social engineering seems to require either marriage, soli- tude, or brief and efficient sexual encounters for which the residents must pay Camden at a rate of 40p an hour for the first 40 hours, 80p for the second 40 hours, and £1.20 an hour there- after. This is a competitive rate compared to the market price, I know, but being a child of the Sixties, I haven't quite managed to shake off the notion of free love. So when the house directly opposite the Poet came on the market – I haven't entirely lost my mind: I'm not actually going to *live* with him – I threw caution to the wind and decided to sell up.

What has become clear in the last few weeks is how right I was to maintain that affairs of the heart should be secondary to keeping as emotionally still as possible. To start with I have pitched myself into the half-lit moral desert of house buying and selling. One thing I know is that wanting anything badly makes a person vulnerable. A shrink once said to me that my problem was my refusal to make myself vulnerable (as in not making the necessary transference on to him), to which I replied I couldn't for the life of me see how volunteering for vulnerability could be seen as a prerequisite for mental health. On the contrary. It's OK to want something, but not so much that it would upset your routine if you can't have it. If anything confirms the danger of desire, it is getting involved with estate agents who, like the most manipulative of lovers, gauge the degree of wanting and then employ maybe-you-can-maybe-you-can't games that propel you back and forth to the edges of hope and despair and make of you their plaything. A lover you could tell to get lost, but an estate agent selling the house across the road from your heart's desire is in sado-masochistic heaven when he tells you that your offer has not yet been firmly accepted and will not be unless you are

prepared to put your finances and psyche on the line with inor-
dinate bridging loans and inconvenient completion dates. If only
I didn't want *that* particular house . . . if only I didn't *want* that
particular house . . . if only I didn't *want* . . . I wake up sweating
at three in the morning. Imagine, caught up in such helplessness
at this late stage of my life. And in any case, what am I doing, all
quiet and in control, free, independent, unbeholden, moving to a
strange town in a draughty fen for a *man*? I know about men. But
Poet soothes me with talk of late-onset passion, of finding and
keeping, of time running out. Not, now I come to think of it,
entirely unlike the methods used by the estate agents. Married
friends encourage the move, partly pleased that I haven't got
clean away with it, but also whispering out of earshot of their
partner that it's a brilliant idea to have two houses and if only
they had thought . . . And even my daughter, just left home and
therefore instantly wise in the way of the world, smiles benevo-
lently and says, 'You might as well, you're not getting any
younger.'

So now I am deracinated, looking into a black hole of debt
('No, no,' my more sophisticated friends explain. 'Mortgage
isn't debt.' Though they have salaries, not publishers) and
mortified in the sight of the god of my principles by my
emotional volte-face. The first few decades of my existence
were really very busy. My whole aim in the second half of my
life was for nothing whatever to happen. It was my intention to
become increasingly reclusive, decaying gently in one place,
newspapers piling up, empty cat food tins encroaching into
the flowerbeds, clothes mothholing, stockings sagging above
my carpet slippers. Just to describe it makes me feel restful,
and perhaps all this will come about, but not quite yet, it
seems.

In the meantime, if you should hear of anyone who wants a
charming four bedroomed flat with a verdant garden just a

stone's throw from Hampstead Heath, previously owned by a careful, a very careful, lady writer who was last heard of going to the bad, you should not hesitate to get in touch with me.

Two

In Cambridge I've graduated from estate agents to solicitors and financial advisers. My flat, on the other hand, has not been sold. It's summer, I'm told. No one's buying, they're all away. Apparently it isn't summer in Cambridge, because I'm not away and I've bought. So a vast loan has been arranged and my cuddly little Cambridge terraced house is being conveyed to me. The only real fear I have in my life is of dispossession. Now I will have two houses from which I could be dispossessed. I understand what Kierkegaard was on about at last. The leap of faith is not towards God, but love (for want of a better term) and housing. One leap of faith begets another, it seems. First I throw myself on the mercy of love and risk betrayal, then on the mercy of the property market and risk penury. Never mind, I can be a mad old bag lady instead of the mad old hermit I had planned to be. Take warning as you skirt around me on the street.

To distract myself, I build castles in Cambridge. Much of the talk between the Poet and myself is about how to arrange our elderly idyll on opposite sides of the road. Will we have keys to each other's house? Well, of course. But must we phone or knock

157

before we enter? No, no, it is as if we live in one house, but separated by a road which is nothing more than a corridor between us. I'm not sure about this, surely some system can be devised to indicate that we're working, sleeping, watching something moronic on the TV or sulking. Traffic lights on our front doors, perhaps, red and green, and amber for 'you decide'. A candle in the window. A particular arrangement of the upstairs blinds. What about coded electric bells, or a pair of whistles whose pitch only the Poet and I can hear? All this is a worry. If my house is his house, and his house is my house, where is the private space we both agreed was essential for mature love to mature further? It begins to look as if one big house with an east and west wing might be more suitable. Sadly, for a poetry making don and a novel writing granddaughter of immigrants, the aristocratic way is not an option. I'm inclined towards a covered walkway across the roofs, a kind of bridge of sighs, but Poet favours a tunnel, a nether world connecting us like the linking of two unconsciousnesses. There you have the him and me of it. If planning permission is a problem we would both settle for a system of pneumatic tubes like they used to have in department stores in the old days. At a pinch email would do. Or there's the phone. Or we could send invitations through the post.

Still, this one house divided into two concept has something to be said for it. It occurs to me that since Poet is a passionate cook and I am passionately not, I don't need a kitchen in my house at all. It could be entirely devoted to my pleasures and needs: a study, a reading room, a luxury bathroom, a dedicated bedroom (maybe two: one for private sleeping, one for sex). But how will he let me know when supper's ready? He could bring it over. Do I want a lover or a waiter?

'Has it crossed your mind,' I say, 'that whenever we talk about this living almost together thing in Cambridge, we always imagine that you are in your house and I'm in mine?'

He's unfazed, explaining that being apart is our difficulty, not being together.

Pshaw, I hiss, or something spelt very like that. I tell him once again that he is in the grip of middle-aged delusion, in love with being in love. And what about when he comes to his senses, and there we are staring angrily at each other from opposite windows?

'But what if I'm not deluded?' he says calmly.

This is very aggravating, because I know he is and all he has to do is agree with me. In any case, as he knows perfectly well, 'what if he's not deluded' is quite as alarming as what if he is. It's all very well countering my what if with his what if, but the fact that there's no certainty to be had this or that side of death, doesn't mean I don't want it. Cambridge has become the land of what if, and I, for reasons that I can't or won't quite put my finger on, am emigrating to it.

'What if,' I mutter, 'after I've moved across the road from you, one of us gets creamed by a lorry as we're crossing it?'

We're both quite overcome by the tragic irony I've just retrospected. We discuss who will play us when Stephen Frears makes the movie (the romantic drama having been transferred to New York and Harvard, naturally). I refuse to have Meryl Streep or Meg Ryan, but I know it's hopeless. The Poet doesn't mind being played by Nick Nolte at all. (He would also like it to be known that he's beginning to develop great sympathy with Mrs Phil Hogan.)

But talking of crossing the road. Do we have to get dressed when we go back to our own house? Will a dressing gown do? Or a bath towel? Can we just skitter across in the buff? It puts neighbourhood watch in quite a different light. I think we'd better probably call a street meeting to thrash out the problem.

Three

Far away on an idyllic Greek island, where the sea is rippling like heavy silk in a light breeze, pomegranates are ripening and the branches of the olive trees are hanging heavy with the weight of their fruit, a phone call from an altogether darker, wetter and more crisis-bound place informs me that there is a crack in my London house.

'Well, of course there is,' I say, uncharacteristically insouciant for a moment from sun-blast. 'It's a house. It's in London. It was built 110 years ago. I'm barely half that age and I've got cracks.'

Then I return to my regular self: oh god, oh god, the house has a crack, the mortgage company will not give me money on it, I can't buy the Cambridge house, I will always live in London (not my London any more), my late ripening love affair will drop off its tree and rot on the ground, I will die lonely, infirm and quite, quite mad. In all likelihood (I'm on a roll, now) my friends will realise the error they have made in ever offering me friendship and blank me in the street, my house will fall down, indeed it will fall down tomorrow, but that won't matter because I have to fly home by aeroplane and you know what that means. Also no one has contacted me from home, so clearly my cats have contracted a fatal disease and died, the pipes have burst in a snap September freeze up, and for all I know, the petrol pumps will have run dry. Well, not the last, that would be ridiculous.

I return to my sunbed by the edge of the sea and flop myself down on it. The Poet smiles contentedly.

'No, it's all right,' I mutter. 'Don't worry. I didn't expect it to last. I've never been a believer in love on a long-term basis, don't know what came over me. We'll just have to put up with the awkwardness of love gone dead for the next week. We're adults. Then we'll go our separate ways. Put it down to experience. Not that I haven't had enough experience already. But never mind. Shall we see if they've got another room I can move into?'

'What?' says the Poet.

'There's a crack.'

'What?' says the Poet.

'A crack. House, life, love, mind. Crack. All over. Finished. Everything. Crack.'

'The house? Well, of course it has. It's a house, in London, it's over a hundred years old. *I've* got . . .'

'It's such a pity that it's all over between us when we've got so much in common,' I wail.

Poet suggests we go for a walk.

'Nope. It's going to rain.' He gazes at the sky: blue as Wedgwood, sun relentless. 'A cloud. See? There, over Turkey. It's going to bucket down. Crack.'

We walk through the village.

'Look,' Poet says, pointing at the base of a house. 'See that carved stone. It's three thousand years old. Some ancient Greek carved it, and some modern Greek used it as building material for his house. Look,' we peer into a disused underground bath house, supported by fluted columns and a breathtaking vaulted roof.

'Roman. Still standing. Look,' we gaze at an abandoned but still gorgeously grand Turkish spa hotel, discarded by the Greeks in the 1930s. 'It just needs a bit of paint and plaster work.'

But I'm not fooled. This is Greece, not north London. Here not there. Now not then. Anyway, I don't suppose the C & G wouldn't give me a mortgage for the Ottoman Spa Hotel if I decided to swap my Cambridge plans for Lesbos. Crack. My plans are in ruins and there's no heritage organisation that will rush in to secure a place in history for my crumbling hope. And I have a lover who is giving an alarming impression of Pollyanna. Crack.

'It will be fine,' the Poet says. 'We get a survey, fix the problem. It's normal, it's just a thing that has to be done.'

But I don't want to do anything. This everything-can-be-dealt-with, it-will-be-all-right-in-the-end makes my heart race in panic. If everything will be all right, then it is not all right now. The present is uncertain, there is doubt, a problem. There is the possibility that everything will not be all right. I can't live calmly in a world of possibility. No plans equals nothing to go wrong. What the hell am I doing having plans? It doesn't suit me.

'And another thing,' I moan. 'Do you realise we have never had a row? Why not? I'll tell you. Sublimation. Suppression. It's not good. Not healthy.'

'All right,' the Poet says. 'You start.'

The next day, another phone call. There is a buyer for the flat. They have cash, contracts can be exchanged in three weeks. Drop the price a little for the brickwork. Fine. A small crack of light opens and the Cambridge house sneaks back into my mind's eye, and me sitting in the study, waving absent-mindedly but happily to the opposite window. I immediately paper over the crack and force darkness back into my head. It's not a done deal until it's a done deal.

'You are the gloomiest person I've ever met,' the Poet tells me.

Returning to London, the plane lands safely, the house is upright and standing solid, the cats are alive and well, Poet and I are still in geriatric love. The phone rings. The buyer has withdrawn, decides it's the wrong area. Oh, and the petrol pumps are dry.

Four

With this house business going on and on (and on and on) I've been given to moments of defeatism. These have been some of the favourite moments in my life: the great rush of relief at ditching some cherished project, of crushing it into a tight ball and pitching it gaily into the incinerator. There is no greater pleasure I know than in uncommitting myself. That's it, I'm not doing it. It's virtually a definition of happiness. I love giving up. So, 'I've had it with houses. I'm staying where I am,' comes easily to me. About once a week or so. To which my friends and the Poet reply, 'But what about love?' 'Not worth it. Don't care. And anyway everyone knows I know nothing about love. It's not what I do.'

But there must be something in this love stuff, because so far I've only thrown the tantrums, I haven't actually cancelled the house selling and purchase even though it's more emotionally distressing than Christmas. Not even when I found myself locked out of the Poet's house this week, completely at a loss in the wild and unfamiliar streets of Cambridge. I might as well have been in the rainforest of Borneo. So far Cambridge has consisted of the

Poet's house, the façade of the house opposite which might one of these days be mine, and the street at the end of the road – the furthest I've made it on my own is in order to visit my solicitor and (more importantly) the Italian deli. Beyond that it's all mystery. A territorial no man's land. Or not my land. I have been driven here and there to dinner parties – they seem to have a lot of them in Cambridge – and to the Poet's college, but I was born without any direction-finding equipment. Drive me somewhere fifteen times and I couldn't begin to find my way to it, especially if thousands of cyclists are throwing themselves in front of you and there are more one-ways than there are streets. I haven't the faintest idea where my new house is in relation to anywhere else, and even less notion of how to get there beyond hailing a taxi, which apparently you can't do in the provinces. I have taken trains all round the States, wandered happily here and there in Paris or Buenos Aires, but Britain defeats me. Home, for me, is about staying in. After 53 years of living in London, I still get lost sometimes, and now refuse to go anywhere that isn't on the 24 bus route. But in London at least there's an underground system and an A to Z if the worst happens and I find myself out.

All I had to do was get to the Poet's college and collect a key, but how to get there? I stood hopefully beside a desultory bus stop for a while and then asked some people standing nearby which bus went into the centre. They looked astonished. 'Bus, what bus? Don't know. Never taken the bus.' Is this because the bus never comes or they never go to any other part of Cambridge? I wandered down the road and found an internet café. I emailed the Poet to email me a cab number and sat with a cup of tea to wait for a reply. Someone who everyone greeted as Bernard sat at my table. 'This is your first time here,' he told me. Dear God, this is definitely not London, I thought, feeling curious eyes swivelling in my direction.

'I can't make it to your poetry reading tonight,' a woman at an adjacent table excused herself to Bernard, looking up from a book.

'What are you reading?' he asked her.

She held it up. It was a history of English literature.

'Researching into the Mountains of Mourne,' she told him with a meaningful smile.

'Ah yes,' Bernard nodded, sadder and wiser. 'The Mountains of Mourne. Yes, the Mountains of Mourne.'

This is not the sort of casual conversation that goes on in my local greasy spoon. I sprinted for the computer to find the return email with a cab number. What am I doing here? I wondered while waiting for the cab to arrive. What do I like about London? Anonymity. I like sitting in cafés and not knowing a soul. I like being on the street in the sure and certain knowledge that no one will say hello to me. At my next door neighbour's party recently, a woman who lived further down the street told me definitively that I didn't live where I had in fact lived for fifteen years, because she'd been living there that long and had never seen me before. 'I don't go out much,' I explained, but she shook her head firmly. 'No, you don't live on this street.'

Going about Cambridge with the Poet is a progress of nodding and smiling every few yards at old friends, colleagues, ex-lovers and the bloke who sold you a deep fat fryer last week. Could I cope with this, or any degree of sociability? Did I want a house in an utterly strange city where everyone knows each other? And all in the name of what people keep insisting on calling love.

When I arrived at the Poet's room, he wrapped me in his arms, knowing that my mental condition was touch and go after the trauma of enforced being out.

'I'll drive you home. You can have a bath, get into bed and sleep. It's been a terrible experience.'

I know it can't last, but there's something very comforting about this love stuff. Perhaps I could get used to it.

Five

I am translated. The house opposite the Poet's is mine. Love has triumphed over estate agents, mortgage companies, surveyors, combative solicitors and my own hard-won insistence on a solitary existence.

Nothing more than a narrow tarmacadamed road separates me from having to admit that I am living with someone. London is my past, Cambridge is my present. The future has been repeatedly defined by the builders and decorators I've contacted as 'not before Christmas', and even that's further than I care to see right now.

Anxious metropolitan friends phone and ask about the state of my spirit/soul/psyche/brain chemistry (depending on their specialisms). I shriek with laughter from the floor of what will be my workroom, what is my workroom as I write this, deskless, chairless, empty of everything but a cushion (squirrelled from the Poet's sofa), a laptop and a phone.

The state of my inner life is for some later, barely imaginable time when I am not finding and negotiating with and co-ordinating plasterers, joiners, carpet fitters, kitchen installers, bathroom renovators, painters and removal vans. There is no time for wondering if I have just made the worst mistake of my life in leaving the only place I've ever known, or if just the one Prozac a day will keep the lurking palpitations at bay.

The mysteries of love pale into insignificance beside decisions about exactly what kind of off-white the walls should be, and whether or not I want to have a wok burner on my new oven (I do, I really do, it turns out). So far the catflap has been fitted – the first priority – a teapot and kettle bought, my floor-level work place set up, and the whereabouts of John Lewis (alias Robert Sayle in these parts) established. I can stroke my traumatised cats, drink gallons of tea, get on screen the book I'm supposed to be working on and then turn it off, and madly order household items I will regret when they are delivered.

All life's other necessities go on across the road in the Poet's kitchen, bathroom, TV room and bedroom. But as to what all this means in any meaningful way, I cannot say. Ask me the drop required for the blinds in the living-room, and I will give you them to the nearest centimetre. Wonder about the relative virtue of twist pile or velvet carpeting and I will provide you with an elegant thesis on the subject. Query the optimum wattage for a fast-flowing shower and I will clear the matter up for you in a trice.

But ask me how I feel about having moved in order to be with a particular person, ask me about love, ask me about the nature of relationships and you might as well be speaking to me in Old Norse. This may be a kind of shell-shock, a deep traumatic reaction, but I've lost all language for things which are not practical and palpable.

There is a kind of reduced dialogue of emotions between the Poet and myself. We sit together, and after a period of silence, one of us will say: 'Are you OK?' The other tenses slightly before offering a clipped: 'Fine. You?' 'Mmm, fine.' This delicate investigation into each other's interior well-being is supplemented sometimes in the middle of the night, when one of us wakes up, nudges the other, and asks: 'Is everything all right?' 'Mmm, fine. Everything all right with you?' 'I'm fine.' So, everything's fine.

Love notwithstanding, we are living or partly living in a hiatus between normalities. At some point, the painters, plumbers and plasterers having left, there will be no choice but to acknowledge that real life has started once again. Right now, life is an ongoing emergency, a waiting time, a series of appointments to be kept, deliveries to be made, when no one can tell what they feel about the way things are, because nothing has finished and nothing has started.

As with the improbability of late love having descended so gratuitously, the Poet and I should be thankful for the experience of turmoil at a time when most people are beginning to go into mourning for the loss of the chance of further turmoil in their lives.

But perhaps what causes our monosyllabic reaction to our new condition is not the chaos of the present, but fear of the return to the regular. What if contentment turns out to be the last thing we want? It's never been a state I've much admired, mostly because I don't think I have come across it much in others (ever, I might almost say), but also because I've always doubted that contentment is very good for people. It is no surprise to me that the fairy stories end with living happily ever after while refusing to give the slightest clue as to what this might be like. What would you think if when you asked someone how they were, they replied 'Happy'? Probably that they needed counselling.

What if, once the carpets are down and there are sofas to sit on, happily ever after awaits the Poet and me? Just as with death, sentimentalists and moralists have concocted fantasies about what happiness might be like, but no one I've heard of has ever returned from that place to confirm or deny the speculations. Well, we'll just have to wait and see. Maybe, in time to come, as your intrepid reporter of the ancient heart, I'll be in a position to report back on the matter one way or another.

Immobility

They said they were going to break my foot in three places, cut and re-tether the bones with small titanium screws each costing £90 (they let you know these things in the dog days of the National Health Service), and that it would be about six weeks before I was able to put any weight on it. Would that be all right?

You mean, I wondered hardly daring to breathe, that I mustn't do anything or go anywhere for six whole weeks?

Yes.

Or cook or visit people or walk in the country? Or shop at the supermarket or go to working lunches or launches or parties? Or visit the gym or use my stationary bike or weed the garden or vacuum the carpets?

Exactly.

Would it be all right? they asked. Oh, it would be wonderful. It would be dreams come true, the pot at the end of the rainbow, El Dorado, Shangri La and any other paradisiacal reference you care to think of. You really mean it? Six weeks of enforced, pre-scribed idleness?

Well, you're not as young as you were, it might take a little longer for the bones to knit.

Six weeks, *for sure*, maybe, dare I hope, more, of living the way I was born to live – and with a medical note.

I've had a problem with my left foot since I was a child. Now, well into middle-age and three minor operations later, I asked the surgeon if he could do anything to stop it hurting when I walked for more than fifty yards. This request that I should be enabled to walk longer distances, a desire so foreign to me that I can still hardly believe I actually asked, was made, let me explain, because of the love that had quite recently come into my life. I had already sold up and moved to my lover's city and we were, in separate houses on opposite sides of the road, still deliciously entranced with each other. The only faint shadow was that my lover likes to walk – on the beach, over the moors, in the fells – and wanted to share this experience with me. Love will make you think anything is possible, so as if in a trance, I sat in the surgeon's office and all disbelieving heard myself request an operation to enable me to go for walks.

I do not do walking. I am an urban person, brought up in the very centre of London. As a child I would reach the bottom step of my block of flats and have my hand out ready, waving for a taxi. Later, in poverty stricken times, I made do with buses and if they didn't stop at my doorstep, I stayed home. Now, I am prepared to walk to get to the car, providing it is not parked too far away, and that's it. This is not because I don't like walking – it's because I like to keep still. I am unable to understand why, if it is not absolutely necessary, I should have to leave my house or, come to that, there's no point in half-hearted confession, my bed.

I can do all I need to do to entertain myself and earn my living without getting up. I can read books, newspapers, letters, journals, write novels, articles, short stories, make telephone calls, daydream, stare blankly into space, panic, worry, watch old movies, remember, misremember, fantasise and theorise all from the comfort of my bed. What should I get up for apart from to wash my face and brush my teeth and make myself ready and sweet for the coming day or night in bed? A static life works for me. It worked for Florence Nightingale and Elizabeth Barrett Browning, why not me? Both took to their beds and found that they could run the world very satisfactorily from a horizontal position. What is the point of verticality, or the advantage of rushing about outside? Experience? Good heavens, I've had a bellyful of that – I'm a wild child of the Sixties, sex, drugs, rock 'n' roll and revolution, school-teaching, marriage, divorce, a child, breakdowns, breakups, books published – enough experience already. Time for a rest. But the arts? The theatre? I've been to the theatre. Parties? I went to one. How can I write fiction if I don't go out and take a long hard look at the world in all its changefulness? Very easily. Hell, I can even turn out a travel book or two while keeping relatively still.

But, of course, there is guilt. My lover leaves in the morning, bending down to kiss me goodbye in bed. He returns in the evening to kiss me hello and I am still in bed, reading a book. And some part of me feels he ought to know how busy I've been during the day. Oh, I've answered letters, paid bills, written two thousand words of my novel and read several chapters of a very dense Lacanian treatise. But why should I care if he thinks I have idled the day away? What if – quite as likely – I have done nothing but sit and stare at the white wall opposite, slept dreamily for an hour or two, listened to gardening programmes on the radio and read a chapter or two of Rex Stout? Overall the books get written, the bills get paid. Daydreaming and idleness are, if you like, the tools of my profession. Indeed, I may have taken up my profession precisely because they are. Why, apart from the fact that he has been rushing around like a wind-blown plastic bag, should he care how I have spent my day, and why should I feel that activity is more worthwhile than stillness? Even so, in an access of love, I ask the surgeon to make me more mobile as if it were the pain in my foot that stopped me going for walks.

And look what has happened as a result of my request – my lying, hypocritical request to be enabled to go for walks. I am obliged to stay still and do nothing that involves moving, foot all broken to pieces, for a minimum of six weeks. It strikes me as a well-deserved present from the goddess of lassitude whose delight in irony is quite as profound as my own. It is confirmation of the promise that to those who have so it shall be given. And so my post-operative days are spent, as ever, in bed, with a strange boot on my foot, a rather Japanese affair, all black and Velcro, that keeps the front of my foot entirely off the ground and raises the heel two inches above my other heel. I can only hobble with the aid of the pair of metal crutches I have been provided with so that I can make trips to the bathroom. For several days I stay still, in some pain, but comforted with strong and dreamy analgesics. My lover, who is a saint, brings me delicious things to eat and news of the world outside. I am not expected to engage with anything except the healing of my bones. I actually have sympathy for my situation. And so it goes on. The pain dies down but the no-weight rule means I have to stay in bed. I can write and read. My lover leaves a tray beside my bed for my lunch, a little smoked salmon and some home-made hummus, and returns in the evening amazed at my productivity.

'Darling, you've written 500 words and read an entire Ross MacDonald. You're marvellous.'

He has only given a lecture, two seminars, marked half a dozen essays and attended three meetings. I am a wonder.

It is true that after two weeks my foot looks like a huge unidentifiable cut of meat on a butcher's slab and when the six weeks are up is still only remotely related visually to a foot. 'I can't walk on it,' I say to the doctor, 'you said six weeks.'

'Did I? Oh no, that was major surgery, you had. These are early days. We'll see you again in a month. In the meantime, don't put any weight on it and keep it up.'

Oh my aged unhealing bones, bless them.

The month passed and last week I hobbled and crutched back to the hospital.

'It's only been three months,' the surgeon says. 'It's healing nicely, but it will be a year before the swelling and the pain stops. In the meantime, take it easy.'

Now, I've got these strange and edgy feelings, as if there is something I want to do. I spend a lot of time imagining beaches, moors and fells. I look longingly at my stationary bike. I dream about the treadmill in the gym. Except to go to the hospital I haven't been outside my house for 12 weeks. Quite often these days my lover gets cross with me for sneaking about the house without my crutches and leaving my boot off in an attempt to get a bit of, well, exercise.

'He said it was going to take time. Be patient. In a few months we can go out for a short walk.'

They say, be careful what you wish for – and they may be right.

HOW IT IS

Keeping Up

The Dictionary of New Words. Oxford University Press 1998

With New Year (anxiety of New Years past, dread of New Years future) breathing hot down my neck, and time itself moving along so fast that it seems to be about to lap me, Oxford University Press has produced a dictionary of two thousand new words. I haven't learned all the old ones yet. It's very stressful. There ought to be a word for that second-half-of-life sense of time accelerating out of one's orbit. The feeling of never quite catching up, of being always slightly then and never quite now, and out of breath with it. Or those nightmares of sitting for exams on subjects you never studied. But I haven't found it so far, if you don't count 'ageing'. Here I am still trying to come to grips with black holes when suddenly I find that *cold dark matter* is on everyone's lips. Being an inept visualiser, I am unable intuitively to grasp that a *buckminsterfullerene* is a 'stable form of carbon whose nearly spherical, hollow molecule consists of 60 carbon atoms arranged in a shape with 12 pentagonal faces and 20 hexagonal ones (a truncated regular icosahedron)'. My heavens, *'nearly spherical'*, a *'truncated regular icosahedron'*, whatever happened to certainty and precision in science? Call it by its alternative name, *footballene*, and light comes flooding in (unless it is just my particular gift to be able to visualise a football).

In fact, this is a new *New Words*, being the second edition of the old *New Words* published in 1991. If you're serious about keeping up, or OUP are serious about providing a record of popular language change, there seems to be a problem. The first edition (now out of print) defines its purpose as 'to take a snapshot of the words and senses which seem to characterise our age and which a reader in fifty or a hundred years' time might be unable to understand fully (even if these words were entered in standard dictionaries) without a more expansive explanation of their social, political, or cultural context'. This is an admirable purpose, and the special use of the word *friendly*, in the phrases *friendly fire* or *friendly bombing* would speak volumes about our age to researchers in the future. In 1991 these were defined as: 'coming from one's own side; especially causing accidental damage to one's own personnel or equipment'. In the new edition, look for *friendly fire*, and you find nothing between *Friday Wear* and *from hell*. Perhaps the aim of the dictionary has shifted between the two editions, so that the needs of the future are no longer taken into account. The second edition claims to 'provide an informative and readable guide to about two thousand high-profile words and phrases which have come to public attention in the past fifteen or sixteen years'. No mention of the future here, but sixteen years ago was 1981 and what has happened to *friendly fire*? Do some phrases grow old before their time? There seems to have been a shift in policy: 'A minority of items covered in the first edition claim a place here because their stories have continued to develop (BSE is an example of this).' From which, let us hope we can assume, OUP have decided that modern warfare is a thing of the past. Luckily, *friendly fire* is listed under *friendly* as a 'special collocation' in the 1973 edition of the OED and the 1993 *New Shorter Oxford English Dictionary*, so the future had better rely on these not so fly-by-night works for its understanding of how we manipulated language in the twentieth century.

Searching the early As in the first edition will give you, for example, *AAA (see Triple A)*, *ABS*, *ace*, *acid house*, *acid rain*, *active birth*, *acupressure*, *Adam* and *alternative*, none of which appear in the new edition. The second edition offers *abortion pill*, *acceptable face of*, *acid jazz*, *acquaintance rape*, *adhocracy* and *alternative fuel*, none of which appear in the first edition. The words both editions have in common include: *abled*, *ableism*, *abuse*, *acquired immune deficiency syndrome* and *affinity card*. Perhaps, in a hundred years from now someone will want to write a historical novel about youth culture (*yoof culture*) in the 1980s; I'm afraid they will have to forego the use of *Adam* ('In the slang of drug users, the hallucinogenic designer drug methylenedioxymethamphetamine or MDMA, also known as Ecstasy') from out-of-print 1991, though they could settle for *love dove* meaning the same thing in the second edition. Contemporaries, however, should beware. A dictionary is, by definition, no way to find out how to be hip (a word not found in either edition, but used, according to the SOED, by both Erica Jong and Shiva Naipaul in the mid-20th century). Be very cautious about casually referring to being *loved-up to the eyeballs* ('intoxicated by the drug Ecstasy') to your young people in the hope of gaining intergenerational respect. Also avoid suggesting a night of *moshing* ('concert audiences express their involvement with and appreciation of the music through energetic physical activity in the moshpit') if you want to retain any standing in any community at all.

The *Dictionary of New Words* is a form of entertainment (*infotainment*) rather than a serious research tool, though there are some (not very startling) indications of the concerns of the late 20th century to be gleaned from it. It looks, from a dip into the newly invented or adapted vocabulary, as if modern society has innovated (*pushed the envelope*) primarily in the areas of computing, business and science, while new forms of old words have had to be coined in the field of good manners (*political correctness*). This will not astonish anyone who has been awake for a reasonable amount of time over the last fifteen years, but the Dictionary provides concise confirmation without launching one into the murky language of social theory, which, time being precious, one might wish to avoid.

However, derivations, especially of slang, are always intriguing. Like jokes, slang surfaces among young people or sub-cultures (a couple of twenty-year-olds told me they were too old to know the current slang, which develops around schools or gangs), often seemingly out of nowhere and suddenly everyone (under twenty) knows them. Once they reach the ears of the over 20s, you can be sure they have been supplanted and their histories and definitions begin to look ludicrous. *Rad*, of course, means 'really good or exciting'. According to the *Dictionary* it originated with Californian surfers in the Eighties to describe a turn 'that was at the limits of control' and this use, specifically by surfers, developed via films, skateboarding and BMX biking into 'the currently fashionable accolade'. It is 'formed by abbreviating *radical* . . . such slang terms of approval often get abbreviated to a snappy monosyllable – in the UK *brilliant* became *brill*'. It's hard to read this history without finding a giggle bubbling up. This is a linguistic version of: if you've got to ask, you can't afford it. (*Accolade*, incidentally, is defined by the SOED as 'The salutation marking the bestowal of a knighthood, at different times an embrace, a kiss, or (now the usual form) a stroke on the shoulder with the flat of a sword', which permits a dream moment when Her Majesty announces, 'I now proclaim you rad. Arise Sir Damien.') *Wicked* ('excellent, great, wonderful'), you may notice, has avoided becoming a snappy monosyllable. It is, we are told after the definition, 'a reversal of meaning' which seems obvious, but dictionaries have to do what dictionaries have to do. Its history is not entirely clear to the compilers: 'There might first have been a catch-phrase or advertising slogan *so good it's wicked* which was later abbreviated to *wicked* alone; however, it is not unusual for an adjective to be used as an "in" word in the opposite sense to its usual one among a limited group of people, and then pass into more general slang.' Anyway, somewhere in the US, sometime in the Eighties. The entries finish with examples from the press or contemporary fiction, in this case a touch prissily from *Time Out* in 1989: 'I've been to loads of Acid House parties. We have a wicked time but never, not ever, do we take any drugs.' So don't worry too much if your youngsters use the word; they may be hopelessly out of date, but at least they're not using. At the other end of the spectrum in 1989, *Blitz* magazine is cited as an example of the word *awesome* among others: 'That night I *freebased* a *fractal* of *crack* and *blissed out* on *E*. It was *awesome*, it was *ace*. It was *wicked*, *bad* and *def*. It was twenty quid. OUCH!' Whoever it was is probably writing for the *Spectator* now. Def, incidentally, is not, I think, derived like yoof. New coinages for death are few and far between, although the medical profession has come up with *gomer* (an acronym for: 'get out of my emergency room', and used of 'a patient regarded as unlikely through age and ill-health to respond to treatments, who is thus seen as unrewarding of effort').

This is where the *Dictionary* is really helpful: in teasing apart the acronyms that comprise a large sector of new words in science and computing. Probably about as much as any non-specialist needs to or can know is given for the word *MACHO* as a 'compact object of a kind which it is thought may constitute part of the dark matter in galactic haloes', but it's entertaining to be told that it is a happy formation of 'massive astrophysical compact halo object' to partner *WIMP* ('weakly interacting massive particle'). This is not just language growing in its own soil, but the comforting thought that scientists as well as discovering things we can't see, also delight in playing language games. Perhaps there's a university department somewhere specially devoted to throwing initials around to arrive at satisfactorily human new names for unseen forces. It's not just physicists, the biologists are catching up: *GIFT* is a technique for helping infertile couples to conceive via 'gamete intra-fallopian transfer'. However, they lose creativity points with a related technique, *ZIFT*: 'zygote intra-fallopian transfer'. Computing, not altogether surprisingly, seems entirely to lack wit in the formation of its acronyms: *LAN, Bit, rom, ram, JPEG, HTML* all point dispiritingly to the *anoraksia* of their coiners, though *snail mail* has a certain charm.

In the world of politics, it is some comfort to find 'Thatcherism' missing from the new wordlist, though *Thatcheronomics* suggests we haven't heard the last of the woman. But what to make of the entry *Blairism* so soon? At the time of the *Dictionary* going to press, it seemed to mean 'a willingness to combine a concern for social issues with an acceptance of many aspects of market-based economies'. At this stage of Blair government, I'd be tempted to drop the first part of the sentence, or at least insert 'professed' before willingness and wait for the third edition of *New Words* to finalise the meaning. *Islington man* is in ('a derogatory term for a middle-class, socially aware person of left-wing views, a resident of North London, and in particular the borough of Islington' – so not Tony Blair then), though with a recommendation to use the formulation *Islington person*.

Things aren't looking good for the businessman, either. He has had to add *karoshi* ('death caused by overwork or job-related exhaustion') to his three-word Japanese vocabulary (*karaoke* is in, but no sign of *sushi* in either edition). *Power breakfast, power dressing, power lunch* and *power nap* take care of the executive's day, but things, I believe, won't be really up to speed until she can

182

set up a power tea beyond the *glass ceiling* with the members of *Emily's list*. *Power Ranger* is, however, not a peripatetic management consultant, but a plastic toy which I'm glad to say I'm sure we no longer have to take cognisance of.

My least favourite new use of an old word is *abuse*, to provide a euphemism for large numbers of disparate behaviours. *Child abuse* simultaneously covers cruelty and incest, two powerful words not much seen these days. *Old age abuse* and *granny abuse* suffices for maltreatment of old people. *Substance abuse* (covering alcohol, drugs and solvents, and anything else that people regularly want to put into themselves) makes the word 'addiction' redundant. *Laxative abuse* politely covers the grimness of the life of someone suffering from anorexia or bulimia. In the sprawling use to which the word been put, there is no sense of proportion (*racket abuse* is what used to be known as bad temper) or syntactic logic (*'safety abuse*, where it is not the safety that is being abused, but those safeguards put in place to ensure it'). A new one on me refers to all that pleasurable eating between meals that I had formerly called greed or even appetite, which now turns out to be *snack abuse*. For nearly all these abuses helplines and counselling are doubtless available, though the more general human problems of cruelty, addiction, sexual predation, and mental illness are not so simply fixed or addressed.

Having got that off my chest, it is clear that the main pleasure to be derived from the *Dictionary of New Words* is, having chosen your favourite linguistic irritation, that it is likely to provide satisfying evidence of language gone to the dogs. Not that it has, of course. Some of the new words are instructive (*Maastricht*, not entertaining, I grant, but informative), useful (where would I be without *cook-chill?*) or amusing (*slaphead* – for bald, I'm afraid). And all the old words remain available in the grown-up dictionaries, ready to be used by anyone intent on making themselves clear, rather than rad.

Getting It

E = mc² by David Bodanis. Pan 2001

For the purposes of plain getting on with things – keeping warm, staying fed, making babies – there is no reason on earth, or off it, why anyone not actively engaged in the world of science should comprehend the underlying workings of physics. All we really need to know is that, accurate or not this week, relativity, cosmology, quantum mechanics don't concern us in our everyday lives. Let the quantum physicist panic because she knows the floor she walks on is almost entirely empty space with a few widely scattered molecules dotted here and there. The rest of us stomp around in blissfully ignorant confidence that – barring unforeseeable acts of God – a floor will continue to do what a floor is supposed to do. Or as the *New York Times* for 10 November 1919 put it, 'Einstein Theory Triumphs. Stars Not Where They Seemed or Were Calculated to Be, but Nobody Need Worry.'

But still. But still. Quantum theory suggests that there is a vanishingly small chance that a kettle full of water on the hob will freeze rather than boil. This is disturbing, if only in a vanishingly small way. And if the stars are not where they seemed to be, then where are they? And to whom did they seem to be where they are not? Are they not where they seem to be to me? Or are they not where they seem to be to someone else to whom they seem to be somewhere quite different because they are looking at them from another point of view? In which case, are they nonetheless where they seem to me to be, or were there those who knew that they were not where they seemed to me to be, but who were as it turned out wrong about what they thought they were right about? And does that make me right? Almost certainly not. But it is an awful thought that people who know something you don't know might after all be wrong, and that when their error is discovered, you will not understand the new solution any better than you understood the old. It's no good being told not to worry, these things are a worry, even if not of such a pressing kind as the question of when the bus you are waiting for will arrive. Moreover, there is always the sneaking suspicion that if you knew what they knew, you would also have a special insight into the arrival of the bus (because things always turn out to be linked in some unexpected way), and you would then be able to conclude that it would be much better if you gave up and went home to bed.

So it has always bothered me to be told that $E=mc^2$ contains a vital truth about the world and not to be able to grasp what that truth is. There are, I know, those who think that science is a special kind of truth that I've no business trying to grasp if I don't have the mathematical tools to understand it, because not understanding it in scientific terms is not to understand it at all, but David Bodanis, the author of $E=mc^2$, is not one of them. As someone to whom science has always been a black hole, I see Bodanis and those who bother to try to explain to the likes of me what they understand mathematically as therapists of a sort. Not to understand something and to know you don't understand it is distressingly akin to being post-Freudian: like being aware of the existence of your unconscious and knowing that it is forever withholding from you what you really need to know about yourself. Actually, to be mathematically illiterate is worse than being an unanalysed post-Freudian, because what is not understood is palpably there in the form of stars or floors, whereas my unconscious exists, if it does at all, in the realm of thought, and can, thanks to its own devious workings and my willed collusion, be ignored.

But scientists are always telling us that $E=mc^2$ is of the utmost everyday importance while at the same time berating writers and artists for taking half-understood scientific ideas and applying them to fiction and works of art. It is, I suppose, some sort of bad thing if poorly digested concepts become common currency, but I rail at being disallowed whole playgrounds full of metaphor and generalisation just because tears of failed arithmetic past spring to my eyes at the merest glimpse of an equation. A little knowledge may be a dangerous thing, but so is a lot of knowledge that only a few magisterial types are permitted by their own obfuscations to understand. Compare and contrast a novel that misapplies quantum theory with the building and dropping of a nuclear bomb.

And what about the extraordinary and inalienable human pleasure of *getting* something that you haven't grasped before? There are, of course, various degrees of getting things. There is the pinprick of light at the end of the hopelessly murky tunnel, when you can see how you might comprehend something if only the fog would clear. Or there is that three in the morning blaze of insight, when you give up trying to sleep, open the *Tractatus* and see exactly what Wittgenstein was on about – though the blaze begins to flicker by the time you turn the lamp off, and is quite dead as you scan the page again by morning light. And there is the bolt from the blue, where you understand with complete clarity what you were sure you would never understand – and what

186

you can't understand now, no matter how hard you try, is how you ever didn't understand it. But, oh, the delight of grasping an idea, the sheer rush of endorphins, the irrepressible desire to leap up and pirouette around the room. What else, apart from sex and drugs and rock 'n' roll, is there in life better than *getting* it? And what is more important in the world, apart from great lovers, honest drug-dealers and fine musicians, than good teachers?

Bodanis gets a gold star for good teaching, and for understanding that with this reader at least there is no level of explanation too low. I've gone the explanatory route of the man travelling in a train with a torch, a watch, a pair of dividers and wellington boots, being observed by a man standing on a platform and another with binoculars on the other side of the galaxy. So this appears like that to him, and like something else to the other, and someone gets older than someone else, or fatter, but what's that got to do with $E=mc^2$ or nuclear fission or even the price of wellington boots? It may be that the man-in-the-train explanation is elementary to someone who already knows what they are talking about, but if you haven't got the basic skills to use the analogy it takes you down quite the wrong alley. I remember reading about Schrödinger's imaginary cat – the one in the box who both is and isn't dead if it has or has not been poisoned and the lid remains shut. Wondering what they would make of the equivocal world of quantum theory, I put this fairy tale to my six-year-old and her friend as a bath-time story. All hell broke loose, waves of bathwater soaked floor, walls, towels and myself as the two outraged little girls flung their arms about and stamped their feet demanding to know who this cruel and evil scientist was who locked cats dead and undead in boxes and was not punished for such behaviour. I feel a little like that with the man in the train. I become more interested in the narrative than the point. Where is he going? Has the bloke on the platform missed his connection? Were they going to meet? And why? Running off together, or plotting world revolution? And why is the guy on the other side of the galaxy so interested in the 11.10 from Euston? Looking for hot tips on privatising the railways of Betelgeuse, I dare say.

Bodanis begins at the very beginning, taking the equation itself as his structure, and nothing for granted as to the possible ignorance of his reader. If you are me, this is not patronising, it is a great relief. E, =, m, c and ^{2} each have a chapter to themselves. E is for Energy. I gave up science decades ago: I really do want to know the history of the concept of energy and be taken back to Faraday, have my hand held through the law of conservation of energy, and be led gently towards Einstein. I'm delighted to learn about the development of the equals sign and what exactly the idea of mathematical equivalence is. And pathetically grateful that mass, the speed of light and the squaring of the speed of light are explained to me step by step, towards the notion that nothing can go faster than the speed of light and how exactly it is that energy transforms into mass and vice versa. 'Visualise the equals sign in the equation as a tunnel or bridge. A very little mass gets enormously magnified whenever it travels through the equation and emerges on the side of energy.' No, I really don't mind being asked to see an equation as a choo-choo train, in fact, on the contrary, suddenly I see the whole point of equations.

So there I am, thinking I get it, and I'm squeaking with pleasure. Bodanis leaves the equation and discusses the development of the idea in the real world. The splitting of the atom and the making of bombs, the discovery of black holes, the creation of our galaxy, the Big Bang. At last I see how they are connected and why everyone makes such a fuss about Einstein's little equation. It all depends on the absolutely limiting speed of light and what happens when any mass is sent across the = of the equation at 448,900,000,000,000,000 mph: the c (constant) squared. I even see why c has to be squared. And then, smug as anything, I turn

188

on the TV to watch *Horizon* where a devastatingly confident young Portuguese physicist from Imperial College pours scorn on the narrow assumptions of his peers and announces that the constant speed of light is not constant at all. Light, he says, travelled faster in the young Universe. Einstein got it wrong. The laws of the conservation of energy may not be unchanging laws at all. The void, he announces with all the clarity of a mystic, which existed before there was anything was not nothing. I no longer know what he is talking about, but it is clear that I haven't the faintest idea what energy, mass, the speed of light, the Universe or even equals means. On the other hand, whether I think I know or I think I don't know, the world goes on in a remarkably similar way, as it does if the speed of light is or is not a constant. Is this relativity?

Relativity is about the only thing left that I think I might understand. In the singular universe of me sitting in my living-room with Bodanis's book, I can grasp his explanation of how everything works. In the parallel universe of the outside world and its neighbouring galaxies, I don't have a clue what any of it means. I both do and do not understand it, just as Schrödinger's cat is both dead and not dead, to say nothing of entirely imaginary. This is not necessarily a tragic insight, or even a bad thing. It confirms what I have always suspected, which is that I should stay home and not wait for buses, and that it is perfectly all right for me to take $E=mc^2$ or any other set of letters and play with them to my heart's content, provided I do not inform the world that I am a competent physicist. Not, as it happens, easy in our category-crazed times. Recently I was phoned by a researcher for *Newsnight* and asked to participate in a discussion of global weather change. Some years back I published a novel entitled *Rainforest*, set to some extent in a rainforest, but mostly inside the psyche of an ecologist studying one. I also wrote a book with the word 'Antarctica' in its title, though it was a memoir, not a natural history. These titles were enough, apparently, to give me an aura of meteorological expertise.

'We'd like your opinion on global warming and its likely effects.'

I quite fancied the idea of babbling uninformed nonsense on TV about forthcoming ice ages or the roasting of the planet, but I pulled myself together and declined the invitation. Remember this next time you see or hear someone pontificate publicly about the state of the world.

On the other hand, at home, armed with Bodanis and other kindly souls, I can pace up and down and chatter to my cats and the four walls on the nature of the Universe. I can turn my half-understood ideas upside down and inside out and half-bake them if I choose. And what harm can I do if I publish them in the form of fictions and fancies, when as far as I can see, this year's truths turn out to be next year's old hats? The hard-core scientists can keep their secret knowledge, and I will continue not to know what I can't know and to do with my lack of knowledge what I will.

The Family Way

It's possible that I'm not the best person to ask about family. Mine was a sorry mess, a ground zero of attempted suicides, mental institutions, dismal disappointments, destitution and love (or something called love) turned nasty. I would veto myself from opinionating on the subject, except for two reasons: the first is that those who claim to be from happy families feel at liberty to praise the institution, so I can't see why mere prejudice should disqualify me. The second is that I don't know anyone, even from families which seem to be models of the genre, who has got away pain and problem free. If they have not been unloved, they have been loved too much. If they were not the first born, they were the last born, or vice versa and contrariwise. If the parents had a deep and profound relationship, their children felt excluded. If life was stable and uneventful, they were ill-prepared for the harsh realities of existence. Coddled or neglected, the result is invariably dissatisfaction and probably several years of psychotherapy to sort it all out. Really, if we had any sense we would take financial steps to assure the provision of shrink fees along with the school fees as soon as a child is in utero. Of course, there's no reason why we should expect a pain and problem-free existence. Freud himself aimed only at returning his patients to ordinary unhappiness. But at some point in recent times we have slipped into a historically unprecedented conviction that a pain and problem-free life is what is to be aimed for above all else, indeed what we are entitled to, and that growing up in the right kind of family is the only way in which we can achieve it. And the right kind of family is?

Do you recall that moment when you were told that you were found under a gooseberry bush? Even supposing you came from a well-regulated and contented family, I'll lay odds that you can remember how your heart leapt at the prospect. Oh freedom, you weren't really one of them after all. Or perhaps you had parents, committed to telling their children the facts of the world as they are, who explained to you the whole sticky inescapable bio-details that proved you were well and truly theirs. How often at night did you fantasise about being a foundling, a maternity ward muddle, adopted, a fairy child, anything rather than accept the flesh and blood inextricable commitment to being one of the family? Such moments of wishful escape happen in the best of families. I even know a man, adopted as a baby, who has spent his life daydreaming that his adoption papers were mixed up, and that he should have gone to a quite different couple.

I ask you to recollect these common, perfectly ordinary childhood thoughts because they fly in the face of our 20th – or what has recently become our 21st – century assumptions, drilled and instilled into us by psychoanalysts, psychologists, sociologists, biologists, sentimentalists and all manner of political and religious creeds. It now goes without saying that the family is sacred, the best way to bring up a child. Indeed, we think of it as the only way. We can no longer imagine an alternative. When families produce damaged goods, we call them dysfunctional. When we fear that civil society has gone to the dogs (and when, at any stage of history haven't we feared that?), governments and moralists huff and puff about failing parents and the loss of family values. We blame the individuals in families that break down, and, depending on our leanings, cite adverse economic, educational or social factors, wayward parenting in a previous generation, collapsing moral and religious virtues, but what you very rarely hear said is that if so many families don't function the way we believe they ought, then perhaps the family itself doesn't work.

The family has become the sine qua non of mental health and well-being. Nice idea, pity it's wrong. The problem, as I see it, is not whether a family is good or bad, but the fact of the family itself; that false, fragile microcosm of benevolent national government, its nuclear arm as it were, on which crushingly unrealistic expectations are heaped. It's true that children have to be assisted in the business of developing physically and mentally into socially acceptable adults; and perfectly understandable that governments should wish to delegate the process to what seems like a manageable unit, yet over the decades the nuclear household has been asked to do more than it is structurally able to accomplish. For one thing, the governments we claim to admire are elected and can be discarded if they do not accomplish what the electorate want. Families on the other hand are totalitarian regimes, self-chosen, and very difficult for their offspring to get rid of if they are incompetent or dangerous. Family is for life, not just for its term of office. Revolting adolescents are simply freedom fighters employing guerrilla tactics in the eternal war of liberation. Even in the best arranged households there is an underlying existential panic at the idea of the impossibility of dissolving the relationship. I come from a happy family: *let me out*. If a family was a dwelling, it would be condemned as unfit for human habitation, and forcing individuals to live in emotionally overcrowded conditions. And if occasionally the family is officially deemed a hopeless disaster, and the child is rescued from it, we assume that at all costs another family must be found to replace it, because love is needed, and love is nowhere else to be found. Even a surrogate family is better than none at all.

Yet while we expect our elected representatives to behave decently, humanely and responsibly, we don't go so far as to demand that they love us. Love, that which will make everything all right, according to our current way of thinking, is the problem at the core of the family fairy tale. It is the panacea, the magical ingredient that when applied makes everything whole, and the family in the past fifty years has been expected to produce love with the ease that it produces babies, as if love, for God's sake, were as simple as the saying of it. We might demand that parents take responsibility for their children, but how can we demand that they love them? Savlon, we can buy at the pharmacy; we can instruct people that is what they need for cuts and abrasions, tell them where to get it, even provide the funds for its purchase. Love, it would seem from the real story of families, is not quite so easy to come by. It's not enough to teach the little ones right and wrong, care for their bodies, nurture their minds, keep them in the right kind of trainers, suppress your instinct to give them a wallop when they near as dammit burn down the house, but you must love them as well, and love them right (whatever that is), or all your efforts will have been as nothing. This *love*, so carelessly, airily, demanded, is, as far as I know, undefined, except by a single sane voice in the wilderness of emotive talk. Only the late child psychotherapist Donald Winnicot has dared risk a practical definition. He said that *good-enough mothering* was as much as anyone could hope for, and that, I think, tells us more about what we can't reasonably expect than what it actually is. And what use is Savlon anyway when you're in the middle of a car wreck?

In any case, this love business is on a hiding to nothing in our post-Freudian times. Psychologists might tell us that love is that without which we can't thrive, but the psycho-daddy of them all, the one whose followers we flee to when the family has done its worst or even its best, made it clear enough that the family is a hotbed of lust, envy and murderous intent. Mummy, daddy and baby are each doing battle for psychic survival. We want, we desire, we rage, we are driven, but love, if you read Freud, has absolutely nothing to do with it.

At present four in ten marriages in the UK end in divorce. In itself this figure hardly makes the loving family the norm, but it tells us nothing about how many of the remaining six in ten marriages have one or two unhappy people staying in them because they believe it's best for the children, or because they don't have the financial ability to set up a life on their own. In 1999 more than 34,000 children under 16 were on the child protection register in England and Wales. And of all the children born in the UK in 1979, the British government estimates that one in four will have been affected by divorce before reaching the age of 16.* I don't have any figures for those individuals in the world who are in therapy, on anti-depressants, or just plain unhappy and unable to make their lives, their loves, their occupations or their dreams work the way they want them to. But my guess is it's just about everyone. A family is the best environment to bring up a child? Really? It might be that in our time and society the family, composed of an adult or two and a couple of kids, is the only practical way to bring up a child, less emotionally fraught kinship systems being hard to keep in place in a post-industrial world. But, look around you, we may be lumbered with our structures and our fantasies, but the family we pour all our hopes into can hardly be called an unqualified success.

*These figures are taken from the Office for National Statistics, on the Government Statistical Service's website of census and surveys, current at time of publication.

Caramel Apples and Cotton Candy

The Celebration Chronicles: Life, Liberty and the Pursuit of
Property Values in Disney's New Town
by Andrew Ross. Verso 2000

Celebration, USA: Living in Disney's Brave New Town by
Douglas Frantz and Catherine Collins. Holt 1999

For a committed sedentary like myself, one of the most striking aspects of the populating of Disney's town of Celebration, Florida was the ease with which people made the decision to sell up and move there. In some cases, they crossed the continent, gave up substantial careers, took the kids out of school, put their property on the market, and signed a financial commitment to buy a plot of land on which not a single brick had been laid, in an alligator-infested swamp owned by a corporation which specialised in producing cartoons and simulations of historical and geographical clichés. Some people just popped in after a trip to next-door Disneyland and signed up for a new existence, others packed up and moved to rented accommodation nearby in order to be on the spot when the lottery for the first plots of land was announced.

You don't have to drive for very long in the States before you find yourself stuck behind a slow-moving house. Not one of those recreational vehicles that might as well be a house, but an

196

honest to goodness two bedroomed, living-room, kitchen and bathroom house that will, when it arrives where it is going, be fixed on elevated bricks and be called home by its inhabitants. At least for a while. The buildings in America may be on the move, but it's nothing compared to the lack of fixity of the people. Even houses that are built in situ, in towns and suburbs, have, no matter what the diversity of architectural style, an air of slightly rackety impermanence, as if their original builders had settled only for as long as it took for word to arrive of somewhere better. People in America move. They always have. They moved to get there in the first place, and then moved again for land, gold, work or just the thrill of going somewhere new. That is the myth, but look at the housing, and it's easy to believe that it is also the truth. The pretext for pulling up stakes and starting again somewhere else has always been to settle down finally in a better place, but surely the idea of transience has become embedded in American consciousness. The United States is a continent of individuals and families on the move, crossing and re-crossing the vast landmass, or exchanging one suburb for another. Ghost towns stand as relics of this tradition, signposted with pride as if their empty, decayed structures tell the American story better than towns and cities presently throbbing with living inhabitants who for the most part have come from somewhere else, or are going there. To be in one spot is a kind of limbo, whereas the ghost town's echo of an extinct past, of people upped and gone, the sense of a place utilised and then forsaken seems to speak of the romantic vigour of those who moved on, more than the waste and abandonment of what they left behind. The itinerant town was an essential component of the making of America. As the tracks were being laid across the wilderness by the railroad companies in their frantic race to bridge the Atlantic and Pacific coasts, supply trains brought the workers and their materials, along with the entire makings of an instant town for the labourers to sleep, eat and play in. These were the original *hell on wheels*, entire prefabricated buildings, broken down into their clapboard parts, like flats for a stage set; and travelling in the coaches behind, the saloon keepers, prostitutes, restaurateurs, gamblers and other essential personnel ready to set up the whole town in a day at the current furthest extent of the railroad. Whereupon life, death, drinking, whoring, gambling, fighting, and doubtless a little quiet poetic contemplation commenced until the railroad tracks had been laid beyond a certain outer limit, when the whole kit and caboodle was broken down, put back on the train and trundled off to the next stopping place.

There is no special mention of this restless tendency in either of these books on the town of Celebration, Florida, but for a European, the rootlessness of Americans is a central curiosity, as well as an unacknowledged factor in judging the degree to which families and individuals were really committing themselves in buying into the Disney dream life. The power of Disney in the psyche of America accounts for a good deal of blind trust, but the way in which people of all ages and classes are prepared to disrupt their lives and go somewhere else underlies and possibly undercuts that trust. Belief that Disney could turn its own fantasy into their reality persuaded people to take large risks. 'People trusted Disney,' said one resident. 'They trusted that Disney standards would ensure that the community they were going to live in would be better than most, if not superbly better than most. I think that is the only reason most people came here.' The original planners of Celebration themselves feared the Disneyphiles they would attract, the ones 'who go to Disney World eight times a year and think that because Main Street is clean they can extrapolate that to a community and think that it is going to be perfect. Those are the people who think their kids will never get a B in school and there is never going to be a weed in their lawn when they move to Celebration.' Though this did not prevent the corporation from blazoning the literature with Disney's name and putting a 30% premium on local property prices for unbuilt houses as an entrance fee to the Disney town. But the risks and the naïveté of those who paid their dollars to Disney were vitiated by their sheer willingness to move and then move on. If the pixie dust turned to dandruff you could always call U-Haul and wash it out of your hair. Ken and Patti and their three teenage children had already relocated from Minneapolis to San Antonio. 'It was two days before the lottery at Celebration, so I flew down and entered it. We didn't really know much about Celebration, but we decided to try it anyway. We figured if it didn't work out, we could always move again. It was a gamble. We'd see how it worked out.'

In 1966 Walt Disney was filmed unveiling his plan for a city of the future. It was that high-tech, old-fashioned future of the post-war era with 20,000 inhabitants living under a vast dome, flitting from skyscraper to skyscraper by high-speed monorail. You can almost see Captain Kirk's thigh-hugging trews and belted tunic. Epcot (Experimental Prototype Community of Tomorrow) would have no slums and no unemployment. This was not an unrealistic daydream on Disney's part because Epcot would be built on the 45 square miles of land Disney had accumulated in Florida, and no one without a job would be allowed to live there. There would be no home ownership, everyone would have to rent their housing from the Disney company. Whether Disney ever planned to build Epcot is doubtful. The point of his speech was to persuade the Florida Senate to approve the creation of the Reedy Creek Improvement District so that the Disney land became a sovereign government with the right to issue tax-free bonds for internal improvements, to construct new rides, sewers and buildings according to its own codes and standards without seeking approval from the Orange County planning department. The company's total control over the environment was ensured. There were in the event just forty inhabitants of Reedy Creek who were entitled to vote and they were all employ-ees who lived in company housing. Even before the Magic Kingdom had fully cast its spell over generations of Americans, the Disney dream had turned the heads of the politicians. Though those heads were not entirely soft. The financial spin-off for Orange County of millions of tourists heading in its direction was deemed to be worth the loss of political control. After which, coincidental with the death of Walt Disney, no more was heard of the fabled city of Epcot, until in 1997 parts of the 1966 film were edited into a video produced by the Disney company to promote the sales of plots of land in the newly planned town they called Celebration. The magic had by now had 30 years to take hold and its powerful grip on the imagination of Americans is indicated by a man in the audience of prospective buyers whis-pering to his companion, 'He hasn't aged at all.'

It depends on your notion of future and past whether you view the shift from Epcot to Celebration as a backward or for-ward movement. Luckily, the movie *Back to the Future* came out in 1985 and elided the two directions, pointing to an underlying anxiety that was at the heart of the Disney conception of the new town. It was necessary to go back in order to improve the future. Something had gone wrong with post-war living arrangements that had turned a hopeful world sour. The source of the problem was town planning and architecture. And the source of that prob-lem was modernism. When Cesar Pelli was invited to design the Celebration cinema he said he wanted to create a modern movie theatre. That was fine, he was told by Robert Stern overseeing the town's look, as long as Pelli understood that as far as Celebration was concerned, modern ended with the 1930s. The future as defined by the brochure from Michael Eisner's Disney Corporation was to be found not in Walt's skyscrapers and monorails, but in a long, lost past of white picket fences and pastel dormer windows, so lost that perhaps it was entirely mythic:

> There was once a place where neighbors greeted neighbors in the quiet of summer twilight. Where children chased fireflies. And porch swings provided easy refuge from the care of the day. The movie house showed cartoons on Saturday. The grocery store delivered. And there was one teacher who always knew you had that 'special something.' Remember that place? Perhaps from your childhood. Or maybe just from stories . . . There is a place that takes you back to that time of innocence. A place where the biggest decision is whether to play Kick the Can or King of the Hill. A place of caramel apples and cotton candy, secret forts, and hopscotch on the streets. That place is here again, in a new town called Celebration.

It was only at the last minute that they decided against providing a backstory for Celebration, a concocted history that had the town built by the survivors of a shipwrecked Spanish galleon or rising from the rubble of General Sherman's march through the South. In fact Celebration rose from a swampy lot at the edge of the Magic Kingdom that was used to relocate alligators once they grew too big for the ponds beside the golf courses and theme parks. It was a flourishing wetland of 10,300 acres, which, if left undeveloped, was in danger of being taken over by the state of Florida for its environmental value. Disney could have created a highly profitable gated community of the kind springing up all over the States for 'white flight' middle-class refugees from what they see as a troubling multicultural world. But Michael Eisner and his Imagineers wanted to try for something with more glory. Walt's (possibly duplicitous) dream of Epcot became a dream of building a neo-traditional community from scratch. Great empire builders in the past have wanted to leave monuments, so perhaps did Eisner who described architect Aldo Rossi's office building at Celebration as 'our own La Défense'. Andrew Ross relates that a few years previously Rossi had broken off discussions with Eisner about designing a building for Euro Disney, declaring, 'I realize I am not Bernini. But you are not the King of France. I quit.'

Instead of a backstory they had the five cornerstones that newcomers were invited to recite at their induction meeting: education, wellness, technology, place and community. The good past as represented by a fleet of famous post-modernist architects was to be combined with the latest in fibre-optic Internet technology from AT&T, medical equipment from Johnson & Johnson, GlaxoWellcome and Hewlett-Packard, and progressive education devised by Stanford University. Celebration was to be an experiment in neo-traditionalism and privatisation on a grand scale. To escape the soulless deserts of American suburbia, dormitories designed for the benefit of the motor and tarmac industries, the new concept was for high density – five or six dwellings per acre rather than one or two – mixed housing, where public space was valued more highly than private enclosure. The houses had small back gardens and porches rather than alienating front lawns, to persuade people to use the communal parks and piazzas instead of retreating behind their own four walls. To enhance a sense of community the houses were within walking distance of the commercial centre of the town and had to conform to design guidelines that regulated everything from the basic house design to the colour of the curtains showing on to the street and what plants might be grown in the yards and on balconies. Buyers signed contracts agreeing to these things and more. No more than two people were permitted to sleep in one bedroom, the Celebration Corporation (TCC) had the right to dispose of any pet which caused complaint, without consulting its owner, and political signs, measuring no more than eighteen by twenty-four inches, were only allowed to be posted in a yard for 45 days before an election. If certain individual freedoms are given up, it is for the benefit of the community as a whole, the rubric goes. In the case of Celebration this ran to political freedom. It was to be a town whose senior officer was not an elected mayor, but the manager of the Celebration Company owned by Disney. The Celebration Company retained a veto on all matters of government and there was no democratic representation in the running of the school, hospital or town hall. This apparently stunning loss of control is accepted by the householders in Celebration. A doctor living in the town explains:

> I'd rather live in a civil than a political society. Here we have a contract with TCC that defines our property rights, and we are not frustrated by bureaucrats with their own agenda. I don't have a contract with politicians . . . What we have here is a deconstructing of government, a rollback of politicization. In a civil society you feel a desire to fit into a community and satisfy your neighbors. In a political society, under the heavy hand of government, you expect your neighbors to satisfy you.

A former teacher who runs the Media Centre agreed.

> I accept this. I'm happy with it. I personally am opposed to elected officials. People who want to go into elected positions, I am suspicious of their motivations.

Andrew Ross, though living in a rented apartment in Celebration for a year in order to write his book, disagrees as he ponders the future of the town based on corporate management. 'There could hardly be a worse way of guaranteeing the public interest in education than by turning it over to corporate hucksters, or even by entrusting it to temporary corporate executives, however sympathetic, who see a way to boost the PR ratings of their employer by doing a few good community deeds. In the corporate world, allying with a well-known brand name is like hitching your wagon to the brightest star in the firmament, at least until the next stock market swing, leveraged buyout, or disappointing quarterly statement. But public trust needs the support of earthly bodies, in an orbit that is dependable, for the long run. When a society allows public education to be dependent on lottery funds or the passing benevolence of toy manufacturers and soda producers, it has already walked away from its democratic obligations.'

Certainly many of the inhabitants of Celebration discovered that when things began to go wrong, the Disney name disappeared overnight from the town sign. The two construction companies licensed by Disney to build and sell the houses were not able to maintain the fabled Disney standards. Houses were eighteen months late, with faulty roofs, sewage systems and air conditioning. Those who could not stand the disruption were offered a deal by TCC, that they could, against their contract, sell their houses before the first year was up, providing they did not go to the press. When the ultra-progressive school turned out not to use books in its teaching methods, and refused to grade its students, assessing them instead with evaluations such as 'not yet', 'listens actively for a variety of purposes' and 'respects human diversity as part of our multicultural society and world', which parents discovered would not get their kids into any decent college, they held secret meetings, for fear of being termed 'negative parents' and shunned by the community, but had no elected voice within the school government. People turned to Disney with their grievances, even writing to Michael Eisner of their complaints, but they received no reply from the corporation which dreaded bad publicity. The fabled fibre optics came to nothing after the relevant division of AT&T was sold off and the company withdrew its experimental equipment.

Nonetheless, the pressure to be a happy member of the community was enormous. Residents of Celebration were watched and watched each other like hawks. The watchers were even within their community. Ross in his apartment, and Douglas Frantz and Catherine Collins in a house that they actually bought in order to write a book about the town. Both parties were open about their intentions and both invested a year of their lives and in Frantz and Collins' case a year of their two children's education as well as $350,000 on purchasing the house. Ross has a tougher take on what it was that made the will to conform so strong. The public silence on the part of the townspeople about the disasters of Celebration, the jerry-built houses, the school, and the intense pressure on dissenting individuals to stop complaining or leave was much more, for Ross, to do with keeping up the property values than with an underlying community spirit. All along a Disney town was perceived as a good investment opportunity, and people paid above the odds and put up with the vagaries of a town not yet fully built in the hope that their houses would rise in price. They had hitched their wagon to Disney's star for more perhaps than the dream value. Frantz and Collins do not make this analysis and seem to have integrated more fully into the community than Ross. They try to write as residents rather than as outsiders, though the line they walk is too fine to be convincing. Neither party intended to stay beyond gathering data for their books; Ross has a sabbatical from NYU, but Frantz and Collins give the impression of wondering if they might. In fact they remained an extra year, leaving finally because despite getting on well with their neighbours, they missed edge and culture. 'The town looked inward, sealing itself off from a world that ended at its borders. It was restrictive, almost tribal, and it left us feeling at times out of touch and uncomfortable in a place where life's edges were rounded and smoothed not by time but by choice.' They note that 'almost none of the houses we visited had bookshelves'.

Celebration had no poor either. The teachers at the school couldn't afford even the prices of the rented apartments in town, while Disney employees, often Hispanic immigrants, paid at the minimum wage of $5.95 an hour, couldn't hope to buy into Celebration. Disney agreed to pay Osceola County $300,000 over three years instead of building affordable housing into their plans. Brent Herrington, TCC's community manager, saw the lack of cheap housing as a plus. 'What happens is, in an affordable house that is couched as an entitlement, you don't have the same kind of personal commitment and pride in your accomplishment in this new home. If people come to a place just because their name popped up when that community had a vacancy, they are not going to have the same commitment to the town. That's the part I think the residents would probably have some squeamishness about.' Both sets of journalists report residents bemoaning the lack of black residents (even middle-class blacks would not buy in to the Disney dream) and the homogeneity, but neither are convinced. A businessman from Celebration spoke to Ross of a recent 'Latin influx' to Osceola County (many of whom would be Disney employees), making a distinction between good and bad Hispanics, 'These are not Latins from Long Island, mind you, they are from south of the border and Puerto Rico.' A woman tells Ross, 'Osceola is a low-rent county with too many ethnics – it's basically a bedroom community for hotel domestics.' Younger people of the boomer generation are more confused about their racism: 'I don't care myself, although this is a white ghetto. I would welcome more diversity as long as it doesn't drive the prices down.' Ross makes the wider point: 'Today, white people are often at their most white when they believe that consciousness of race is not natural . . . white-skin privilege abides and goes unexamined when it's no longer "natural" to think about someone's racial background and is perceived to be racist to do so. As Malcolm X pointed out, "racism is like a Cadillac. There's a new model every year."'

Ross regularly provides the wider analysis, while Frantz and Collins better capture the texture of life in Celebration, but both, having been neighbours of those they are writing about, are remarkably gentle about the fantastic absurdity of the Magic Kingdom dream that brought the residents of Celebration together, and the intellectual process that lies behind both the decision to live in and the decision to build a community out of sentimental escapism.

After all the quality of dreaming matters. There are dreamers and dreamers. Great dreamers, on the whole, are saints or sinners (the Marquis de Sade, Simon Stylites), variations on innocence, whom we revere or abhor, while your everyday small-scale worldly dreamer (the bloke down the road who wants to build a conservatory, the woman saving up for a breast enhancement) is a more mundane figure for whom we are more likely to feel contempt. The degree to which we admire or despise dreamers depends mainly on the size of the dream and the distance of the dreamer from our own lives. Grand dreams about peace and social justice and the like are accorded great reverence, probably because we don't believe the dreams are remotely achievable but we're glad someone is wasting their time on them. It salves our conscience and gives us an easy object of admiration. We are very pleased that Martin Luther King had a dream, and that Nelson Mandela held to his dream through twenty-five years on Robben Island, mostly because we are grateful that we don't have to do it ourselves, or watch our children's lives being sacrificed to their principles. Impractical dreaming that amounts to something in the world we positively venerate, at least in retrospect. But then very often what we call admiration is, on closer examination, a special form of contempt.

But what of those who simply dream of having a notionally nice life and who are in the fortunate position to buy into it when an ersatz version is offered to them by a corporate dream-maker?

This is very difficult for the liberal observer because to admit contempt for ordinary dreams goes terribly against the grain. As soon as the news broke of the Disney Corporation building a 'real' town to be filled with real people that took an idyllic homely past as its theme, the press and academia groaned their disdain. It was OK to despise Disney, the progenitor of the saccharine Mouse, who has become a synonym for all that is false and tacky. But what about those who choose to take up residence in the Magic Kingdom? What follows is a customer's review from Amazon.com of Frantz and Collins' almost excruciatingly balanced account of their stay in Celebration:

> Written by left leaning, snivelling reporters. They are critical of Disney's handling of the wetlands, yet the authors bought a house in the middle of the wetlands. They snipe about Disney not giving away part of their profit margin to accommodate low income people, yet didn't rent out their 'granny flat' to an underprivileged person. As true liberals the authors see corporations as responsible for everyone's welfare . . . It would be nice at least once to hear them thank Disney. Thank you Disney for your vision. Thank you Disney for risking your capital. Thank you for fighting the political battles to make Celebration possible.

Utopia, these days, is a Mickey Mouse business.

Movie Monk

The New Biographical Dictionary of Film
by David Thomson. Little, Brown 2002

Nobody's Perfect: Writings from the 'New Yorker'
by Anthony Lane. Picador 2002

Paris Hollywood: Writings on Film by Peter Wollen.
Verso 2002

I think it is two years since I've been to the cinema. This is something of a mystery to me, like love gone wrong: in fact, it is love gone wrong. Was the love misguided in the first place, have I simply aged out of the way of love, or has the beloved altered beyond all recognition? Naturally, lovers whose love is depleted are inclined to think the last: it makes them feel better, less fickle, less hopeless, that the loss is not their own fault. But it's always best to doubt such self-serving conclusions. Generally, things are one's fault, unless it can be positively proved otherwise. Anyway, sit me in front of *Bringing Up Baby*, *The Wild Bunch* or *The Conversation* and I'm ravished. It's not the films I love that I've fallen out of love with.

So, the cinema. I don't go any more. Not for lack of opportunity: there is an excellent cinema barely five minutes away with multiple screens and a grown-up programming policy. I'd be free to go in the afternoon all alone (an old movie-going treat) or in company of an evening. But I don't. I notice a film that I think might be good, and then shake my head at the idea of actually going to see it. The risk of disappointment is too great: I would rather wait until it comes out on VHS or DVD and buy it or rent it from MovieMail. That way, when it turns out to be, at best, only half-good, I won't have got cold, or wet, or cross with myself for being too demanding or not demanding enough. What a way to be a film-lover.

Films were everything to me in my teens. I'd bunk off school to get to the first afternoon showing of the first day of *8½* or *Pierrot le Fou*, hunkering down in the red plush seats of the Academy cinema, along with, though at a proper distance from, a couple of severe film buffs, a woman in dark glasses trying to distract herself from an affair gone wrong, an Oxford Street shopper in from the rain and a pervert or two hoping for some Continental movie action. I spent whole days and nights at the NFT catching up on what I'd missed in previous decades (Bogart weekends, seven hours of *Les Vampires*, an all-night marathon screening of the *Apu* trilogy), and every Hollywood musical and melodrama shown on TV was another opportunity to fill in the gaps. Watching movies of any kind in any way was the purest pleasure. Good, almost good, bad. I dreamed that one day it would be possible to own films and watch them at home. Be careful what you wish for.

Partly my reluctance to go to the movies comes from a newish but unshakeable sense of the absurdity of sitting in a darkened room with dozens or hundreds of other people, all facing in the same direction. I imagine the roof being taken off the cinema and a baffled child giant looking down on us and wondering what kind of thing the human race could be. But minor psychoses aside, the terrible thing is that I don't miss going to the cinema.

Audiences chatter, eat, drink, wander about and are reliably over six foot when they sit in front of me – it was always so, but now either they do it worse and taller, or my tolerance threshold has sunk to sea level. What I do miss however is wanting to go to the cinema. Only very rarely in the last decade or so (the reissue of *Nights of Cabiria, Happiness, The Usual Suspects*) have I felt that the movie I was seeing was worth putting up with the irritation and effort of going out. Am I feeling the way people feel as they get older about a world that no longer seems to be addressed to them? Movies, after all, aren't made with me in mind any more. Do I just resent that, or does it really make for poorer movies?

There is one reliable cinematic pleasure that remains to me: I indulge in reading about movies with undiminished enthusiasm. David Thomson has written about his disappointment with contemporary cinema, about how the franchise movie and the blockbuster are killing Hollywood and his hopes, and because I am one of the legion of Thomson's devoted fans, it cheers me up to hear it. If he thinks so then it's not just me feeling jaded: maybe there is an objective difference (or else we are of a similar age and therefore suffering from the same nostalgia syndrome). In a review (in the *New Republic*) of Anthony Lane's book *Nobody's Perfect*, Thomson, aged sixtyish, compares a non-exhaustive list of the movies available for Pauline Kael to review in the 1970s with those reviewed in the *New Yorker* by Lane, aged between 30 and 40. Here's his 1970s list: *Bonnie and Clyde, The Godfather* (1 & 2), *The Conversation, McCabe and Mrs Miller, California Split, Nashville, Chinatown, The Long Goodbye, The Last Detail, Shampoo, Mean Streets, Taxi Driver, The Conformist, Last Tango in Paris, Carrie, The Fury, The French Connection, The Exorcist, Klute, The Parallax View, Jaws, Close Encounters of the Third Kind, Annie Hall, American Graffiti, Star Wars, Harold and Maude, Two-Lane Blacktop, Five Easy Pieces, The King of Marvin Gardens, Badlands.* These are the movies reviewed by

Lane that Thomson lists: *Indecent Proposal, Sleepless in Seattle, Speed, Wolf, Forrest Gump, Pulp Fiction, Braveheart, The Bridges of Madison County, Crash, Con Air, Contact, Titanic, Godzilla, Ronin, Meet Joe Black, The Phantom Menace, Gladiator, Mission: Impossible 2.*

A couple of interesting films in the second list, and a couple of uninteresting ones in the first. It's not quite fair because Thomson has left some seriously good movies out of the later list (for example, *LA Confidential, The Usual Suspects, Thirty Two Short Films about Glenn Gould*), and a few others (*Nil by Mouth, The English Patient, The Truman Show, Shallow Grave*) that someone might feel it was worth crossing the road for; but in general his argument that Lane's evident talent has had little to work on and is condemned to dissipate itself in being wickedly witty about lousy films holds true. (Not that wickedly witty doesn't provide great pleasure. On Woody Harrelson in *Indecent Proposal*: 'The whole thing needs a leading man with snap and vim, instead of which it gets Woody Harrelson. Admittedly, it's an awful part, which calls for little more than unfocused emoting, but then Woody trying to emote looks like anyone else trying to go to sleep. At one point, he has to give a lecture on the inspiring joys of architecture, rising to the contention that "even a brick wants to be something." He should know.') Thomson's point, in his review, is avuncular, if a little smug: Lane, who has claimed Thomson as a mentor, is suffering from being born too late.

Thomson is besotted with the cinema: Lane would be if he could. As it is, he is largely obliged as a film reviewer to keep his pen poised for deadly lines (on *The Bridges of Madison County*: 'There's a hunk of baloney devoted to Africa, all about "the cohabitation of man and beast", but worse is to come: at one point . . . Clint Eastwood wears a pair of *sandals*. Whatever for? You don't see the Dalai Lama packing a .44 Magnum'). As if he knows the world of contemporary film isn't enough to detain him, a third of Lane's book consists of literary essays, and another third is devoted to profiles of a few directors mostly long gone and others not notable for their movie credits – Karl Lagerfeld, Walker Evans, Ernest Shackleton and Lego. In Thomson's view film ought to be enough to detain a film-loving writer, but it isn't. Perhaps Lane is merely keeping his options open and, who knows, doesn't want to be a writer exclusively on film. The diversity is admirable, but it blurs the focus of Lane's book.

Thomson's *Biographical Dictionary of Film*, first published almost thirty years ago and now in a revised fourth edition, is constantly proclaimed a cult book, and movie-lovers await new editions in the way *Star Wars* fans anticipate back stories. It functions like a prototype of hypertext. You check out one entry and find you have to follow up others, each of which gets you fanning the pages to find further references. Try 'Cary Grant' and see if you can manage not to read about Hawks, Hitchcock, Hepburn, Mae West, Capra; except that having got to the Hawks entry, you are deflected on to Elisha Cook, Montgomery Clift, Boris Karloff, and each of those will send you off on another mystery tour . . . I have spent whole days leafing through names and chasing the shadows disappearing through Thomson's pages. If someone could only make it into a film, then cinema would have achieved its apotheosis. Actually, Thomson himself has already turned it into a novel, *Suspects* (1985), which pretends to be a biographical dictionary of an array of fictional characters from great movies: the likes of Richard Blaine and Ilsa Lund, George Bailey, Travis Bickle and Norman Bates, who turn out, in the interstices of the entries, to have entangled lives and a dark plot all of their own. If only Howard Hawks wasn't dead and had made a movie of *Suspects* we could all die happy and go to deconstruction heaven.

Though the characters in the *Biographical Dictionary* would claim not to be fictional, they are utterly at the mercy of

Thomson's wayward and wonderful opinions and his ornate and seductive prose. Philip French considers Thomson's prose too baroque and his opinions not disinterested enough for his taste. But if you were in the business, you would be furious at being left out of the *Dictionary*, even though the risks of inclusion are great. Thomson quotes from Lars von Trier's third manifesto:

> There is only one excuse for having to go through, and force others to go through, the hell that is the creative process of film. The carnal pleasure of that split second in the cinemas, when the projector and the loudspeakers, in unison, allow the illusion of sound and motion to burst forth, like an electron abandoning its orbit to generate light, and create the ultimate: a miraculous surge of life.

Thomson concludes: 'We could note several things from this: that one man's carnal ecstasy may be another's imagination; that sometimes there are no excuses; and that the language of self-inducing cinematic exultation is oddly akin to the rhetoric of fascism.' Sheer joy. And as for Roberto Benigni's god-help-us-all Oscar-winning *La Vita è Bella*:

> Despite the enormous effect *Bambi* had on me as a child, I have had difficulty digesting Thumperism – I mean, the philosophy that if you can't say anything nice, don't say nothing at all . . . There are candidates for honest badmouthing, reaching from one's relatives to the alleged leaders of your world. And there is Roberto Benigni.

In spite of loathing Benigni's previous efforts Thomson would have been inclined to omit him from the *Dictionary*, but:

> Then came the thing called *La Vita è Bella*. I often echo that sentiment myself, but if there is anything likely to mar *bella*-ness it is

not so much Hitlerism (I am against it), which is fairly obvious, as Benigni-ism, which walks away with high praise, box office and Oscars. I despise *Life is Beautiful*, especially its warmth, sincerity and feeling, all of which I believe grow out of stupidity. Few events so surely signalled the decline of the motion picture as the glory piled on that odious and misguided fable. I am sure Mr Benigni is kind to children and animals. I am prepared to accept that he is a model citizen and a good companion. Still, *Life is Beautiful* is a disgrace.

Thomson's views should be available to any off-planeters who happen to find themselves viewing *la vita* through Benigni's sickly viewfinder.

Not that my devotion to Thomson's *Dictionary* depends only on those of his opinions I agree with. *The Piano*, a film I abominated, 'is a great film in an age that has nearly forgotten such things . . . The sense of place, of spirit and of silence is Wordsworthian . . . No one has better caught the mix of sensitivity and ferocity in the human imagination.' An imaginary argument ensues on reading this, which Thomson wins (even though he's quite wrong) because he loves films better and is a more generous person than I am.

French is right: Thomson has no distance from film. He responds directly to what he sees and puts it down on paper. It sounds most of the time as if he really minds. That's what makes reading him so exciting. Here's where Lane's excellent wit and easy prose fall short of Thomson's passion. When Lane writes of his admiration for *Titanic*, you do a double-take, and instead of having an argument, pass on, shaking your head and wondering if his other judgments were as solid as they seemed to be. If Thomson had liked *Titanic* (he didn't), I'd have bothered to stop for a fight.

In *Paris Hollywood: Writings on Film*, Peter Wollen makes no mention of *Titanic*, and one would rather hesitate to mention it to him. He writes as an academic, which does not mean he loves film any less than Thomson, but does mean that his love isn't as evident. His essays sometimes cover the same ground as those of the other two, but he is not doing the same thing. When he writes of Howard Hawks it is not with the perplexed adoration of Thomson who would take ten Hawks movies to his desert island and let the rest of the directors go hang, even though Hawks's macho values worry him: 'a moviemaker for boys never quite grown up'. Wollen writes an informed and magisterial article about why it took so long for the mandarins of film criticism to admit Hawks to 'the canon', but it's much less a piece about Hawks's movies and their understated qualities than a historical overview of the debates between critics writing about Hawks.

Similarly, Wollen's essay on Hitchcock is written 'against compartmentalisation', with the purpose of discrediting the idea that the director's oeuvre can be neatly divided into his English and American periods. He argues that in 1919 Hitchcock was working for the American-owned and managed studio Famous Players-Lasky and that in his Hollywood years a class-conscious Englishness is central to his work. You feel that it is a contribution to a debate about Hitchcock that you haven't been part of but which must have been going on somewhere, between critics, and Wollen argues his case efficiently, but it doesn't make you rush to your video shelf to check the movies out. He writes careful, well-ordered pieces: on *Blade Runner* and its relation to economic writings on the World City Hypothesis, or on the importance of the canon and the necessity of it being rewritten from time to time. 'Looking back on those years, I can see now that "auteurism" was the last major and explicit attempt to rewrite the film canon.'

We are in a different realm of film-writing from both Lane and Thomson: a world where a debate is going on between cognoscenti far away from Hollywood, even though Wollen has the Chair of the Department of Film, Television and New Media at UCLA, and even though he, of the three writers, is the only film-maker. Yet he is the one who seems to have kept his gloves on: the other two appear to have rolled up their sleeves and got their hands dirty. It's a different way, perhaps, of loving movies, but he never, as Thomson does often and Lane does sometimes, finds himself daydreaming his way through the screen into the movie, like Buster Keaton does in *Sherlock Jr*. Wollen keeps his place in the auditorium; but then someone's got to stay there and keep watch.

Thomson, on the other hand, for all that he might tick Lane off for dangerous slickness, is himself sometimes at the mercy of his writing talent. Mind you, his apparent deviations from the point have a mad method to them. He riffs with an almost crazed meticulousness about Hoagy Carmichael as Cricket in *To Have and Have Not*. 'He sits at a piano that manages to be set aslant to everything else in the world. He has white pants (they might be cream or ivory) with a dark stripe in them, and it could be crimson or dark blue against the cream (this is Martinique light). And in the shirt there is the same pattern of vertical dark striping on a pale ground, except that the stripes are twice as regular.' But from that beginning he gets to the heart and soul of Hawks's movie. He rants about Madonna; after a list of her various film involvements up to *Dangerous Games*, he writes: 'The burden does not lighten . . . then all the ads said she was Evita – no matter that she managed hardly any emotional involvement, and again seemed incapable of understanding the nature of acting. Still, nothing before had been as fatuous as *The Next Best Thing*.' He rambles about Kim Basinger: 'I don't always "get" Kim Basinger. I mean, why did she ever buy that small town in Georgia, and why is she virtually the only actress who's ever been sued successfully for getting out of a movie (*Boxing Helena*)? Why marry Alec Baldwin? Is she, even, that beautiful? Well, the paper didn't catch fire, so I'll press on.'

Thomson refuses to line up with the Hitchcock devotees (Lane among them):

> The method, despite its brilliance, is equally private and restrictive. To plan so much that the shooting becomes a chore is an abuse not just of actors and crew, but of cinema's predilection for the momentary. It is, in fact, the style of an immense premeditative artist – a Bach, a Proust or a Rembrandt. And beside those masters, Hitchcock seems an impoverished inventor of thumbscrews who shows us the human capacity for inflicting pain, but no more. Such precision can only avoid seeming overbearing and misanthropic if it is accompanied by creative untidiness. In the last resort, his realised blueprints affirm film's yearnings for doubt and open endings.

Contentious? Irritating? Dubious? Yes. What a relief to have something gristly to gnaw on. Thomson urges Lane to give up his Atlantic-hopping and move full-time to America if he really wants to be 'more than a brilliant movie reviewer': 'It is the best advice I can offer. And I think it might be fun – as in fun to run a newspaper, the sport that made Charles Foster Kane famous, and that destroyed him.' The romanticism oozes out of Thomson, but I see him more as a mad movie monk, huddled decade after decade over his ever-expanding *Dictionary*, scratching his illuminated prose in the flickering light, murmuring to himself about distant memories, cackling at his own jokes and wondering why there is such a shortage of young fellows willing to join him in the monastery.

Get On With It

The Knox Brothers by Penelope Fitzgerald. Harvil 1990

In the decade after the war, and long before Harry Potter, I learned what an English family was supposed to be from the books I found in the children's library. There were the Darlings of Barrie's *Peter Pan*, the Christopher Robins and James James Morrison Morrison Wetherby George Duprees of A. A. Milne, Edmund, Lucy, Peter and Susan of C. S. Lewis's Narnia stories, Great Uncle Gum's Fossils in Noel Streatfield's *Ballet Shoes*, the long-suffering humans who were the source of *The Borrowers'* wherewithal and the Bastables from E. Nesbitt's *Treasure Seekers*. None of these children came from backgrounds anything like my own, but they were, I had no doubt, the real thing, and me and mine an aberration from the norm of proper middle-class English life. The families of the children from the books were not rich or aristocratic, some indeed were suffering genteel poverty, a falling away of a style of life they had once been accustomed to, because of the changing times (war-time shortages, post-war austerity, the loss of parents through war or carelessness), but they all exhibited similar standards of speech, behaviour, education and mutuality that I learned to think of as distinguishing elements of an English upbringing. I could taste and smell those rambling, underheated, over-corridored houses the siblings (almost always more than one of them) ranged around, and heard their effort-less elocution as they called to each other, although I lived in a centrally heated two-roomed city centre flat, alone with just my mother and father, both of them the children of heavily accented immigrants. I knew exactly how it should be, but I also knew how alien I was from it; as alien in my actual life in England from real English life as I was from the world of fairy and folk tales that were the other source of my reading. This is part of the reality of growing up in a class-bound society, where the slightest shade of rank could be discerned from a single syllable or the quality of a walk. The problem was not that I wasn't middle class, but that I could not fit myself into any of the official degrees of Englishness, since even second generation Jewish immigrants were then out of the loop. However, I knew from reading and from the very air I breathed, it seemed, precisely how the system worked. And, of course, I fervently wished I belonged, not just because belonging is what children wish to do, but because after all whatever hardships or heartache the characters had to suffer, they counted enough to inhabit story books. It wasn't just that they had substance, but that they *were* the substance of the country I inhabited and the imaginative life I led, as mythic to me as the fairy-tale princes and princesses, but real too. I believed in them, most of all because they seemed so utterly to believe in themselves.

This conflation of fairy tale and a perfect English family appears in the introduction to Penelope Fitzgerald's memoir of her Edwardian father and his three brothers, as she recalls how each Knox brother counselled her on her wedding day. She doesn't begin 'Once upon a time', or entitle it 'The Four Wishes', but:

'Evoe, my father, muttered to me on the way to my wedding, "The only thing I want is for everyone, as far as possible, to be happy." Dillwyn: "Nothing is impossible." Wilfred: "Get on with it" – also "Why should we not go on, through all eternity, growing in love and in our power to love?" Ronnie: "Do the most difficult thing."'

Imagine coming into the world and having ready-made, not on paper, but in the flesh, these four benevolent, brilliant, quirky spirits watching over you. You would, of course, want to notate and celebrate such a family, to make a story book of their lives and utterances. And reading it, I experience in myself an immediate return to my childhood voyeurism, and a confusion of envy and derision at the familiar echoes that retain such power, even now I know there is a price the proper English family has to pay.

Evoe – Edmund – became the editor of *Punch* and a famous wit. Dillwyn was a distinguished classicist who became the prototype of the eccentric code-breaker at Station X in Bletchley Park when he found the key to Germany's Enigma coding machine. Wilfred settled to being an Anglo-Catholic priest, living a quietly saintly existence devoted to poverty and told only a single lie in his whole life. Ronald, a Catholic convert, was chaplain of Oxford, a translator of the New Testament, as well as a writer of detective fiction and popular newspaper columns.

The Knox boys (there were two sisters: Winnie, who gives sweetness and succour to the brothers, but who doesn't count in Fitzgerald's mind as extraordinary like the boys; and Ethel, who is somewhat backward and simply doesn't count) were the sons of an Anglican Bishop, himself a descendant of rectors, chaplains and the odd Quaker, going back to the eighteenth century. On their mother's side, there were vicars and a grandfather, Thomas French, Bishop of Lahore, who was more of a wandering fakir and seems to have been revered as a saint by Christians and Hindus alike. Fitzgerald's story of her uncles' lives begins at the time called Edwardian when England was still a place of empire and certainty, and God was another term for good-breeding. The story continues, however, through two world wars and the social turmoil they brought, when even the children of the establishment had to find their relation to modernity. Penelope Fitzgerald, a fine novelist, wrote the book in 1977, completing this new edition just before she died earlier this year at the age of 84, and it is clear from the moments when her own voice calls through the quiet, admiring, pellucid narrative, that she has her own uneasy relation to the contemporary world. The sense of a lost world is palpable on every page.

The family story has the inevitable trajectory of nursery brilliance transforming into academic highflying, an essential English eccentricity, and final eminence in whatever field the boys chose. Mixed in with this mellifluous progress are a series of difficulties in the form of personal tragedy (the early death of their mother, the death of wives and beloved friends) and excruciating moral and religious choices which shake but fail to rupture the family affections. Their childhood in large draughty rectories was exemplary. They learned and recited the whole of Bradshaw's *Railway Guide* along with Macaulay's *Lays of Ancient Rome*. They forbade any one of them from speaking a language all the others didn't understand, though Ronnie threatened to learn Sanskrit and Welsh. Dilly was an erratic but brilliant cricketer, and so was not permitted to make more than one hundred and fifty runs a game. They invented rules of life and play so recondite, no outsider could hope to break in, and the family game-playing developed naturally as if it were training into the poetry, code deciphering, translating and theologising they were to do for the rest of their lives. In the Thirties, when spending eighteen hours a day deciphering German code was not enough, Dilly contrived a new five-line verse form he called a Pentelope. Each line had to end with a word of the same form, but with a different vowel, which had to come in their proper order, a, e, i, o, u, or the equivalent sounds in English:

Just look at my father
And mother together!
I fancy that neither
Would very much bother
If rid of the other.

He was accused of creating a form that was too rule-bound to handle genuine emotion, so on A. E. Housman's death he produced a Pentelope obituary with echoes of 'They told me, Heraclitus, they told me you were dead . . .'

Sad though the news, how sad
Of thee, the poet, dead!
But still thy poems abide –
There Death, the unsparing god
Himself dare not intrude.

The family affection for each other became degrees of socialism in all the brothers which meant even the most religious of them expected goodness to have some positive effect on the ills of the world. Their brilliance, of course, went without saying. Of the four, only Eddie failed to get his Oxbridge first (although as the editor of *Punch* he was awarded an honorary D. Litt.), while Ronald, the youngest, was one of those golden ones who in each generation is regarded by both students and masters as the most brilliant boy who had ever been at Eton. At the age of four Ronnie was asked what he liked doing and replied, 'I think all day, and at night I think about the past.' Doubtless in Latin. Dilly, the second eldest, was the only one who went to Cambridge where, as a classicist of note at King's College, admired by Lytton

Strachey and best friend of Maynard Keynes, he became the only confirmed atheist in the family.

Not wanting to risk the immortal souls of the two youngest to the air of the godless Fens, the Bishop insisted that Wilfred and Ronald went to Oxford, where religion did indeed grip them, but caused more heartache (the Anglo-Catholicism of Wilfred, the eventual 'poping' of Ronnie) for the Bishop than Dillwyn's defection, which is glossed by Fitzgerald as 'nothing less than faith by an appeal to reason'. According to his niece, Dilly found Christianity a two-thousand-year-old swindle inducing human beings to be afraid or hopeful. 'If the swindle could be proved, that would "save his reason", and Dilly always hoped that it might be. Yet his attitude was always to defy God for what He had done, or reprove Him for not existing, rather than ignore Him because He didn't.' This is Fitzgerald being her usual tartly witty self, but also excusing her atheistic uncle by not quite believing in his disbelief. Penelope Fitzgerald is not just a narrator of the lives of her father and uncles, but a commentator whose passing thoughts about her subject and the state of the world place her firmly in the Knox tradition. She defends Wilfred's moral guide, Billy Temple, President of the Workers' Educational Association and Archbishop of Canterbury-to-be, from contemporary accusations of comic idealism, stating roundly in her own voice that 'church history should be judged, not by whether it is successful, but by whether it is right or wrong.' Right and wrong are clear to Fitzgerald as they were to her uncles. Speaking of the 'plain but good' upbringing of Christina Hicks, Eddie's wife and her mother, she tells how as children she and her sister would write down a list of all the things they wanted but couldn't afford, then they would burn the piece of paper. 'This is a device which is always worth trying,' Fitzgerald advises her reader. She takes a firmly humane view of the doctrinal anguish Ronnie's tendency to Catholicism caused his father: 'Surely one would think it must have been as clear then as it is now that if human love could rise above the doctrines that divide the Church, then these doctrines must have singularly little to do with the love of God.' But she keeps sentimentality where it belongs. On the subject of the perfect hard sauce or brandy butter the brothers craved at Christmas, but which only Merton College made correctly and then lost the knack of producing, she is severe: 'Perhaps perfection should be left where it belongs, in childhood.' She never, apart from her wedding wishes, refers directly to herself, but the novelist in her cannot help but regret the thoughtlessness of the younger generation of which she was part. Ronnie, the indulged child, became an indulged man, taken in and cared for by wealthy Catholic families. The younger generation, she says, 'felt he was in danger of getting a little like one of the recurrent characters in the glossy period films of those days, a clerical figure shyly entering the salon – "Why, Abb. Liszt, have you been writing anything new?" All this was quite unfair. They did not understand the priestly life, and underestimated the amount of happiness necessary to someone of fifty.'

What comes across is a departure from the modern notion of biography, where emotional distance and the use of popular psychology are supposed to provide bold insights into the shadowy motivations of those lost to the past. Instead there is frank affiliation with standards and ethics that bed her characters to their time, an acknowledgement that things have changed but no glee in filleting period from personality, and an understanding of the power of the past on a life without the dulling determinacy of the full Freudian project. It is, in a word, an old-fashioned account of time and place and people into which the time and place and character of Penelope Fitzgerald, the next generation, is cunningly and quite appropriately woven.

SEX . . .

Good Vibrations

Solitary Sex – A Cultural History of Masturbation
by Thomas W. Laqueur. Zone Books 2003

Some things, you would think, have been going on forever, but everything has its starting point. Didn't Philip Larkin tell us in *Annus Mirabilis* that sexual intercourse began in 1963 (though you may feel – and he would likely have agreed – that he was not the best person to consult on such matters)? And prior to sexual intercourse? Masturbation, naturally:

> *Up to then there'd only been*
> *A sort of bargaining*
> *A wrangle for the ring,*
> *A shame that started at sixteen*
> *And spread to everything.*

Now Thomas Laqueur, in a compendious and witty analysis of the subject, would have us know that masturbation had its beginnings, too, though on a more global timescale than Larkin's self-scrutinising view. It was a lot later than you'd think: Laqueur's thesis is that masturbation began in 1712, give or take a year or two. He is not, of course, suggesting that no one had thought of or performed the act of solitary sex before that date, any more than Larkin is implying that human beings had no idea how to get their genitalia together pre-1963, but, according to Laqueur, masturbation was quite specifically invented as a profound cultural concern in an anonymous pamphlet published in England entitled *Onanism*, which coincided with the early days of the European Enlightenment. No coincidence actually, Laqueur says. Cultural historians permit few coincidences. His history searches for the meaning behind the brouhaha caused by *Onanism*, with its bold new claim that masturbation debilitated the body even unto death and the mind to madness, and the bandwagon response to it of quacks, medical men, educationalists, clerics and *philosophes* alike.

In a comprehensive survey of attitudes to masturbation before the early 18th century Laqueur suggests that the subject had very little of the weight that was to be attached to it. For the Greeks it was a matter of hygiene – in the interests of maintaining a healthy balance of bodily fluids, Diogenes was applauded by Galen when he relieved himself by hand while waiting for a prostitute who turned up late. In antiquity, masturbation was either a joke about those sad enough not to have a partner in their sexual activities (no change there), or it was a useful outlet. Overheated pubescent girls were advised by Albertus Magnus to rub their clitorises in order to preserve their chastity. The problem in Jewish law was the spilling of seminal fluid – the seed that Yahweh made so much of in his promises to Abraham. The hapless Onan, unwilling husband of Tamar (and martyr, it would seem, to coitus interruptus rather than masturbation), is endlessly debated by the rabbis in Talmud and Midrash and their labyrinthine discussions are followed with mild exclamations of panic by Laqueur, looking for a single thread in a world where single threads come always in delightfully intricate bunches. 'But just when we think we recognize the vice whose history we are tracing, we are brought up short. Immediately after Rabbi Yosi's citation of Genesis 38.10, Rabbi Eliezer is reported to have asked, "Why is it written, 'Your hands are full of blood'? . . . These are those who commit adultery with their hand." Aha! But this is followed by the Tannaitic authority, who specifies that "you will not be subject to adultery, whether committed by hand or *by foot*.'" Christianity, on the whole, was against masturbation, in its grudging recognition of the sanctity of marriage ('It is better to marry than to burn'), but more in the sense that masturbation belonged to a group of sexual behaviours that were 'contrary to nature', that is, non-reproductive, such as sodomy, homosexuality and bestiality. Burchard of Worms in 1007 suggested 10 days on bread and water for masturbation, whereas sodomy drew a penance of 10 to 15 years. Even if Laqueur is not entirely convincing that pre-Enlightenment masturbation was inconsequential, he makes a plausible case for it being at least not a major source of anxiety before the 18th century.

The pamphlet, *Onanism*, was written with the purpose of describing a new medical condition for which the author and his doctor associate (himself) could, for a fee, provide medicine. Again, not much change. Just last January the *British Medical Journal* criticised research funded by drug companies which detected a new condition called Female Sexual Dysfunction, the treatment for which, say its manufacturer, Pfizer, is Viagra. A good way for Pfizer to sell 50% more Viagra, but a bogus illness, says the *BMJ*. What Thomas Laqueur finds when he considers the overwhelming response to the scurrilous pamphlet designed to enrich its author by playing on the fears and salacious fancies of its readers, is that solitary sex had come into its own (it is almost impossible to write about the subject without making even unintentional *double entendres*) as an autonomy too far in a world that was suddenly debating the nature of self-governance

231

after the decline of religious and state authority. 'As the purchase of natural restraints and a seemingly natural hierarchical political order underwritten by God and the heavens seems to wane, the importance of individual reason, restraint, transparency, sensibility, imagination, and education waxed. How the individual was to become part of the new social order is the great problem of eighteenth- and nineteenth-century moral philosophy and political theory.' The new social order demanded society and sociability; a commitment to the exterior world, an acknowledgement of its overriding importance because of its material reality. No daydreaming, now. Obedience to Nature replaced the old forms of obedience, and ensured that civil society remained orderly. Masturbation, on the other hand, requires nothing and nobody else. It is the supremely self-sufficient act, done in private, needing no resources beyond what is readily available – the body and an imagination, and having no natural breaks on its implementation. It is freedom gone mad, radicalism unfettered, the releasing of the beast in humanity – which was apparently quite a different thing, to those expressing concern at its unnatural state, from acting in accordance to Nature. It was not the sex so much as the solitariness of solitary sex that worried people; after all, the Enlightenment approved of sexual pleasure. But if pleasure is to be highly valued, and if it could be obtained whenever one wanted, without the constraining factor of the willingness or availability of others, then why should anyone ever do anything else beyond what is absolutely necessary for survival? Bang goes the social contract. Bang goes empire. Bang goes capitalism. Masturbation is, as Laqueur says, 'the crack cocaine of sex', an 'equal opportunity vice'. It was the dark underbelly of Enlightenment, liberty beyond reason, mental activity in the service of its own satisfaction, and worst of all there were no witnesses to police it. The terrors of excess, of unlimited interiority, 'the derangement of sociability' were too much for the likes of Rousseau, Diderot, Tissot, Voltaire, Kant and later Freud. The answer to uncontrollable pleasure was to instil fear and guilt.

Of course, Foucault has already claimed this political territory. Laqueur agrees that masturbation corresponds almost uncannily with Foucault's theory that authority incites (or excites) the desire and then controls it by medicalising and professionalising it – the highly respected physician Tissot followed the original pamphlet with a best-seller of his own, providing acres of detailed masturbatory behaviours, describing the terrible consequences and then offering cures. But, Laqueur (a bit of a showman, inclined to elaborate on other theories only to knock them into the shadows) says that political control is no more than part of the story. Masturbation also came of age at the time of an exploding 'commercial credit economy that magically promised undreamed-of abundance, shakily linked to the concrete reality of real goods and services'. The insatiable lust for orgasm meshed neatly with the crazed desire for wealth, especially if it came from nothing – the tulip mania, and other greed-driven speculations offering chimerical riches. The relationship between self-induced (the imagination and the hand) sexual pleasure and fantasies of wealth based on nothing more than dreams and paper is clear enough. In a new economy that depended on the desire for more, the self-pleasuring, ever-renewable bottomless wealth of masturbation was both caricature and a dangerous emblem of the disappearance of the market. The masturbator needs no credit, she keeps unlimited cash under the mattress.

And on the bedside table lies a novel. Laqueur surveys the role of fiction, that hothouse of privacy and imagination, and finds that it is everywhere blamed for women's masturbatory practices. Pictures (designed for men) show women reclining exhausted, other-worldly in their recent pleasure, with a fallen book beside them. The remnant of this that bookish children suffer from adults ('Take your head out of that book and go and *do*

something') relates directly to the fear of what the solitary reading of words on a page might bring a person to.

Then along came Freud. Organicist and social conformist that
he was, at first he concurred with the notions of physical damage
that masturbation was believed to cause, but masturbation was an
irresistible addition to his theory of socio-sexual development.
The innate polymorphous perversity of infancy required masturbation – the finding of the organs of pleasure that would come
to be so important later in life. Whereas before children had to be
policed in order to prevent them playing with themselves, now it
was a proper part of social development towards civilisation
which necessitated masturbation so that it might be given up at
puberty in favour of heterosexual desire. Easy enough in boys,
who were, as it were, only practising, but a true giving up for
girls, who, Freud claimed, had to relinquish their 'masculine' clitoral self-penetration for the passivity of becoming vaginal
receivers. Not to do so was to become a stunted form of human
being. And then, of course, there was the guilt, the primary guilt
for the primary addiction, that drives us all on, sublimating and
transforming itself into work and art.

Which brings Laqueur to the mid-twentieth century – 1963, in
effect – when all of a sudden, so it seems, feminism and the gay
movement turned masturbation on its head, declaring not so much
that it was after all a supremely social act, but that its solipsism
fitted perfectly with the new creed of self-discovery. Only experiment, and what better to experiment on than oneself? Feminists
proclaimed masturbation vital in the search for self-value,
countering the normalising strictures of Freud by declaring the
clitoral orgasm the only one that counted. Books appeared called
The Sensuous Woman, and *Sex for One: The Joy of Self-Love*, and
they were not intended for the rapacious male gaze, but as radical manuals for women. Liberationists of every kind celebrated
masturbation as a route to self-knowledge and a new utopian

acceptance of our bodies. The Me Generation took the most Me activity to its heart. Now, Good Vibrations, a sex shop, promotes an annual National Masturbation Month. The internet globalises masturbation by providing easy access to pornography with websites devoted to the activity. The gay *Melbourne Wankers* and the *San Francisco Jacks* sites, among others, endorse group and solo masturbation with pictures and discussion groups at the touch of a button. What Rousseau called 'books to be read with one hand' are now supplemented by chat rooms for single-handed typists.

Even so, the demons remain. Laqueur closes his excellent history of the creation of modern guilt by pointing out that Clinton fired Jocelyn Elders, his Surgeon General, for seeming to endorse masturbation, and that Christian.Net advises worried young men against the activity, suggesting that it's a substitute for healthy relationships: 'God is explicit on this topic: "He who chases fantasies lacks judgement."' Masturbation is on our screens in *American Pie, Something About Mary* and the not-wanking contest in *Seinfeld*, but it always contains the troublous history of solitary sex. These days the guilt may be ironised, but it's still there.

Pot Noodle Moments

The Sexual Life of Catherine M. by Catherine Millet.
Serpent's Tail 2002

Unless you are one of those without a television set or who only
very occasionally watch opera on BBC 4, you will surely have
noticed an advertisement currently playing between the acts on
the commercial channels. A man and a woman are sitting at a
table finishing a sandwich. He is guiltily unsatisfied with the
neat, respectable snack/sex they've just had. 'I do love Kate,' he
whispers to a friend on the phone. 'It's just those sandwiches. I
need something filthy, like a kebab.' His mate advises him to get
himself a Pot Noodle. Cut to dark alleys, garish neon and gaudy
young women outside 'Live food' shows. Our man asks one if
she does Pot Noodles and receives a slap round the face. Some
things a girl won't provide. He keeps trying and failing until
eventually he finds a woman willing to give him what he wants.
She looks round shiftily and whispers, 'Round the back.' The
two of them are on a bed, each guzzling their Pot Noodles and
groaning with extreme pleasure. 'It felt so wrong – and yet it felt
so *right*,' the man intones in a voiceover. The advertisement ends
with a hero shot of a pot of Pot Noodles and a woman's voice

straight out of EastEnders declaring, 'Pot Noodles: the slag of all snacks.'

'Ah,' as Coward almost said, 'the power of cheap food.' The food/sex correlation is hardly new, but there is something novel about dragging the analogy into the gutter rather than escorting it through the doors of the Ivy. The bland current assumption that both food and sex are commodities to be traded up by those with social aspirations is nicely overturned. You may love Kate but you hanker for a slag. And there's the hint of a solution to the dilemma in the ad which as well as making the connection between food and sex is also perhaps offering them as alternatives, suggesting that the lower appetite might be assuaged by substituting filthy eating for filthy fucking. You can have your cake and eat it, *and* hang on to the doily.

There is a Pot Noodle moment in Catherine Millet's otherwise supercool anxiety-free sexual autobiography. In a sauna she has sex with numberless men and even as she goes to the shower has her clitoris 'aggressed and . . . nipples pinched'. A 'little masseuse' works afterwards on Catherine's aching body and carries on a pretence that she doesn't know what has been going on, that her client is just another stressed modern woman in need of a relaxing massage. Catherine M. enjoys the play-acting: 'After all, I was no more the debauched little bourgeoise she must have taken me for than the steadfast one we were inventing.' Because Catherine M., you see, is an intellectual, the editor of a respected French art magazine *Art Press*, and even though she spends her nights servicing queues of men in the Bois de Boulogne ('should I count only the men that I sucked off with my head squashed next to their steering wheels, or those with whom I took time to get undressed in the cabins of their trucks, and ignore the relay of faceless bodies behind the car doors . . .') she does not like to be confused with a 'debauched little bourgeoise' or, to freely translate, a slag. Catherine M. is more of a Marks & Spencer take-away sushi – the courtesan of snacks.

A slag is someone who will let anyone do anything they want to her, do anything for them and do it for nothing. She belongs round the back of the bike sheds, her hair is lank, her eyes are usually dull, and she is not expected to be a high-achiever academically. She's dumb and she's easy and she's not just cheap: she's free. But not a free spirit. That's another kind of sexual woman, much more up Catherine Millet's street. Catherine M. will let anyone do anything they want to her, do anything for them and do it for nothing, but no one could say she's thick. I think we're back to the old duality. If sex is just a bodily event, that's slag; if you think or better still write about it, that's freedom. No review of *The Sexual Life of Catherine M.* fails to mention that by day she lives and works comfortably in the world of intellectuals and that the book is *well-written*. It is suggested that Millet's project in writing about her sexual encounters is related to her intellectual concerns. Writing about pleasure, she says, is a work of art and she anatomises her sexual experiences and responses as a cubist might the visual field. We are in the thought world of 'paradoxical solitude' among the writhing bodies, 'jouissance', and the existential desire of participants in the orgy to achieve 'annihilation of the senses'. (There is a problem here because the translation indicates very little of the apparent clarity and stylish simplicity that Millet's prose was praised for in the original. Either it was done in a great hurry, or the translator had only a passing acquaintance with colloquial English. Phrases like 'with retrospect' and 'That is, I, as I was want [*sic*], would jerk my hips rhythmically' don't give you confidence, but often the writing is so muddy that you just hope it's the translation rather than the author: 'But space is only ever an immeasurably large balloon with a hole. If you blow it up too fast, it will readily turn on you and deflate just as quickly.' Even with a dictionary and a lot of thought I can't understand 'Is it because people were less interested in my bosom that it is more lymphatic by nature . . .?' And can you make a picture of this shot of Catherine M. on video? 'Later, on the screen, I will see myself taking on the shape of an upside down vase. The base is my knees which I have brought up to my face, my thighs are squeezed up to my trunk forming a cone which gets wider as it reaches the buttocks, and then narrows at the neck after flaring widely on each side – would that be the curve of the iliac bones? [Christ knows] – leaving just enough room for the plunging rod.' Somehow, in order to take Catherine M.'s effort seriously, you really want this to be a bad translation.)

To be clear, Catherine M. began at the age of eighteen to have sex with multiple partners when her first lover suggested it, and has continued to make herself available to groups either at private encounters or public places as arranged by her current lover. In between the organised gang bangs she is prepared to have sex with anyone (preferably men) who suggests it. Her sexual encounters have been innumerable, but she declares that from eighteen to the present day there are just 49 men whose faces or names she could recognise. At some orgies there were 150 people and she 'would deal with the sex machines of around a quarter or a fifth of them in all the available ways . . .' In such circumstances, you don't ask for a formal introduction. She has both personal and doctrinal reasons for her activities. She claims that she has always been socially awkward and finds the usual ways of getting to know people excruciatingly embarrassing. What she calls the preliminaries, the flirting and the banter that precede most sexual encounters, are, apparently, beyond her. Getting straight down to sex avoids the social encounter at which she is so inept. But alongside her personal difficulties, she is contemptuous of preliminary rituals. She expresses great moral disapproval of one group who insisted on dining at a restaurant before they got down to the serious business of sex, and she thinks it 'obscene' to tell salacious stories at an orgy. She deplores play-acting and delay. She preferred the 'soirees curated by Eric and his friends . . . the inflexible sequence . . . their exclusive goal; there were no outside factors (alcohol, demonstrative behaviour . . .) to impede the flow mechanics of bodies. Their comings and goings never strayed from their insect-like determination.' Catherine M. has very decided views on how a sex object ought to behave. At one orgy a young woman waved her arms and legs around under her heaving throng of men and made a lot of noise indicating her pleasure. 'I observed this sort of extrovert behaviour with placid indifference. One of the participants expressed their admiration, saying she was "really going for it", and I thought this was stupid.'

In some ways, Catherine M. is perfectly understandable. She is a 'Sixties' libertarian expressing the ideal of freedom with her body, transgressing norms, despising the bourgeois evasion of desire. She takes her radical philosophy from Bataille, and admires Pauline Rëage's über-underling O for her perpetual readiness for sex, her propensity for being sodomised and her reclusiveness. Millet is an absolutist, despising those opportunists who take time out of normal life for a little promiscuity. 'I believed that fucking – and by that I mean fucking frequently and willingly whoever was (or were) the partner (or partners) – was a way of life. If not, if this thing were only permitted when certain conditions were met, at pre-determined times, well then it was carnival!' Certainly she is a very rigorous, not to say humourless libertine. She acts out her paradoxical freedom paradoxically by being completely available, by refusing nothing and seeing herself as a heroine of abjection. Feminism is rejected as another subset of morality, as a drag on the will. But even the will is a drag on the will. What she wants or does not want is to be subsumed by absolute indifference and the great overarching project of finding the perfect negation of ego. Numbers are only part of it, where and how she is used and in what part of her person must also be a matter of sublime disinterest. Everything is permitted and pleasure is not in itself a goal. 'I paid no . . . attention to the quality of sexual relationships. In cases where they didn't give me much pleasure, or they even bothered me in some way, or when the man made me do things which weren't really to my liking, that wasn't reason to call them into question.' She will admit to an inclination for self-abasement but true freedom must go beyond disgust for Millet. Disgust raises one 'above prejudice', breaking through taboos to the clear air of unmediated liberty. This is what she sees herself as doing primarily, but it is hard to read her account of providing anal relief for one man she depicts as an aesthete who lived in filth amid his books and papers, never brushed his teeth and who she describes in terms of sewers ('dirtier than is usually acceptable for intellectuals who often neglect their physical appearance'), without feeling that her inclination towards self-abasement has the edge over her passion for putting radical philosophy into practice.

Contradiction abounds in her account of herself. As well as being a fighter on the barricades for freedom, she describes herself as a resolutely passive woman, never having any goals other than those set for her by other people, but being absolutely dependable and unwavering in the pursuit of those aims. She insists that this is her character, even in the world of work, getting on with the job 'more like a driver who must stick to the rails than a guide who knows where the port is'. So she has no ideals, she says, in work or love, only obedience to the will of others. Her lover (Claude, Eric, Jacques over the years) set up the venues and kept watch as men held her splayed out against walls, or on floors while they made use of her. She consciously performs – is performed on – for the pleasure that her lover takes in watching her being used and for the delight she takes in feeling herself become nothing more than an object. But there is pride in this, and, of course, a sense of power over the men who are physically

241

beholden to her and the watching man who depends on her submission for his pleasure. She is at one and the same time a passive
masochist; a powerful enabler; a victim of her pathology; a seeker
after unbridled freedom of spirit. Even in its insect-like formu-
lations, sex is a complicated business. There isn't one story to tell
and, though I suspect she would like to, Catherine M. either
doesn't or can't keep it simple.

In fact, the great open space of sexuality permits all the possibilities of abjection, power, narcissism, pleasure-seeking, dour
determination, creativity and mechanisation. It would be very
hard to devote such a great deal of life and thought, time and
effort, to it as Millet does without getting them all pretty much
confused. The reason why everyday pornography is so linear is to
keep a single idea afloat in an ocean of polymorphous potential.
Sexuality gets out of hand; it runs rampant with meaning unless
you keep to a very firm remit. The sexual story can transform
from pumpkin to princess to swan with injured wing and back
again in the blink of a thought. It is a nothing, an empty arena,
that might be everything. And everything is more than we can
cope with. The obsessive, fetishistic, single account that pornography provides is what keeps sexuality within bounds. Here is the
danger of writing about the sexual life, you lose the boundaries
unless you keep perfectly only to detail. At times Catherine
Millet seems to be attempting to do this, but over and over, like
a painter who writes explanatory notes over her picture, she tries
to explicate, to flesh out the doing with her intellect, and then the
sexual life is shown up for the kaleidoscopic and random playground of ideas it is. She has complained because reviewers have
not seen that *The Sexual Life* is not the entire life, but she herself
spills over her own boundaries. Ideally, the sexual life of
Catherine M. would have been just that, but the person behind
the sexual life can't manage it. On the one hand she tells us, 'I
have always thought that circumstances just happened to mean

242

that I met men who liked to make love in groups or liked to watch their partners making love to other men, and the only reaction I had . . . was to adapt willingly to their ways.' If this is ridiculously disingenuous, it's par for the course for determined erotica. But she cannot leave it there. She needs us to know about the world outside the sex; she has to give us the sexual life in relation to the social and psychological life: 'Given that, in other ways, I obviously had to comply with all sorts of constraints (a very demanding and stressful job, a destiny determined by poverty, and, the worst shackle of all, the baggage of family conflicts and rows in relationships), the certainty that I could have sexual relations in any situation with any willing party . . . was the lungfuls of fresh air you inhale as you walk to the end of the pier.' There goes the purity of the lover of freedom and here comes consequences and motivations. And just a small injection of reality opens the account of Millet's sex life to questions that a mythic pornographic depiction would not stir up. The Catherine M. of the title might not be precisely the Catherine Millet who wrote the book. You begin to doubt the prodigious numbers, and one woman's capacity for exhaustion, nor her tolerance for pain and discomfort, and her uncommon resistance to any sense of either despair or the ridiculous in these endless anonymous copulations. You have to question her assertion that she has never suffered any kind of clumsiness or brutality, or wondered at the absence of unpleasant diseases. Of course, you wouldn't if it were a fiction, you would collude with the form. But the documentary nature of Catherine M.'s account of her sexual life left me with all manner of practical and philosophical queries. As a fiction, her purely sexual story would be enough, but as autobiography it makes for an unsatisfactory case history and raises huge questions about the limits of tolerance of the human spirit and how much the boundaries of the self can be stretched before the individual explodes.

Perhaps it's merely sentimental to assume that the source of the self is so frail that it must be damaged or deranged by such copious invasion. I suppose it's sentimental to suppose even that there is a source of the self. But Millet's notion of the annihilation of self sounds in reality too much like a psychic retreat from violation. She never feared being found by the police in public places. 'I would only have been put out if I had been caught in the act exhibiting myself on the public highway. The body discovered by the representative of the law would have been no more or less than the body penetrated by the stranger in the Bois, not so much an inhabited body as a shell from which I had withdrawn.' Later, she explains how she 'endures all the risks of coitus . . . the eccentricities of each partner and the minor physical discomforts. This can be put down to an ability to programme the body independently of physical reactions. A body and the mind attached to it do not live in the same temporal sphere, and their reactions to the same external stimuli are not always synchronised.' Which rather than nirvanic ecstasy seems more like closing her eyes and thinking of France. And when she tells us 'for a large part of my life I fucked without regard to pleasure' and concedes that 'for someone who has known so many partners, no outcome was ever as guaranteed as when I sought it alone', you begin to wonder if you are not reading an old-fashioned morality tale after all.

What is exhilarating about Millet's book is her impeccable lack of guilt. In spite of a Catholic upbringing and her reading of Lacan she claims to be quite free from sexual (as opposed to social) anxiety. You cheer her on and hope it's true. It would be nice if someone had got away scot free. But there is nothing Dionysian about this freedom. Her project is to write about her sexual activities as plainly as if she were a housewife describing her domestic round. In this she perhaps succeeds too well. It's perfectly true that sex can be humdrum, and it is sort of heroic of

Millet to devote her life to proving it. Certainly the book is not pornography. It sets out to make sex smaller than it seems to be, whereas what Susan Sontag calls literary pornography contrives to do the opposite. The upshot (and the point) of *The Story of the Eye, The Story of O*, and Sade's writings is the fact of death. There is in all of them, and most other erotic works, an underlying rage against the inescapable loss, a nihilism that comes from the knowledge of the impermanence of the flesh and consciousness. Fetishism and grim repetition battle against the necessity of decay and destruction, and entropy always wins. This structural movement that gives us sex but reminds us of something else is entirely lacking in Catherine Millet's book. There is no real sense of transgressing anything more than a few social rules, no battle with the way things are and have to be, and as a result it is dowdy by comparison with Bataille's ability to shimmer the absurdity and despair of being human through the limited possibilities of the flesh. Somehow guilt is so much more sexy.

My Little Lollipop

The Truth at Last: My Story
by Christine Keeler with Douglas Thompson.
Sidgwick and Jackson 2001

Christine Keeler votes Conservative. She would, wouldn't she? Having seen off the Macmillan Government in the 1960s, exposed the squalid underbelly of upper-class public life and fired the starting pistol to begin the sexual revolution by revealing that 'You've never had it so good' was actually 'You've never had it so often', she reckons she knows what's what about the world of politics and power (though sex and men are not really her thing). She has nothing but contempt for Blair's New Labour: 'just a bunch of control freaks, just more ardent, more determined to bring in rules and take away our freedoms. What I have learned most is that those who would lead have agendas rather than feelings or emotions.'

Christine Keeler also has an agenda. You get to an age when the truth seems all-important, she says. In her case the age of truth would be around 59 because today 'it makes me shudder when I understand the cumulative effect of the years of lies on which history has been created.' As a result of this insight she has been moved to study: 'now with that scholarship, hindsight and, of course, my day-to-day witnessing of events as they happened . . . I feel able, at last, to tell the whole truth.' It must also be disturbing to have reached such a stage of maturity and have to confront the fact that for forty years you've been famous for being the tart who was accidentally instrumental in getting Labour into power after 13 years of Tory Government. (She didn't think much of Wilson's lot, especially that 'ugly' George Wigg, the one 'with the ear of Harold Wilson' who, in addition to being apparently genetically modified, she 'always thought looked like a pervert'.) She has a place in history, to be sure, but not one that's likely to be welcome in her scholarly middle years as the mark she will have made on the world. As both a lover of truth, and a misunderstood victim of a cover-up by powerful men to protect each other, she aims to set the record straight with her recollection of the events of the Profumo Affair.

Christine Keeler bemoans the fact that she can never escape being Christine Keeler, but actually she is no longer Christine Keeler. She has changed her name through two marriages and deed poll, and also, like the rest of us have or will, she has grown into an older woman who looks back on her former self with a mixture of pride and embarrassment. From being 'innocent and warm-hearted' when she arrived in London in 1959, she became, she explained to her son Seymour, as he was growing up, 'wild and naughty'. But she emphatically denies ever being 'the common tart' she was painted as. She was not, she insists, a prostitute 'in the sense that most people understand the word'. The sense in which I understand the word is that it describes a person who offers sex in return for money or the equivalent in goods. 'It's true that I have had sex for money but only out of desperation,' Keeler elaborates, distinguishing herself from those who do it because it's such a laugh. In fact, she goes so far as to say that she thinks she 'might have been one of the most moral women of that particular, frenzied decade'. Her friend Mandy Rice-Davies was the 'true tart': 'There was always shock on her face whenever she thought she might have to do more than lie on her back to make a living.'

Visiting the Twenty-One Room, 'a glorified knocking shop with overpriced drinks and rooms to rent upstairs', Keeler met a Major Jim Eynan. He wanted to go to bed with her in the afternoons, she says, 'and, for nearly two years, he often did. Ours was a commercial situation for Jim always advanced me some money for rent or helped out financially in other ways.' Keeler may or may not have been the most moral woman of the 1960s (my vote would go to Elizabeth Taylor for her belief in the sacred bond of marriages), but the looseness of her definitions is problematical for someone claiming to offer the whole truth. Apart from the moral issue, her assertion that she was never a prostitute is important for her other big claim: she would have it known that she was, in fact, a spy. Not exactly a treacherous spy, not a willing betrayer of her country, but the innocent and warm-hearted victim of an evil spy-master, Stephen Ward, who passed himself off as a playboy but was in fact at the centre of an international espionage ring. In her salad days, Keeler was not a prostitute, not a popsie (a word whose absence from the world I've missed these past thirty-odd years), not a good-time girl (except in the sense that she just wanted a good time like any healthy young thing) but a pawn – no, that's *pawn* – in the Cold War.

Stephen Ward, you may recall, was osteopath to the great and the good. There was almost no one in society he didn't massage. When he wasn't manipulating them, he was sketching them, having discovered a talent for making likenesses. The Duke of Edinburgh, Princess Margaret, Lord Snowdon, Archbishop Makarios and Adolf Eichmann all sat for portraits. He was an invitee at all the fashionable parties, and a man who specialised in providing fun for his friends. Keeler met him when she was a showgirl and moved into his flat, though they never had sex, not with each other. He took her to dinner parties where lords and ladies hurried through their desserts so that they could undress and orgify before Keeler had to leave for her parading and hostessing duties at Murray's, a classy strip club. She accompanied him, stopping sometimes on the way to pick up girls waiting for buses, to the cottage in the grounds of Cliveden, made available to Ward at weekends by Lord Astor, who with his friends, including John Profumo, the Minister for War, would chase a minutely towelled Keeler and others around the swimming pool. But all this, says Keeler, was a front for Ward's real activity, which was spying for Russia on the British establishment during the months before and after the Cuban Missile Crisis.

Profumo was besotted with the stunning Keeler, but she was not all that interested in him. She has always, she says, been 'cursed by sex I didn't particularly want'. Ward insisted, demanding to know how anyone wouldn't be interested in getting so close to power. She obeyed, and was taken in the official car for a tour of London, visiting the War Office, Downing Street and 'I'll show you the Army barracks, too, where I inspect the men.' Who could resist? Keeler was also sleeping with a Russian attaché called Eugene Ivanov, a regular visitor to Ward's flat, as were Roger Hollis, head of MI5 and mole extraordinaire, and Anthony Blunt. They spoke freely in front of Keeler, she claims, about nuclear warheads. They weren't worried about her apparently. Ward knew she was safe. 'The only gossip was about fashions, the new French and Italian underwear, ladders in stockings. There were no tights or La Perla and naughty knicker shops then . . . Clearly, I was not a candidate for spilling Stephen's secrets and he didn't see me as a threat.'

On the contrary. Once Profumo had become a regular visitor to the flat, Ward entered Keeler's bedroom and paced about.

'That night in the bedroom, between drags on his cigarette, Stephen just asked me straight out to ask Jack what date the Germans were going to get nuclear weapons.' Keeler expresses surprise. 'This seemed so bold. I had dropped off letters to the Russian Embassy' – to Ivanov – 'this was different. This was gathering information. Spying. Properly. Or rather, improperly.' She refused: 'I became afraid and begged him not to ask me to do such a thing, that I couldn't betray my country.'

Myself, I regret her refusal, since the account of her under-cover work would make for fascinating reading. Imagine, if you will, the Secretary of State for War and 20-year-old Christine Keeler in bed, relaxing perhaps after their exertions.

> 'Jack darling, that was . . . just . . . mmm.'
> 'It certainly was, my little lollipop.'
> 'Umm, Jack . . .?'
> 'Mmm, what is it, Popsie?'
> 'Jack . . . you know Germany?'
> 'Mmm.'
> 'Well, you know – oh, what are they called? – uh, nuclear weapons?'
> 'Yes, sweetie?'
> 'I was just wondering . . . you know . . . when do you think Germany will be getting some?'

I have gathered over the years that people in very high and very low places are a great deal more stupid than we expect them to be, and that sheer incompetence accounts for much in national and international politics, but I can't help wondering how masterly a master spy Stephen Ward could have been if that was how he approached Cold War espionage.

Keeler is insistent, however, on Ward having been at the dead centre of political intrigue, rather than just a dilettante at that as well as everything else. Her wish to retrieve her past is understandable. Much better for the amour propre to have been Mata Hari than a party girl who bedded Tory peers and the slum landlord Peter Rachman ('I never knew about the terror tactics with tenants who didn't pay rent or were difficult . . . There was something deeply hurt in him from the beatings in the concentration camps and he would never ever get over it'). She is enraged that Stephen Ward was found guilty not of espionage but of living off immoral earnings. Where's the justice in that? she cries. Certainly, Stephen Ward, Christine Keeler and Mandy Rice-Davies were punished for causing trouble for the toffs, while the toffs slunk away. She told Lord Denning, whom she trusted as a decent older man like the father she never had, that Ward was a spy, that she'd met Hollis and Blunt in his flat, that they'd discussed nuclear warheads and the like, and even that President Kennedy was in danger (immediately after the Missile Crisis, Ward had said: 'A man like Kennedy will not be allowed to stay in such an important position of power in the world, I assure you of that'). Denning covered it all up, Keeler says, on behalf of his friends in high places. He smothered the spying with tales of sex and smut.

Life for Christine Keeler has been up and down. She got £23,000 from the *News of the World* (pushing half a million in current money) and another £13,000 from the *Sunday Pictorial*, but spent it, ending up living in a council flat with her youngest son. Her elder son and her mother no longer speak to her. She did time in Holloway, ostensibly for perjury, and she was banned from Vidal Sassoon's salon when the respectable society women complained about having to share a backwash with her. In 1967 she became a 'silicon pioneer'. Her breasts were checked 'early in 2000 and I am glad to report everything is well and where it should be'.

We have much to thank Christine Keeler for. The rumours at

the time were delightful, confirming everything we'd always suspected about the sanctimonious, repressive establishment.
Profumo, of course, resigned for lying to Parliament (in effect for
being found out), and for sleeping with a call girl who was sleeping with a Russian. He has spent the intervening years doing
rather public good work in the East End of London, and being
invited to the Queen Mother's dos. Keeler's done her bit for society too, working for Release, having become interested 'in trying
to prevent young people going to prison for smoking drugs which
I thought were harmless'. Unlike Profumo, she wasn't asked to
join in the Queen Mother's 100th birthday celebrations. It's perfectly understandable that she felt aggrieved when in 1995
Margaret Thatcher invited Profumo to her 70th birthday party,
saying, 'He is one of our national heroes. His has been a very
good life. It's time to forget the Keeler business.' Oh, let's not.
Let's remember the foolishness and arrogance of the privileged.
Let's go on giggling at them as they hang on to their sagging
trousers and mouth pious platitudes and fawn on vicious old
ladies of the Far Right.

Larkin's Lesbian Period

*Trouble at Willow Gables and other fictions by Philip Larkin,
edited by James Booth. Faber and Faber 2002*

Life is too short to read Philip Larkin's juvenilia. Reading
Trouble at Willow Gables and *Michaelmas Term at St. Brides* is up
there with stuffing mushrooms: there is a part of me which, as
I read – or stuff – has precognition of the moment of my death
and the very last conscious thought which is the blinding aware-
ness of the precious hours wasted on Larkin's schoolgirl stories
or mushrooms when I might have done something more positive with them such as sleeping or filing my nails. Actually, I've
never stuffed a mushroom in my life. That much sense I've got.
I have no idea whether James Booth has ever gone in for fancy
cooking. No time probably. He has his hands full of Larkin. He
is a Reader in English at Hull University, and after a false start
in 1981 (*Writers and Politics in Nigeria*) he has devoted himself
to the cause of Philip Larkin. *Philip Larkin: Writer* in 1992
was followed by a collection of essays *New Larkins for Old*
(2000). He is secretary of the Philip Larkin Society and edits its
newsletter *About Larkin* (it's a joke, d'you see?). Now he has
edited and introduced these mostly unfinished and unpublished

fictions that have been lying around in the archive. It's what some literary academics do for a living, I know, hanging on the every word of their chosen one, but when it comes down to scratching about at the bottom of the barrel of the 21-year-old Larkin's doodlings during the summer after leaving university, it's time to head for the kitchen and get the mushroom scraper out.

The trouble with making a career around Larkin is that the output is quite small, and others, Andrew Motion and Anthony Thwaite, have already picked the meat out of the life. What's left after a couple of books of literary criticism wouldn't amount to a serious life's work for a mayfly. Or shouldn't. There is, however, an unmistakable reverential quality in the scholarly apparatus. The artefacts with which the acolyte is working are so precious as to require the minutest description of their physical reality. They are relics, touched by and touching the life of an exceptional being, like a sliver of the true cross.

> A typescript (recto and verso) of 16 sheets, less flimsy and of smaller size (224 × 173mm) than the paper used for *Trouble at Willow Gables* . . . The title and author's name are underlined using the red typewriter ribbon, the first letter of "WHAT" is typed over in red, and a short red line has been typed below the date. The verso of the title-page is blank; thereafter the pages are numbered in the centre at the bottom – 1 –, – 2 – etc. The essay ends at the bottom of p. 29 which is not numbered but has the final ornament ———ooOoo———, with the O and os in red. The verso of the final sheet is blank. The sixteen sheets are made into a booklet by two staples a little over a centimetre in from the left edge.

We are not told what width lies between the staples. There must be some priestly secrets or the keepers of the truth would have no function at all.

The above describes the typescript of a spoof essay, *What Are We Writing For?*, written by Larkin in 1943 in the guise of Brunette Coleman, a Lesbian writer of girls' school stories. The entire oeuvre of Brunette Coleman (the nominal shadow of a real Blanche Coleman, an 'all-girl' band-leader of the day) consists of a finished 120-page novel, *Trouble at Willow Gables*, an unfinished sequel *Michaelmas Term at St. Brides*, the essay mentioned above on the glories and sorrows of writing girls' school stories, and seven poems called *Sugar and Spice*:

> *The cloakroom pegs are empty now,*
> *And locked the classroom door . . .*

By the end of 1943, Brunette Coleman's day was done.

> *And even swimming-groups can fade,*
> *Games-mistresses turn grey.*

It was not Brunette who was offered and turned down the laureateship (though some might regret this), nor did she write *Jill* or *A Girl in Winter*. She existed mainly, it seems, to keep a few Oxford friends – Bruce Montgomery (Edmund Crispin), Diana Gollancz and the dreadful Kingsley Amis – amused. Brunette's work was read aloud to Montgomery and Gollancz after evenings at the pub, and its progress discussed in salacious detail in letters designed to persuade Amis that Brunette's puppet-master was a bit of a lad. Many writers and non-writers have dabbled when young with a bit of porn or pastiches of childhood reading. It's a kind of youthful arrogance, like playing Bach as twelve-bar blues instead of doing five-finger exercises. But James Booth would have us see the Brunette Coleman year as something more. For one thing, he claims, Larkin tried to get *Trouble at Willow Gables* published, or so he surmises from the literary agent's stamp on the front of the document wallet containing the manuscript. Larkin took his girls' school stories seriously, it is suggested. This, of course, justifies the archive burrower in his publishing and analysis of the material. But there's another thing about being young: you are crazy to be published. Anything that gets finished is, you reckon, worth having printed. Later, many of us are relieved not to have published evidence lying around of what we were capable of before we got properly going. Let this be a lesson, at least, to anyone who hasn't got around to chucking out the crap they wrote in their teens and early twenties. There will – given the hordes of English graduates with a living to make and only limited numbers of jobs available at Accenture – be someone out there ready to publish a great fat volume of the stuff. Get rid of it now. It's too late for T. H. White, whose illustrated spanking novel is soon to see the light of day, but you've still got time.

But you will be wanting to know about the pornographic content of these works, because if not that, then what on earth is the point of them? This is an interesting question – or as interesting a question as I can come up with given the material I'm working with. According to Larkin, Coleman represents his 'lesbian period' (A side question: is a male-female transsexual who becomes a lesbian woman more cunning than confused?). Booth sees it as a case of transgendering, the outflowing of, as Larkin describes it, 'the dear passionately-sentimental spinster that lurks within me'. Her presence, for Booth, is confirmed as he remembers that Larkin 'conducted an interminable fussy-solicitous correspondence with his mother, and relished the works of Barbara Pym and "Miss Read"'. As if reading Barbara Pym were not evidence enough, Booth suggests that Larkin also retreated into the feminine in face of the war (didn't want to go into the army) and his father's fascism (seems rather to have come to terms with that later). However, psychologically interesting as this may be, Booth insists that Brunette Coleman is 'just as importantly, a creative amalgam of diverse *literary* influences'. Such as? Um, the impact of 'Yeats's poems spoken by women ("A Woman Young and Old") is audible in such poems as "Wedding-Wind" and "Deep Analysis" and, less directly, in the Brunette works.' Much less directly, I should say. Bruce Montgomery wrote to Larkin 20 years on and wondered if it had occurred to him that 'quite the best of your earliest poetry is in *Sugar and Spice*'. This, Booth would like to believe, is not a whimsical judgement, because according to him those 'parodic, and self-parodic, elegies are technically among the finest poems Larkin wrote during the decade, with an assured delicacy of tone far beyond anything in *The North Ship*'. Just as 'Larkin, the mature poet, was later to transfigure the clichés of urban folklore and advertising in poems such as "Essential Beauty" or "Sunny Prestatyn"', so he turns 'well-worn schoolgirl clichés into moving elegies ("Now the ponies all are dead")', and 'the intimate domestic triviality of the schoolgirl world with its "seniors", "juniors" and "sewing-classes" stands as a poignant metonymy for Life . . .'

But enough of poetry, tell us of the pornography, I hear you cry – sorry, the Brunette style is catching. Well, there isn't much. There is one rampant lesbian senior, Hilary ('a big girl, with a strongly-moulded body, damp lips, and smouldering, discontented eyes') who has a crush on Mary, a sporty junior who causes the words 'strong tawny young lioness' to roll around in Hilary's head, who almost has her way with her as Mary nods off over cocoa and biscuits. There is a vigorous punishment scene when an innocent Marie is unjustly caned to within a yard or two of her life by the Headmistress while being held down by two burly prefects ('Then she began thrashing her unmercifully, her face a mask of ferocity, caring little where the blows fell as long as they found a mark somewhere on Marie's squirming body.'). There is a mixture of the above two incidents when Hilary beats up and then nuzzles Margaret, a more guilty junior ('Lust had turned into anger, and anger into cruelty, and now cruelty, partly sated and partly still hungry, was turning into lust again. With a smile she stroked Margaret's cheek where her blows had landed, and felt under her hand a solid body.'). One of the maids gets titillatingly tied up by Marie as she makes her escape from her locked room, and there is a moment in the second novel, in which the girls have gone up to Oxford, when Mary (the sporty junior, remember?) finally melts willingly into bed with the still damp-lipped Hilary ('Mary gave a pleasurable yawn, and rolled over so that her head lay on Hilary's lap. "I'm so tired," she murmured. "So terribly tired. Do put me to bed." For a second her tawny eyelashes lifted over her grey eyes, and she gave a little wriggle, and stretched. "I'm so tired, I shouldn't notice even if you put me in the wrong bed."'). But it can hardly be called pornography. All the details (and details, surely, are what matter in pornography) are cloaked in coyness. Not a breast, not a clitoris is seen or mentioned. It's true that runaway Marie tears her trousers and her naked bum would be visible if she didn't hold the seat of her pants together, and that Margaret also runs away, barebacked and knickerless on a local horse, making a note to herself that it is quite pleasant, but that is as far as anatomy goes, if you don't count the short gym skirts that fly up when chasing healthily after the hockey ball and reveal a lot of leg.

It's pitiful pornography, and feeble erotica, but it does provide something for the male gaze to rest on. The words offer little but pictures for the imagination to take in and manipulate. Once you've got Marie under the cane, the male observer is free to embellish and impose his own private schoolgirl fantasies. Larkin provides the numbers which the reader (and he himself, I suppose) is free to join up into the scene of their dreams. There are the bare outlines of classical pornography in the innocent heroine wrongly accused and punished, and the hierarchical structure of the school where each echelon suffers at the hands of those above it and makes suffer those below it. Pauline Réage and the Marquis de Sade would recognise the architecture of these pieces, but where Réage and Sade offered precisely detailed illustrations (or instruction) of the experiences of *O* and *Justine*, Larkin sketches a mere outline and then walks away with a snigger. Which is to be judged the more obscene depends entirely on the mind which reads them.

Or perhaps it's just not worth wondering about these efforts at all. Plenty of people who didn't turn out to be Philip Larkin wrote smutty stories, and thankfully the rest of us are not required to be bothered with them. Surely scholarship has better things to do? There is indeed a strong sense that Booth hasn't got enough to keep his mind occupied. Otherwise why would he bother with footnotes informing his readers that Hugh Walpole was a 'popular novelist', Benny Goodman an 'American clarinet-tist and bandleader (1909–86); nicknamed "the King of Swing"', and that Myfanwy's comment 'Ours not to reason why' is an inaccurate reference to '"Their's not to reason why/Their's but to do or die . . ." Alfred Tennyson, "The Charge of the Light Brigade"'? Is he trying to educate those readers only interested in pornography, who, he perhaps supposes, have no background information about anything at all, or does he imagine that Larkin's avid readers are too young to have heard of Benny Goodman? Or is he just trying to justify the time and fill out the pages of the very little he has to work with?

After the works of Brunette Coleman there are some desultory attempts to outline and write a third legitimate novel. According to Larkin, his ambition was to be a novelist 'in a way I never wanted to "be a poet"'. Nothing happened after he finished *A Girl in Winter*. Larkin commented, 'I tried very hard to write a third novel for about five years. The ability to do so had just vanished. I can't say more than that.' He suspected that he dried up because novels 'are about other people and poems are about yourself . . . I didn't know enough about other people, I didn't like them enough.' He worked on *No for an Answer* and *A New World Symphony*, both dealing with his relationships with women and his wish not to be engaged to and with them. He had abandoned both by 1953, either, suggests Booth, because he sensed his 'superego' was too much in control, or because he feared the wrath of those he was writing about (would that be his superego not enough in control?). Whatever the reason, he abandoned them. They were not finished or published. Now they are, after a fashion. They are fragments, not worked on, not finally drafted, not even worked through. Scholars might pick them over for whatever theories they may have about the relation between the life of the author and his literature, but these poor pieces of unfinished stuff qualify as neither. Booth suggests the present publication of them 'makes it possible for readers to make their own judgement'. This is all very democratic. But one of the things a writer does *as a writer* is to make his or her own judgements about what has been produced and whether it should be made available to the judgement of others. An unfinished work is not a work. An abandoned work is no one's business. And readers have enough to read, surely, without having to flog through the half-chewed thoughts of writers trying to decide what they are going to become. There isn't much that's flagrantly exploitative about Brunette Coleman's drivel, but there certainly is about the publication of these sad ramblings.

. . . AND SHOPPING

Supermarket Sweep

It was my good fortune recently to receive some vital shopping wisdom from Sir Robert, Daddy of all the Sainsburys, Lord of the Wing. 'Never, my dear,' he said, leaning on his cane. 'Never buy anything you don't passionately want.' Passionately wanting wasn't the problem. I *wanted* the John Davies sculpture I was looking at; it was money, not irresolution, that made me pause. But it did seem very sound advice, worth applying not just to Art, but to life's more menial purchases.

It's not so easy: I've tried but cannot love cornflour and low fat spread. Bourbon biscuits, on the other hand, I can love. Or at least I could until I and my young but expert assistant sat down Easter Monday to perform consumer research on them. I'd accumulated packets of Sainsbury's, Budgen's, Peak Freans, Crawford's and two curiosities from Gateway – Butler's and Baker's Selection. We drew up a table with, after much discussion, essential categories: separability (you know how you have to open them up and then scrape the chocolate cream with your teeth?), total taste, cream alone, looks, packaging and nostalgia quotient.

Crawford's won, with Peak Freans just behind (the cream was

messy round the edges so scored low on looks, though it got maximum marks on the nostalgia quotient, because my fellow taster
had been brought up on them), Baker's Selection was off the
scale, verging on the disgusting, Budgen's were only all right,
and Sainsbury's didn't fare well at all, I'm afraid, Sir Robert.

None of that, however, is as interesting, or sad, as a formerly
undisclosed result of consumer testing: neither of us will ever
look a Bourbon Cream straight in the eye again. It was some
time before we were quite well. And then, a further problem:
what's to be done with six unwanted, opened packets of Bourbon
biscuits each with two taken out? I suggested our next-door
neighbours, but my companion balked at this. After all, we have
to go on living next door. How were we to explain this bag of
half-eaten goodies? She mooted putting them outside the front
door for whomever might pass by. I rejected this. What if the
postman refused to make deliveries ever again? The birds won in
the end. But what are we going to do about the remains of next
week's Pickled Onion survey?

Every few weeks or so I dream I'm running along a narrow road
with a high brick wall at the end, being strafed by low-flying
aircraft. I see it as evolution's way of preparing me for my
moment of death. Practice makes perfect, I tell myself, untan-
gling the sweat-sodden sheets. And in terms of what the shrinks
call 'feeling tone', surely the weekly supermarket visit is practice
for what happens next. Not hell, exactly, but that halfway house:
purgatory. My dictionary defines purgatory as: a place or condition of suffering or torment, esp. one that is temporary. See?

It begins, as the end must, with the loss of light. You drive
through a barrier (Take a Ticket/Abandon Hope), down a
snaking path to the underground car park. Daylight and radio
waves fade. The message is clear: there's no going back. There is

only that slow circling cruise in search of the last empty slot, knowing all the while it will inevitably be filled by the car in front. The sense of futility mingles with the smell of burning fossil fuel: you know what kind of place you're really in. You leave the final familiarity of your car, for a dream-like journey (escalator, lift – call it a ferry ride) which ends with an explosion of light, noise and movement, and you emerge into the hubbub of Hades.

There's pity, at first, for the suffering you see (this isn't hell; you haven't lost your humanity). You weep for the half-conscious creatures, moving in inexplicable ways, stopping and starting, reaching out over and over again, changing direction as they realise they've taken a wrong turn. Then you're among them; one of these lost souls. It's now that the learning process begins. You must hold on to your knowledge that this is not it, not for-ever itself, but only a version of infinity.

Submission is the key. This thing has a time and necessity of its own. Reign yourself. Every path must be trodden: short cuts will only mean having to retrace your steps. You *cannot* avoid the tinned soups. You *must* contemplate every brand of yoghurt. Don't even think of skipping the condiments. It is the only route home. Get the alpha rhythms going, lower your heart rate, mutter your mantra in the knowledge that what must be gone through must be gone through. This is *not* your life draining away, but practice for ever and ever. Go to the supermarket in the right frame of mind. You will be everlastingly grateful.

———

I'm a bit of a worrier. Years ago, a friend told me how her toddler, the same age as mine, 'almost choked on half a pea'. *Petits pois* immediately disappeared from my menus until, months later, she explained it was half a *penny* which had caused the trouble. Naturally, I banished small change for fear my small charge might come to harm. I worry a lot about chicken sandwiches, too: look what happened to Mama Cass. Mayonnaise is an indispensable home safety requisite.

I like making mayonnaise. Once I discovered mayonnaise never curdles if you use *two* egg yolks, it became one of my antidotes to anxiety. The drip, drip, drip of oil, and the magic of emulsification helps soothe my terror that at any moment the sky will open, and me and mine will be deluged with heavenly garbage. But there's great truth in the old saying: *you can't make mayonnaise every time you want a chicken sandwich*; so there has to be a pot of the ready-made stuff handy.

Once there was only Hellmann's and it seemed wildly transatlantic. But I never really liked it; there was an undertaste that reminded me of the acrid salad cream my wicked stepmother used to hand round to adorn the slice of damp ham, uncut tomato, and two wet lettuce leaves that the old witch called high tea.

A handy ex-husband, just back from France, still with the taste of the real thing in his mouth, nominated himself to test my collection of mayonnaise. I would have double-checked his findings, but I decided against it after seeing him dip a well-sucked finger into each jar. 'It's the undertaste you've got to watch for,' he explained knowingly. It wasn't accidental we were married once.

He declared Sainsbury's French Mustard Mayonnaise by far the best, though it was a little too mustardy. Marks & Spencer's mayonnaise 'captured the lumpiness of the real thing' which apparently meant it was excellent, but Waitrose's was 'awful, tastes chemical'. Crofter's, Gateway's version, was artificial and salty: 'Don't bother.' 'My God!' he said, after the first fingerful. A meditative silence followed. He had some more. 'This is . . . a totally different experience. *Very* interesting. You don't want the rest of this, do you? Incidentally, I noticed Marks & Spencer have started selling caviare. I wonder if you shouldn't do a column on it.'

Bad news for ex-husbands this week: an empty space where the caviare used to be in the Camden Town Marks & Spencer in London. 'I suppose no one bought it,' the cashier said. Made sense to me. But we were both wrong; they'd sold out. Celebrations at the proclaimed end of the recession, maybe? It's all right, though, since it gives me a chance to complain about the sinister forces of infantilism which have swept the supermarkets over the past few years.

I'm speaking of the pre-pubertal vegetables that are on offer these days in the nursery sections of almost every high street store, though Marks & Spencer started it, I think, and even have a special area labelled Baby Vegetables. There seems to be no end to the parade of new and unthought-of vegetables cut off well before their prime.

The latest I've noticed is the Baby Brussels Sprout. What *is* a Baby Brussels Sprout? How small can a sprout get before the authorities move in to protect it from being untimely ripped from its stalk?

For those of us who don't have wide-eyed furry toy animals sitting on our pillows, the increasing cuteness-level of doing the weekly shop is becoming lethal. I have a barely controllable urge to pulverise cherry tomatoes with my fist wherever I find them, and one of these days I'm going to get done for infant leek abuse.

But it's not only an aesthetic problem. What about the flavour? The fact is baby corn doesn't *taste* of anything, certainly not of corn. Just as the sense of seasonal has disappeared, so the notion of ripeness is vanishing.

Isn't the point of growing plants for them slowly to absorb sun and nutrients from the soil, until over time they transform those raw materials into their own substance and taste? Won't someone please open a Grown-up Vegetable department, where weighty cabbages, carrot-sized carrots, and marrows big enough to stuff exude the taste of having been allowed their allotted span on the planet?

I'm that person people avoid standing behind at the checkout – the one with the trolley overflowing with *everything*. You can hear them thinking: she looks quite good for a woman with such a large family; or, what does she know about the future that we don't? In fact, mine's a maximum two-person household: I just have the fantasy that if I do it all now, I won't have to do it again tomorrow. This goes for all aspects of life, but the day when there's nothing more to be done because I've done it all never comes. Someone pointed out to me that the condition I'm after is death. *That's* when there's nothing else to do. Doesn't stop me filling my trolley, though.

There are people with a more reasonable attitude to life, who actually like shopping for groceries. You can tell by their strategically filled hand-held baskets – just what's required for tonight's carefully thought-out dinner – and the fact that they keep going back for more. For them, Tesco's superstore in Covent Garden is Mecca. It specialises in the premium and super-premium products of the Tesco range, the manager explained. 'Superpremium?' 'Peking duck with all the trimmings.'

It's bright and airy, designed not to offend those who've popped in after a trip to Emporio Armani, and caters for the youngish media and PR types working in the area, burdened with fashionable tastes and high mortgages, but not half a dozen children screaming for Hero Turtle crisps. Unlike the out-of-town superstores, it sells more champagne than beer, fish than meat, smoked salmon than ham.

The Covent Garden shoppers don't buy the slightly incongruous range of novelty birthday cakes for their children, of which they have none, but for each other – awfully amusing . . . And they do say it's *the* singles' meeting place, so if you're lucky you can get tonight's dinner *and* someone to eat it within one trip. It's all a bit life-enhancing for my taste, but if you're that way inclined, it's positively superpremium.

The Season, they said. What season? I asked, displaying my ignorance. I've never watched boats sailing or horses running, though, when I was small, my dad took me dog racing at White City. I couldn't understand why, if it was called dog racing, the fluffy white rabbit always won. 'I wanna bet on the rabbit,' I'd nag. However, I was once taken to Glyndebourne at an impressionable age and had to flick spilled caviar away before I could sit on the grass. Not long after, I was fomenting revolution outside the American Embassy.

Luckily, I've mellowed, and been blessed with a few good friends (and an ex-husband, whose time had come, at last) prepared to form a caviar-testing working party. The Stoly was retrieved from the freezer. I'd acquired Beluga from Fortnum's (a gold standard to work from) and Sainsbury's; Sevruga from Marks & Spencer and Waitrose; salmon eggs from Waitrose again; lumpfish roe from Fortnum's (lead standard), and from Londis up the road. 'OK, get stuck in, and think of Ascot,' I directed my team.

We all ached to discover Londis's lumpfish to be every bit as good as Fortnum's Beluga (a delightful saving of £76.81), and thereby puncture the white-walled tyres of pretension. No such luck. Fortnum's Beluga dematerialised to cries of 'Oh, my God', 'Tastes of oysters', 'Tastes like sex', and 'More!' The lumpfish roe received only unpleasant noises I can't spell. Worse, Sainsbury's Beluga at £23 less than Fortnum's did *not* please: 'mushy', 'no comparison'. Better off with the Sevruga, we decided, at around £18. Marks & Spencer's very satisfactory; Waitrose, unfortunately, not so: 'crass,' said ex-hubby (though, fearing a banning order, he'd like Waitrose management to know he liked their salmon eggs).

After that, things are a bit hazy, in a vodka-coloured sort of way. There's a note on my pad saying, 'Nice for what it was, but it wasn't what the other stuff was.' It almost certainly means something, though, so far, no one has been able to remember what.

When they write the definitive history of the fall of the radical Left, there should be a chapter on the insidious role of the supermarket.

Like capitalism, supermarketism is inescapable because it gives you the impression that you're in control. It seems as if you're wandering freely, making choices between a magnitude of products, whereas it's *moving round the aisles*, not what you buy, that makes you a frozen prawn in the manipulators' hands. The orientation and order are theirs, and once we're all going in the same direction, they've got us.

The radicals of the Sixties and Seventies thought that they could tame the tiger. Heard about the ultra-radical commune that attempted to mix Marxist-Leninism with running a computer company? Its inspired strategy was to subvert big business by infiltrating its own revolutionary programs into the system. It's bold enough to make Trotsky's toes tingle. But even communes have to shop, and it was their downfall. They made a computer program which generated a weekly shopping inventory listing everything they needed in the order it appeared on their local supermarket's shelves. Triumphant at having beaten the system, they marched single-mindedly round the aisles, taking each item as they passed it. Right to left, no stopping, so no distracting temptations. They'd buy only what they really wanted in the minimum time possible, and thus undermine the real purpose of the supermarket, which is to make us spend as long as possible buying as much as possible.

It all went wrong when their local supermarket rearranged the order of the shop. You know how they do? And you thought it innocent? One day the commune's shopper put a hand out for pesto and found a Victoria sponge in the basket. It was the beginning of the end. They re-programmed the computer; and then it happened again . . . and again. Ever since, they've been locked in a perpetual battle, fighting hopelessly to keep their shopping list up to date, as the store continually rearranges its shelves. They've no time for world revolution now. There's just no end to the cunning of capitalism.

———

Wearing a Robertson's golly badge once signified, to those in the know, that the wearer was no longer burdened by her virginity. You can't send off for a metal golly any more, however much you wish to announce your newly-acquired status, but Golden Shred marmalade – one of the Robertson's jams whose labels you had to collect – is still on the shelves.

In a trip to my local Sainsbury's, I wondered what had happened to the other half-remembered groceries of my 1950s childhood.

Since food nowadays is all rigatoni and fusilli, tiramisu and syllabub, salami and saucisson, I assumed that they had all but disappeared. In fact, it seems that I had simply allowed them to slip from my consciousness. Hidden between the rows of modern products, the foodstuff of childhood remains, and I discovered the past with small yelps of glee.

Revamps such as Heat 'n' Serve Microwave Jam Roly-Poly with Custard didn't interest me. All that sort of thing is ersatz nostalgia, not the real thing at all. I am talking about Brown and Polson's Blancmange Powder (five flavours to a box), side by side with Bird's Custard Powder. Neither looks a day older than they did in 1953, when they were sweet treats until usurped by the upstart Angel Delight (that's still there, too).

I fell ecstatic on tins of Spam, which brought back fondish memories of wet summer holidays and Spam sandwiches from a café in Russell Square where hopeless magicians always showed the cards up their sleeves.

There were tins of Heinz spaghetti, soggy red worms to be vacuumed up with as much noise as possible, and Soft Herring

Roes which, spread on toast, defeated me, but not the sophisticated palate (so I was told) of my father.

Even Potter's Malt Extract is available: a tablespoonful a day
of that blackish viscous gloop was supposed to keep me healthy,
though it can't have been much better for me than the sherbet
flying saucers I used to buy, four-for-a-penny.

I have grown up now, and put away childish food. Thank God.
And, no, I didn't eat the Spam.

———

I once knew a woman who went crazy while drying a lettuce. She
was whirling wet leaves round and round in the salad basket,
when, just like that, everything caught up with everything else
and she and the lettuce came to a grinding halt. Since when, I've
daintily dabbed salad dry with kitchen roll, though I believe I'm
in more danger of coming to a standing stop at the supermarket
checkout than dealing with a wet lettuce.

I can't find *checkout panic* described in any textbook of psy-
choneurosis, but I know I suffer from it. Having given up on
(and been given up by) psychotherapy, I've tried various self-
help strategies to avoid the nightmare build-up, as plastic bags
refuse to open, and the mounting heap of jars and packets swells
rather than diminishes, no matter how fast you chuck things into
the carriers. The items stream ineluctably towards you, and suddenly you're Minnie Mouse in a new version of *The Sorcerer's
Apprentice*, while, behind you, customers click their tongues and
look at each other.

I've tried to take control, dumping armfuls of shopping on the
conveyor and racing to the other end before the first products
arrive, but the assistants are on to that, and put their foot down
on the accelerator. For a while I only bought what came in easily-
baggable packaging, but I got weary of eating, and washing with,
frozen spinach.

In France, packing is automated and your shopping falls off the end of the belt into open bags, which drop into your trolley when they're full. My solution is anti-social, but it's this or catch the ferry every week. Here's my tip. Always choose the cucumber they missed with the pricing gun. Place it in the exact centre of your goods on the belt. Look self-righteously aggravated as the supervisor carries it off to find out the price. Now, pack at leisure.

―――――

I've played tennis only twice in my life. The first time, I held the racket in my left hand; the second I held it in my right. I didn't manage to hit a single ball on either occasion, and since it was before the days when using both hands was a possibility, I had no alternative but to give up all thoughts of winning the Grand Slam, and retired gracefully from the circuit.

It's just as well, because I turned out generally to be a natural spectator. Even so, I look forward to Wimbledon like no other event in the year. It's not a love of *tennis*, you understand (I can't tell a half-lob from a triple lutz), nor of quintessential Englishness, but a more sinister delight in long, afternoon vigils sitting cross-legged on the sofa, consuming favourite secret snacks, and watching the psycho-drama of gladiatorial combat. The thrill is in the see-sawing, inner drama of a sudden, inexplicable collapse or resurgence of belief when a match, virtually won, is lost in a single moment of foundering faith. It's the personal battle with triumph and despair of individuals doing something I couldn't care less about, that I rejoice in. I'd have made a good Roman.

Nothing could be further from a strawberries-and-cream experience than Wimbledon fortnight. The tastes I require to accompany the tragicomedy of tennis are the darker pleasures of salt, sour and bitter. New green pickled cucumbers, rollmops and gentleman's relish, from Waitrose. At Marks & Spencer's, it's packets of crudités with sour cream dip, courgettes-and-cheese keftethes to dunk into a tub of houmos, and a jar or two of pickled onions. Then Sainsbury's, for tins of Kalamati olives, bunches of radishes to eat with sea salt and Normandy butter, and, for the Men's Final, in the hope of five long sets of tantrum and heartache, a cauldron's worth of Rayne's Smatana to pour, icy cold and sour, over a mixture of diced cucumber, chopped onions and excessive amounts of garlic. Eye of newt is optional.

———

Background disappointment, like background noise, is always with us. I don't mean the grand, universal disappointment of realising that you've reached the future you were heading towards and none of it has turned out to be quite what you'd hoped. I'm thinking of subtler, more insidious, everyday disappointments: a letter that doesn't arrive, a phone that isn't ringing, a frock that looked stunning in the fitting-room tried on at home, the first sip of coffee made from the beans whose smell made you gasp as you took the lid off the grinder.

It's important, then, to notice those few things which regularly and repeatedly do live up to expectations, and to make sure you know where you can get your hands on plenty more of the same. If you've got a lover who fits the description, fine, but failing that, or (you should be so lucky) in addition, I find Assam teabags are a particularly reliable hedge against life's little disappointments.

All the brands of Assam I've tried deliver what they promise on the packet. Waitrose's does have a 'strong, full flavour'. Sainsbury's is 'malty, deep bronze, strong and refreshing'. Twinings' Assam is 'dark amber, full bodied, rich' and also 'malty'. And now Marks & Spencer has brought out its own 'rich, smooth' and, yup, 'malty' version. St Michael's Assam is best of all, though personally I'd substitute 'nutty' for the ubiquitous 'malty', if only for a change of prose. My one complaint is that they're sold in dinky packets of 20 – I suppose on the dubious grounds that good things come in small packages. This is barely a day's supply to those of us seeking a source of consistent pleasure which never disappoints, and who need to be sure that, whatever the state of our sex lives, we can at least get a decent cup of tea whenever we want.

———

Several readers have pointed out that the Robertson Golly remains in vibrant health and can still be acquired everywhere. 'You should read the labels,' one lady chided, quite rightly.

In an attempt to pull my socks up, I've been reading everything and anything in print – which is how I found myself staring at a notice by the escalator at Marks & Spencer. I know now why I don't examine the world with too much attention: some things don't bear thinking about. The notice warned that anyone caught stealing would be banned from *all* Marks & Spencer stores *for life*.

Is that a nightmare, or what? Naturally, I wouldn't dream of stealing, but the notion of becoming an Marks & Spencer outcast grabbed me by the throat and hung on. How does it work? Do they issue an ornate document like a papal bull of excommunication? I suppose there'd be some kind of protocol where you'd stand, head hanging in shame, in front of all the shop managers, having your store-card cut in half and flung at your feet. Then they'd take your picture (front and side view), and distribute copies to the stores to be posted at entrances and checkouts for all to see.

Once, when I was very bad at primary school, the Head stood me in front of the assembled pupils and teachers and announced that no one was to speak to me for a fortnight. At seven, I was strong enough not to let anyone see me cry but I don't think I could manage not to blub at the Marks & Spencer banning ceremony.

Imagine, no more crème caramel or gooseberry fool; no more

luxury taramasalata. Come to that, no more knickers. For life. I
live in terror, now, of becoming one of those menopausal
shoplifters. I've asked my doctor, but he says it's too soon to tell.
So I'm starting a collection of disguises: wigs, eye-patches, beards
and moustaches. If the worst happens, I'll be ready.

———

There was an interesting little drama at my local supermarket
recently. I'd got no further than the soft-fruit section by the door
when, out of nowhere, half-a-dozen uniformed men flashed past
me and disappeared out through the entrance into the High
Street. It was a weekday morning, there weren't many people
around; mostly women, middle-aged and the broad social mix
still found only in local supermarkets, which *do* cater for everyone. Or almost everyone.

We all stopped shopping and stood beside our trolleys looking towards the door. Moments passed and then the security
guards returned, frogmarching a struggling man; a streetperson,
filthy, tattered, matted hair and beard, in his twenties, maybe.
Two security men had him in a double half-nelson, while the
others formed a phalanx around him, ready for a breakaway. He
was protesting his innocence and asking them to let go of his
arms.

The shoppers around me began to look at each other and, like
a Greek Chorus, a low muttering started. 'Shame.' 'They ought
to let him go.' 'He couldn't have taken much . . . he was probably
hungry . . .'

Nothing to do with justice, this. No one doubted he had stolen
something, but it was a matter of *fairness*, I think. A sense of
some big bully hitting on an already wounded victim. Someone
called out: 'I'll pay for what he's taken.' But the security guards
had their officious, blank faces on, and disappeared with their
prisoner into the back of the shop.

Of course, I and my fellow shoppers were in the wrong – none of us would have condoned the man breaking into our house, or stealing our purse. We'd have called the cops. Large organisations must have the same right to protect their property. But, despite logic and law, the fact is I was glad that a sense of the outrageous unfairness of things was still strong enough to override reason. It's one of the things I like the most about human beings.

———

Anyone troubled by thoughts of the afterlife, and their likelihood, or otherwise, of having one, could do worse than make regular visits to the supermarket. They are, of course, very useful for shopping, but their function as spiritual gymnasiums shouldn't be overlooked. I can think of few situations which offer as many opportunities for practising virtue, all under the same roof.

Abstinence, for example: go to Waitrose and only buy necessities. Ignore the Cappuccino Chocolate Cake and Häagen-Dazs. Don't buy onion bhajis or, if you do, don't eat half of them by the time you get to the checkout.

Work on laziness: no ready-washed bags of three different kinds of exotic lettuce, or pre-julienned carrots. Buy organic cos and fat leeks with earth in every crevice. Avoid trimmed sugar snap peas and miniature cauliflower in a microwave tray. Only buy loose fruit and vegetables, so you have to queue to get them weighed.

Love your neighbour: shop on Saturday afternoon and take every opportunity (even if you're still there on Sunday) to back your trolley up the aisle you've just struggled down, so that your fellow shoppers can make easy progress. And *smile* as they pass. Pretend you feel nothing when the children behind ram you. Gaze indulgently at the high spirits of the younger generation, and indicate to their mother your admiration for the tremendous job she's doing bringing them up.

By the time you've reached the checkout, you should be feeling pretty other-worldly, but don't relax yet. Choose the longest queue and watch those in front of you unload their goods without making a single judgment about what they've bought. Finally, as your turn comes, turn to the man behind and suggest that, since he's only got a basketful of shopping, he should go in front. When the woman behind him looks at you, then at her watch, don't hesitate. Insist you're in no hurry, of course she can go first. And smile, smile, smile.

It's too late for me, but, selfless as ever, I was thrilled to see the signs above three of the tills in my local Marks & Spencer announcing their SWEET-FREE CHECKOUT. My toddler has long since grown beyond her sweet compulsion (these days, her demands are all for balsamic vinegar and elderflower tea), but I still feel solidarity with the rest of you, engaging in grim head-to-heads during the long wait to pay next to a bank of Rolos, Mars Bars and Crunchies.

Everything I know about psychological warfare was learned at sweet-saturated checkouts, holding a small clammy hand in mine. It was where I understood that I would do anything (even sacrifice my child's teeth) for a quiet life, and where I finally came to terms with the reality of failure and my feebleness of character. And it was where The Offspring learned that when Mum says 'No!' she means 'All right, if you promise to keep quiet, and only this once, unless you pester me enough next time, in which case you can have some then, too.' Funnily enough, she's turned out to be a really nice person with a full set of teeth, but I think that must be a happy accident.

A problem still remains, though, if only some of the checkouts are going to be sweet-free. It's fine as long as the kids can't read, but, after that, the problem's just been shifted back a stage. Let's hope the new English curriculum isn't *too* successful, or, next thing you know, the supermarket aisles will be cluttered with early readers and their distracted parents doing battle over which queue to join. Perhaps the signs could be in French, or, better still, what about running simultaneous courses in Mandarin for prospective parents while they are learning pain-free panting at natural childbirth classes? Then again, maybe pain-free panting would have done the trick at the checkout.

It might be worth a try. Mustn't grumble, though – things are undoubtedly improving. Is there any chance, I wonder, of a balsamic-vinegar-and-elderflower-tea-free checkout?

———

What do you *feel* about your local Tesco, Waitrose, Safeway or Sainsbury's? Nothing is not an acceptable answer. I won't believe you. Food is one of the two most emotive facts of our lives. It's the earliest connection we make with other people. *Feed me* and *love me*, any shrink will tell you, are virtually synonymous demands.

Moreover, we're naturally inclined to attribute personality to the inanimate world around us – a hangover from the days when we had the good sense to reckon ourselves no more and no less than everything else on the planet.

Put the two tendencies together, and you come close to explaining why we can't help having a relationship with those powerful organisations which provide our sustenance; at a cost, of course, but that's right, too. Unconditional love from a nurturing parent may be the ideal, but we all know reality better than that. The breast is never offered entirely gratis. Free love and free lunch are equally unobtainable. The best we can hope for is a fair price, and that, I think, is what determines our love–hate attitude to supermarkets.

We want to feel they have our best interests at heart, and they encourage us, designing clean, wholesome surroundings, like the kitchen of a good mother, with essentials at basic prices, but treats, too. They show us, on television, how to cook the ingredients they provide. They remind us of their family origins, and their decent, not to say paternal, attitudes to their customers and staff. This is why, when huge profits are announced during a recession, angry articles appear, accusing them of exploiting a vulnerable, captive public.

We're delighted when car manufacturers boost their profits, but when the food retail families come top of the wealth index, we become resentful, because we all know that parents make sacrifices in hard times so that the kids can thrive. The *feed us/love us* syndrome makes very inconsistent capitalists of us all.

A curious summer combination of me holed up for a week in a monastery, and the daughter-with-the-sweet-defying-teeth spending 10 days in France, has meant I haven't darkened the supermarket door for over a fortnight. Two weeks of occasional trips to the deli and the corner shop, and an injudicious use of the home delivery pizza, have left me with a gloriously empty fridge and a touch of hyperagoraphobia (as in: fear of the supermarket-place). Doubtless, you can get treatment for it, but there isn't time before my young Euro-traveller returns and wants to know what's for dinner.

I'm hoping she'll enjoy the results of my self-help strategy for getting back to trolley-pushing. There should be months of interesting eating in store with the new categorical shopping system I've devised. Alphabet shopping alone will take care of 26 weeks. So, next week, it's aubergines, anchovies, Angel Delight and Aberdeen Angus; the week after, black pudding, biltong, Bath buns and Bombay duck. Mmm, delicious. The last three weeks might prove a little more troublesome, though I've eaten worse combinations than Yeastrel, yoghurt and Yorkshire pudding. And there are much worse things to eat than zwieback, zucchini and zabaglione.

After that, it's geometrical shopping. Rectangular foodstuffs to ease ourselves in: sliced bread, butter, German salami and Mr Kipling's cherry slices – a down-to-earth week, and an orderly relief from all that foaming, formless zabaglione. Round food, and the world's our melon, with no end to spherical fruit and veg, plus the occasional haggis. Things are very cheese-and-biscuity when it comes to triangles – processed cheese portions, wedges of Brie and oatcakes. After that, it gets tricky. Octahedrons are off the menu, and a week of starfruit and starfish doesn't appeal.

On to colour co-ordination: radishes, radicchio, Bloody Marys and borsch. Custard, pineapple, corn-fed chicken, camomile tea. Pumpernickel, burnt toast, squid-ink soup. Faint heart's pumping faster now. I'm shopping-ready and raring to go. Oh, and if you've been wondering about week 24 of alphabet: we're eating out.

—◆—

I don't know what got into me, but one morning last week I woke up filled with a sense of well-being. I ignored the small, knowing voice in my ear warning me that nothing good could come of starting the day in such a buoyant mood. 'Nonsense,' I said. 'You'll see,' sneered the small, knowing voice.

The inner glow stuck around, seeing me serenely through the arrival of a parking fine and the discovery that the day before yesterday's milk was sour. I didn't even bawl out the cat for biting my ankle to amuse himself while I opened his tin of food. Ominously at one with the cosmos, and humming 'On The Sunny Side Of The Street', I set off for the supermarket, tootling around the aisles, smiling at my fellow shoppers – dripping with the milk of human kindness. Recommitting to planet earth, I stocked up only with what was recycled, unbleached, whole, brown and organic.

Trolley and soul were bulging, positively iridescent with goodness and purity, as I reached the checkout, where I remembered milk. I left the trolley at the bottom of the aisle and went back to the dairy cabinet, stopping to reach for a bottle of cooking oil for an old gentleman who was even shorter than me. We passed the time of day. Nice morning, aren't the peaches lovely? No hurry. If only people stopped to chat more often, we're all made of the same star-stuff, after all.

And when I got back, my trolley had gone. Some rat-faced pig had taken my shopping through the checkout. The manager tried to look sympathetic, but no crime had been committed. They'd paid. 'But I *shopped*,' I wailed, 'what about grocerynapping? Piracy? Supper-rustling? Alienation of muesli? It's not fair, nice or decent.' He shrugged. 'That's human nature for you.' The small voice told me I only had myself to blame for getting up on the right side of the bed. It won't happen again: in future, I will get up properly grouchy or not at all. Thomas Hobbes, forgive me for ever doubting you.

— · —

So the big three supermarket giants are joining forces to beat off Costco's plans for building discount shopping stores, where you pay an annual fee to join and then get your goods considerably cheaper. They are muttering about it not being *fair*, because Costco's stores count as warehouses and don't need planning permission the way Tesco and friends do. But the great argument against shopping clubs (which flourish in the US) is that 'the British public isn't ready for them'.

Historically, purveyors of food-and-drink-stuffs have often had their chocolatey fingers on the pulse of moral and social welfare –

think of the Frys and the Cadburys. Look how nice the Booker and Whitbread companies have been to novelists – the way, each year, Booker gives six lonely, unsocialised writers the chance to go out to dinner and meet people.

Now, though, their concern is extended to all of us, and I, for one, appreciate it. Sainsbury, Safeway and Tesco have got together and are paying their lawyers to go to court on my behalf to protect me against the exploitation of cynical companies who plan to make a profit out of saving me money. Someone's got to look out for my interests in a hard, commercial world. It's all too easy to save money by buying everything more cheaply, but will it be good for me? Am I ready for such a step? Have I reached the point of maturity where the money I have saved will be beneficial? Or will it spoil me? Only Tesco knows.

And if the supermarkets know all that, perhaps they know other things that might help me:

Dear Mr Wait and Mr Rose,

I have met a gentleman. He is unmarried, good-looking, intelligent, witty, and a wonderful lover. Oh, and filthy rich. He's asked me to spend a fortnight on his yacht in the Caribbean. Should I accept?

Dear Ms Diski,

No, you are not ready. Decline the invitation and find yourself a poor, plain, train-spotter. Believe us, we have your welfare at heart.

———

Supermarkets first arrived in this country in those not-so-long-ago days when post-war austerity had come, through force of habit, to be linked with right living. The supermarkets, along with launderettes and more than one television channel, infiltrated themselves into a world where coffee bars, garlic, folk music and disposable lighters were seen as sure signs of moral decay.

It was the magic word *convenience* which won us over. Time and motion studies were everywhere, showing housewives how much effort they expended unnecessarily – whisking eggs by hand when an electrical gadget could do it in a tenth of the time, and traipsing along high streets buying different types of food from lots of specialised shops. Gradually, a new sense that life did not have to be a grim and continual grind seeped into British consciousness.

Better still, convenience went hand in hand with *cheapness*. Cornflakes cost less in the supermarket than in the corner shop, in addition to the time saved by not having to wait for personal service.

Isn't it funny, then, how the development of supermarkets seems to have gone into reverse? They've moved increasingly upmarket, towards the exotic in small packages, with prices rising to the point where a Marks & Spencer PR man cheerfully agreed when I suggested that larger families, or those on a limited income, would not be likely to shop in his stores. Nowadays, they've got specialised butchery, bakery, fish and deli counters with real assistants cutting, slicing and weighing the cuts you point to – and a waiting line at each section. As to the concept of time-saving, how many lunch hours and Saturday mornings have you spent queuing at checkouts?

And my corner shop is filled with people who seem pleased to stop and pass the time of day chatting to each other, while a neighbour tells me she never bothers with the big stores; the local street market's much cheerier, cheaper and more convenient.

———

Praise be – the ex-hubby's back from France again and available once more to convey his Francophiliac thoughts to the nation. 'Hi, Rog. Bread!' I said, when he phoned. 'What we need over here is Balladur,' he told me. 'Really? Sliced, is it?'

It turns out that M. Balladur is the prime minister of France, and has just decreed that French bread can only be called French bread if it's made from scratch in the actual *boulangerie*. If French bakers want to use ready-kneaded, frozen, half-baked dough to make their baguettes, they still can, but they can't call them French – unless they send them to Britain.

It is true that none of the baguettes I bought from the super-markets tasted like the ones I used to buy in Paris in 1970, but then bread isn't the only change I've noticed between then and now. The thing about real baguettes is that they don't have any bread in them. They're just crust with a bit of air inside. The ex-hubby protested: 'But it's tasty air.' Which is true. There's plenty of bread inside the Sainsbury baguette (frozen, part-baked dough from France, finished at the in-store bakery), but it doesn't taste of anything much.

The pages of *Larousse Gastronomique* rustled in the background, and the current Missus came on the extension with the answer: 'It's fermentation that gives it the flavour. Kneading, proving, leavening and time.' Isn't that always the way?

Marks & Spencer doesn't import dough, but buys bread in from specialist bakers. It's freshly made here, and not frozen, they said, which, I suppose, makes it more genuine French bread than frozen French bread from France. It's nice, but still not Paris-in-1970 quality.

But at least French bread, wherever it comes from, looks edible. I had a very distressing experience this morning with the sun-dried-tomato-flavoured ciabatta I thought I'd better try, just to be fair to the Italians. I don't know about you, but I really don't want to wake up in the morning to red bread.

———

The funny thing was that I was asking about bread for last week's column when, all out of the blue, the young man in a suit let fly on the subject of beggars. They hang around outside the store, he fumed, his voice rising in fury, and bother the customers. He's right, there are always Big Issue sellers outside his shop. But the one who is probably responsible for the store manager's rage, sits on the pavement with a cardboard notice announcing: *Yes, it's just another bloody beggar* . . .

There's no call for it, the manager told me, when he gives stock past its sell-by date to local charities. Such as? The Simon Community and the London Zoo. Do I catch a hint of irony? No, I don't. Irony doesn't seem to be the strong point of supermarket managers. Still, it's a free street. But they are not entitled to bother our customers, he insists, why don't they go to the Simon Community? Or the zoo, I suggest.

No criticism of the Simon Community or any other charity, they are vital and entirely admirable. I only wonder about the way they are seen as a means of organising poverty out of sight.

Customers leaving high street supermarkets carrying bags laden with bargains – mangoes marked down to £1.09, custard apples for a mere 99p – *should* be asked for money by those who don't have any. We ought to be bothered into having to make the choice to give or not, by a face-to-face meeting with someone in need. It's a simple experience of reality, removed from a tax-exempt standing order to a charity, which keeps us well insulated from the fact of poverty.

To be asked for money by another bloody beggar outside a supermarket is a form of street tax which, though voluntary, requires us to make real-life decisions about our relations with others. You could always say no. Either way, you'll agree with another store manager who told me, straight-faced, 'We don't like our customers to be harassed, they've got enough on their plate already.'

After two million years of human evolution – from homo erectus just bright enough to stand and wave his fist, to homo sapiens with gigantic brains capable of thinking up quantum physics and the electric nail varnish dryer – I stood waiting in the checkout queue at Sainsbury's.

I'd been to Marks & Spencer to get the week's cooking-free food, but I needed shampoo, conditioner, Anadin, bulgur, fresh ginger (concessions to the food-conscious offspring), and the bananas I'd forgotten. So I'd popped into Sainsbury's, grabbed a trolley, dashed round the aisles, and was now standing at the express checkout with my six items.

'It says Baskets Only,' a voice said, behind me.

I turned to see a woman in her early sixties glaring at me.

'Sorry?' I said, baffled.

She pointed to the sign. 'Baskets Only. You've got a trolley.'

'I've only got six things in it. Aren't express checkouts for people buying just a few things, so the queue moves quickly?'

'This is a Baskets Only not an express checkout.' The woman's eyes were alarming. I've seen my cat look more benevolent while stalking a moth. 'If you had any conscience or decency, you'd go and join the right queue.'

'But,' I spluttered, doing a quick count, not quite believing this was serious. 'You've got 10 things in your basket and I've only got six in my trolley.'

'The point is, this is a Baskets Only queue.'

Naturally, being England, everybody nearby became fascinated with the corners of the ceiling and the ingredients of their marmalade.

'Look,' I said, trying to compromise. 'What would you say if I took my six items out of this trolley and put them into one of those empty baskets? Would that be all right?'

'If you did that I'd say you were a very dishonest person.'

It was my turn. I bought my six items and turned to the

woman behind me, knowing she felt wronged and cheated and that the world was full of people who broke the rules and got away with it. I said goodbye and hoped her day would improve. But I knew it wouldn't.

———

The ex-hubby had been growing increasingly excited. The night before the big day, he called to make sure my alarm was set. This was the culmination of the Holloway Road supermarket wars. Past Marks & Spencer, past Safeway, beyond the Sainsbury's which the week before had folded its tent and slunk away, there it was: the new Waitrose on the site of the late-lamented Jones Brothers. Ex-hubby wasn't having any of that. 'But I liked Jones Brothers,' I muttered. 'Don't be silly,' he said.

Men-in-suits from head office stood in nervous groups in the great entrance hall, all columns and monumental plants. 'It's like the Roman senate,' ex-hubby said, awestruck. I thought the cream and green tiles made it more like the toilets of the Roman senate, but I didn't want to criticise. A brand new supermarket is a thing of wonder. For two weeks, the manager, Geoff Bee, and his staff had been stocking the shelves with military precision. No tin stood proud of its rank, every potato had its place in the great potato design. I lost touch with Mr Bee, who, recognising a fellow enthusiast, swanned off with ex-hubby, but I caught up with Rog and Geoff, as they were now calling each other, at the fish counter – a swirl of crustacean arrangements. I stood open-mouthed, while Geoff and Rog discussed life in the John Lewis Partnership. Geoff met his wife 20 years ago when he was in charge of the China and Glass department of John Barnes and she was a Christmas temp.

There are discounts galore, not the least of which was the great Multi-Value bargain no shopper should miss: buy 10 fresh oysters and you get two of them free. That'll pull the punters in.

And, if you purchase a whole salmon, Mr Bee will lend you one of his two fish kettles, and you can't say fairer than that.

Ex-hubby pronounced the whole venture a triumph as Geoff beamed and, surely, Wallace Wyndam Waite and Arthur Rose, now in the great supermarket in the sky, are quietly proud as well.

ANGRY-ON-A-SOFA

Election Diary 1

When I opened my copy of the *New Statesman* last week I realised there had been a terrible misunderstanding. It promised, as part of its election coverage, 'Jenny Diski on the campaign trail'. When the Poet saw it, he came to find me, because by then I was lying down with a cold compress on my head, moaning softly.

'I'm sure that what I said yes to was: "Jenny Diski on the campaign *sofa*". I thought I was going to be the election apathy correspondent.'

The Poet agreed that it didn't seem likely that I would have signed up for anything that meant I had to go out. He knows me quite well by now, since middle-aged passion swept over us and I threw up the giddy life of suburban London to buy a house directly opposite his in Cambridge – or Not London, as I call it. Six months on, builder free, all money spent, we continue to be love's antiqued dream, still excitedly anticipating our first row, the tarmac between us beginning to show signs of a well-worn path. But romantic soppiness notwithstanding, I have retained my essential character, reverted to type so far as a social life or outside world is concerned, and go out as little as possible. Beyond the carpet and blinds departments of Robert Sayle (which is Cambridge for John Lewis), my new city is a mystery to me. I've given up my car, and I certainly don't walk anywhere. After my uprooting exertions, I planned to stay home. Love and work; work and love. No need to go out. So you will understand my alarm at seeing the words 'trail' and 'on' so closely associated with my name.

However, it is true that I have been a little worried about representing myself as one of Blair's apathetics. *Angry-on-a-sofa* would better describe my state, both now and in the past four years. Perhaps the Chinese have a single word for it. *Passive-aggressive* almost does it. *Sullen* is closest of all. In fact there is little at the moment that quite so stokes up my recumbent rage as Tony Blair's sanctimonious and self-serving misrecognition of anger and helplessness as apathy. His contempt for his electorate is, I suppose, no different from any other politician, but it is so badly concealed, so ineptly spun. When, for example, did you ever hear a genuinely humble person describe themselves as humble? I object as much to the crudity of the deceit as I do to the deceit itself. I understand that politicians lie, but please, lie better. So when I don't vote in this election (the first time I haven't voted, the first time I haven't voted for Labour), I would like it to be clearly understood that, apathetic though every bone in my body is inclined to be, my failure of civic responsibility is in reality a symptom of chronic disgust.

Actually, it's not true to say I never go out. Not long before the 1997 election, I went to a dinner party. I found myself seated next to a minister in the shadow cabinet. Back in the Eighties, he had been a right-on right hand man of Ken Livingstone during the glory days of the GLC, now, in '97, he was a card-carrying Blairite with the scent of office powerful in his nostrils. He asked if I was excited by the expectation of a Labour victory at long last. I said my feelings were mixed. I rejoiced, of course, at the prospect of the end of Tory government, but even by then, dismay had set in about New Labour. We had heard nothing from them about dealing with child poverty, about poverty in general, what they were going to do about the loss of council housing stock, the deterioration of the National Health Service, the demoralisation in schools – that is to say, nothing that sounded remotely like a commitment, nor even the will to remedy these catastrophes, nothing about a redistribution of wealth, nothing about the necessity of raising income taxes to fund the recuperation of the welfare state.

The soon-to-be cabinet minister looked at me and nodded sagely. His eyes were quite moist with sincerity.

'Trust us, Jenny. Just wait and see. There are things we can't say in public now. We must get elected, and we won't if we frighten the electorate with talk of raising taxes. Believe me, we care profoundly about the poor. But be patient. For the time being, we have to keep our counsel. Once we're in power, every-thing you talk about will happen.'

I queried this. Surely, if getting into power was so important, wouldn't staying in power be just as imperative? When would it finally be OK for New Labour to come out as socialist? My dining companion's mood changed. The eyes went from moist to furious. The sincerity from apparent to real.

'We will do whatever we have to do to get elected. We must never, never, be publicly humiliated again like we were in '83. Nothing like that must ever happen to us again.'

That was authentic. Excuse me, I said, but your humiliation, unpleasant though it must have been, is not the point. The point is decent social policy. I couldn't care less about the bruised egos of the party and its officials, what I really wanted was to hear someone saying what is right, someone holding to the idea of social justice firmly and rationally so that they gained people's trust, and then doing what needed to be done. He looked at me as I guess I once looked at a fifteen-year-old pupil who asked me whether the Second World War was before or after the eighteenth century; that is with hopeless pity at my irremediable condition. He gave it one last try.

'Listen, we're living in the real world, even you creative types know that. When you write a book you consider what your readers will want, don't you? You're no different from us. We want votes, you want to sell as many books as possible. You write your novels with the market in mind so you can have a best-seller, isn't that so?'

'Well, no,' I said. 'As a matter of fact . . .'

But the upcoming New Labour government minister had quite lost interest in me, and was already deep in conversation with the diner to his right.

So here we are, four years later, four years of New Labour government later: two million children are living below the poverty line, 250,000 children in the poorest households are worse off than in 1997, lone parent benefit has been abolished, a single parent who can't work gets £52.20 income support and £27.55 in child benefit, and the only taxes that have been raised have been those which hit the poor harder than the rich. Rather than supporting the very needy in our society, public money has been spent on socially divisive advertisements against benefit fraud and the setting up of a shop-your-neighbours-hotline, while government figures acknowledge that between £2bn and £4bn of benefit entitlement is unclaimed. Oh, you know. Gordon Brown calls child poverty 'a scar on the soul of Britain' and Blair whines that he can't be expected to do everything in just four years. Give him another four, he says, and we'll see how much better things get.

It seems the buzz word for this election is going to be 'meritocracy', as in the Prime Minister's speech at his constituency last weekend: 'We are meritocrats.' Fine. And those without merit? Those unable to shape up to Blair's vision of personal achievement? Those who, brought up in poverty, suffering lower standards of health, housing and education as a result, cannot rise to the top of the heap, and those who just don't fit the mould of New Labour civic worth, what of them? Are we back with the deserving and undeserving poor. Is the ghost of Samuel Smiles wisping around our heads as we boldly go where we have been before under a different name?

And if you think I'm pissed off, you should hear the Poet, who can work up a rant against New Labour worthy of an old time firebrand preacher. 'So you're not going to vote either?' I slide into a brief lull as he takes a breath. There's a sigh, a terrible sigh, as he joins me on the sofa.

'I'm going to vote Labour, of course.'

'Because?'

'Because everything else remotely electable is worse.'

Which is what I call apathy. It's beginning to look to me as if us apathetic stay-at-homes are the nearest thing to a radical movement (or lack of movement) we're going to get. Indeed, if someone were to form an Apathy Party, I'd be out there on the hustings, campaigning with all the insufficiency of energy I could muster. In the meantime, I am so discouraged by the Poet's despondent voting plans that I am moved to rise from my sofa, after all, and find myself, most reluctantly, shuffling towards the dreaded campaign trail to find out if it is most dismally true that the least worst is as good as it can get.

Election Diary 2

You know how they always say – about Christmas, for example – that when you actually confront it, the reality turns out to be better than your worst fears? Well, like many things they always say, they're wrong. Not just about Christmas – which is invariably as bad as my worst fears, but also, I can now tell you, about confronting the reality of politics. What I've discovered, having been roused to investigate the world beyond my sofa by the Poet's pragmatic-apathetic in-lieu-of-anything-better plans to vote Labour, is that things are uncannily as I had feared and my options more dire than I imagined. Still, I have made a bit of an effort, and that, as they used to say in the bin when examining the sorry basket thing I had made, is something at least.

I began with the party most likely to succeed, at whom most of my anger is directed. The Labour candidate in Cambridge is Anne Campbell, a ladylike smiling sort of person with a 1992 majority of a whisker, and a 1997 majority of more than fourteen thousand. Lord Falconer of the Dome was at her adoption meeting to commend her to the faithful – and faithful was what the 40 odd people were who sat in the Labour Party headquarters trying not to notice anything significant about the fact that the roof was leaking and the rain was pouring in, filling the buckets that had been intended to be passed around and filled with donations. There were no dissenting voices, just cheers and foot stamping affirmation. His Lordship warned against the cynicism of the voters (the word apathy has been banished), explaining that they couldn't expect to do as well in Cambridge as they had in 1997. The need to be pragmatic while in power had disappointed some people, he smiled knowingly at those who had kept the faith. In her speech Ms Campbell declared herself humbled at being chosen yet again (as well she might having pledged herself against student tuition fees and then voting in favour of them as an elected MP), and said she knew that some people were worried about changes that had occurred in the Labour Party. But society had changed and now there were many white collar workers who had moved up from being blue collar workers who must be retained for Labour. This was an interesting insight into how new Labour is abolishing class – everyone is a worker (vote Labour . . .), only the colours of the shirt collars change (. . . even though you can now afford a washing machine). As ever, only the language changes, finessed into a New World euphemism. Blair uses old fashioned words like reform and radical in that nasty new-fangled way that Margaret Thatcher did, to mean privatisation and the sanctification of capital. Thus far no surprises. And no shame.

In search of dissenting voices, I went to the Socialist Alliance meeting in a local internet café. Howard Senter is amiable and has a rare sense of humour for what I remember of 1970s International Socialists. The Poet was an International Socialist back then until IS declared itself the Socialist Workers' Party because they judged the time for world revolution had come. The Poet, clear-eyed versifier that he was, begged to differ about the imminence of world revolution and was promptly expelled, very likely causing disillusion and psychological damage one can only guess at. There were twelve people, including myself, at the Socialist Alliance meeting. Old habits die hard, and when I explained that I was from the press, the chairperson booed and the secretary, a member of Militant, thought I should be excluded from the meeting because he couldn't talk freely. He was reminded by Mr Senter that this was a public meeting and they were seeking election, not, at the moment, fomenting revolution. I was allowed to stay and plunged back thirty years to my teaching days in Hackney and the meetings, the endless meetings, where Any Other Business twinkled in the increasingly far distance while we squabbled (as if we had all the time in the world) over matters of doctrine and points of order and amendments to motions about motions and invariably failed to get to the substance. Ah youth, I thought nostalgically, but no, here it still was, the old'uns and the young firebrands together, still not managing to agree what kind of demonstration exactly (legal or illegal) was required at the local detention camp for asylum seekers, let alone what day it should be on, nor whether people with 4 by 4s would be welcome as SA voters. But never mind the inefficiency and the nitpicking, look at the policies: renationalising the railways; taxing the rich; defending asylum seekers; raising pensions; an end to homelessness; raising the minimum wage to £7.40 an hour; scrapping student tuition fees; cancelling Third World debt; and last, but not one of my absolute favourites on account of the scope it allows for an overweening sense of superiority, saving the planet. Apart from the last, yes, yes, yes. And if they don't explain how this could all be achieved, or even pretend that they are likely to save their deposit let alone a whole planet, at least they are saying what I want someone to be saying. Some days later, at the press launch of their manifesto, I was the only member of the press. I tried very hard to look like a crowd as Howard Senter and the other officials behind a table delivered their prepared speeches directly to me. Then it was off to the Market Square for a 'stunt'. What kind of stunt? I asked as we walked to the Square. Howard didn't know. No one had told him. Did anyone know? Howard didn't know who knew, but he hoped someone would tell him once we got there. But once we had got there, it seemed everyone had assumed that someone else was dealing with the detail. After a bit of foot shuffling, they put up a few posters on a market stall and stood around looking like interested bystanders while Howard gave an off-the-cuff speech about cheap principles up for sale. A couple of Americans stopped for a second to photograph this example of British democracy in action. A group of kids hanging out wanly on the corner cheered or jeered (it was hard to tell) at inappropriate moments before wandering off to find a more exciting way of bunking off school. Here at least there was a photographer from the local free paper, so I felt a little less lonely. Nonetheless, on behalf of the fourth estate I received their message and pass it on to you, and on behalf of disappointed socialists everywhere I wished them the best of luck. They were, as far as I could see, the only option short of flatly refusing to be fooled by the whole idiotic charade of Western democracy and not voting at all. Apart from voting for the Liberal Democrats – don't make me laugh – where else can I put a cross that tells Labour exactly what I think of it?

Still, I went, grumpy and embarrassed, to the Lib-Dem meeting on the insistence of the Poet who is a completist. After all, I don't know many people in Cambridge, no one need know where I'd been. But as it turned out, this really was a meeting, not a rally of the faithful. After a speech or two, there were questions. Quite searching questions. People who had voted Labour all their lives, new and old Liberal Democrats, students and public service workers demanded to know of David Howarth what his policies were on MDS, refugees, GM experimentation, mental illness, patenting DNA, the reform of the common agricultural policy, affordable housing, class sizes, funding the National Health Service, an ethical foreign policy and the financing of care of the elderly. And David Howarth's considered, intelligent, humane and left-leaning response to these questions was, I was astonished to discover, not a million miles from just what I wanted to hear. He was even willing to say what he really thought.

'Will you fight to dismantle the WTO?' asked a fervent woman in natural fibres.

But he wasn't against the WTO as such, only the way it operated. The Green policy of abolishing international trade in favour of regional self-sufficiency was clearly nonsense. This time the word reform made some sense.

'And will you,' demanded one elderly lady who had earlier been telling her friend how many pro-lifer candidates each party had. 'Will you be promoting marriage through the tax system and in schools?'

'No,' said Mr Howarth. 'I don't think I will.'

My hero.

But, Reader, beware. Take me as an example of what can happen when, against your better judgement, you go out. You discover, to your horror, that you are a Liberal Democrat. Don't tell me being a Lib-Dem is better than my darkest fears in the lonely watches of the night: LibDem'ness was the darkest fear even my darkest fear couldn't confront.

Election Diary 3

Thank God it's over. I hate portraying myself as an outraged citizen, especially when that is exactly what I am. The little shards of sincerity (fury, disgust) that get through in spite of myself when confronted with the mimsy farce of democratic representation make my insides curdle. Now I can return to the cleaner, more invigorating nothing-surprises-me-baby cynicism me and mine have missed so these past weeks. How odd that Blair should have disparaged cynicism when it is so effective at keeping genuine rage at bay, but like his concern for disappointed Guardian readers, he couldn't care less about the underlying anger of those on the left who don't agree with him. Remember that car sticker in 1992: *Don't blame me, I didn't vote for Thatcher?* I want one: *Don't blame me, I didn't vote for anyone.* If I hadn't gone soft and fallen for the Poet, I'd still be in the Hampstead and Highgate constituency and could have voted for the Nun of the Above Party whose candidate is a bloke in a habit offering the only choice I could wholeheartedly have put my cross against. As it was, the Poet and I took to our bed early on election night and spent the sleepless hours singing well-loved hits of the Fifties and reciting favourite nonsense poems such as is suitable for folk slipping ineluctably into terminal apathy.

At least I can stop pretending to be a woman about the world, get back on the sofa and revert to my day job writing fiction. And thank God for that too, I say, because whenever I encounter it, real life, or non-fiction as they call it in the bookshops, is so riddled with cliché that I'm ashamed to put it down on paper. 'Mummy,' I once said during a pause for breath in the middle of a family tempest. 'This is like living in a storybook.' My mother abandoned the venomous argument she was having with my father and turned on me in a howling fury, and quite rightly, because what it was actually like was living in the world. Having experienced the unbearable triteness of being for several decades without really coming to terms with it, I finally realised that if one can do nothing about the bad taste storybook narrative of existence then one must write a world of one's own, where there might be the possibility at least of surprise or originality. The only escape from the stage-managed banality of real life is to make it up. But oddly I still sometimes forget, and convince myself that there is some point in going out into the world in the hope of finding a better perspective than the one I get on the sofa. Well, look what happens. I only offer the following story because it actually occurred; I wouldn't dream of including it in a novel because I would be accused (correctly) of using the worst kind of sentimental symbolism.

One afternoon last week, I accompanied Anne Campbell, Cambridge's sitting Labour candidate, to the gates of a local primary school to leaflet what they called 'the mums' picking up their kids. There were four or five people in the Campbell entourage handing out balloons and stickers to the kids – 'Mum, dad, vote for that nice lady who gave me the pretty balloon' – while I hovered in what I hoped was a journalistic fashion to watch and listen to the response of Campbell's constituents. For the most part the parents manoeuvred a path through the mêlée and out of the gates that avoided the electioneering, though it was difficult and caused arguments because what kid doesn't want a balloon and a badge to stick on their jumper? Behind me someone grumbled that we were in the way (which we were), it was crowded enough coming out of school. Another woman swerved sharply aside after throwing a poisonous glance in our direction and snapped impatiently to no one in particular, 'I can't be doing with all this.' But a couple of women did make a point of approaching their previously prospective and now current Member of Parliament. Both of them were polite to the point of apology at daring to mention their complaints: neither could make ends meet, one as a single parent with two small children who found she couldn't juggle the earnings, benefit and childcare cost conundrum in a way that gave her enough money to live, the other who had just given up her job as an NHS booking clerk not considered under Labour legislation a 'key worker' worthy of the new and hardly princely living allowance ('It's not only doctors and nurses who keep the hospitals going,' she pointed out). Anne Campbell like any true politician has perfected the public, sympathetic smile. 'Yes, I can imagine it must be very hard. I'll be doing my best for you when I get back to parliament.' The women thanked her, apologised again and went away. I stopped the one who had left her NHS job and asked if she was satisfied with the response she got. Of course, she wasn't, but neither was she surprised. I asked Anne Campbell if she thought she had given either of them hope of a solution to their problems.

'When I'm in Westminster I talk to several senior cabinet members every day.'

'But the NHS has just lost another member of staff.'

'You know, we can't just wave a magic wand . . .'

You ask a question about policy, and you get an answer about magic.

Finally it was quiet, most of the parents and children had

dispersed, and we were left standing in a small group while parliamentary candidate Campbell and the County Council candidate discussed with their supporters how valuable the exercise had been and how visible the red balloons were bobbing down the road. As they did so, I gradually became aware of a noise that I realised had been going on for some time. I looked across the narrow street and saw a girl of seven or eight sitting alone and disconsolate on the pavement. She was crying noisily, sobbing in a way that was supposed to attract someone to her predicament. I waited for a moment to see if anyone else would notice. She sobbed louder, heaving and hiccuping her distress. Nothing. No one turned, no one seemed to hear a thing. I crossed the road and squatted down.

'What's up?'

'I don't know where my mummy is . . . she's never late . . .' And she scared herself into an even greater upsurge of choking tears. Do you remember the terror of finding yourself eight years old and abandoned in the universe? Someone was late picking you up from school or a party and you knew without a doubt that you had to make your own way in the world from now on, but that you were too young and you didn't know how; that the worst thing in the world, the thing you feared the most, the only thing you feared, had now actually happened. I murmured unhelpful things about traffic jams or watches being wrong and after a bit of coaxing took her back into the school, past the still chatting self-congratulatory huddle of candidates and Labour party workers, to find the school secretary and get her to phone around. When I came out, Anne Campbell noticed me.

'Oh, have you been to look round the school?'

'Not really.'

She wondered if I'd be wanting to accompany her that evening knocking on doors. I thanked her but said I thought I'd go home.

'Seen enough, have you?'

I had.

A Long Forgotten War

Promise of a Dream: A Memoir of the 1960s by Sheila Rowbotham. Allen Lane 2000

A year or two ago Germaine Greer, discussing the shortlisted artists for the Turner Prize, ended huffily by saying that if this is the way the world is now, she was delighted that she wouldn't have to be part of it for very much longer. Time was she would have leapt on the barricades and given the world a piece of her mind, explaining exactly what it had to do to shape up. Of course, the fact that she has to complain now about the world gone to wrack and ruin means that back then, at her most gladiatorial, the world took not a blind bit of notice and went on its way, impervious. It's a generational thing, disappointment; part of a cycle of anger, action and failure that is as inevitable as hormone fluctuation, but which seems to have taken us postwar baby boomers quite by surprise. It was there to be read about in classical and modern literature, in histories, in drama, poetry and the defeated mutterings of our own grandparents and parents. But our time was different, we thought, and we seem still to think, because even now we can't work out what happened.

I recently heard a radio interview with a sixth-former who

had been invited by the United Nations to take part in a young people's conference on the state of the planet. She announced that her concern was to right the mess (war, Third World poverty, ecological catastrophe, global capitalism) that her parents had made of the world. It was a moment before, astonished, I realised that she meant *me*. No dear, I thought, that's not right. It wasn't me, it wasn't us. It was them. It was our parents who made the mess that we set to sorting out in the 1960s. I remember it distinctly. 'We're just trying to sort out the mistakes you made,' I announced to any baffled elder who asked. 'It's not as simple as that,' they would mutter as our lips curled in contempt and we went off to demonstrate, take drugs, right wrongs, foment revolution, do it all differently. We had a dream, and according to Sheila Rowbotham, it was to be more than the promise of a dream. The old meanwhile turned towards each other, panicked and took us at our word. But that's part of the deal. Becoming the older generation is, it turns out, difficult enough; there isn't time to be philosophical about youth. In any case, we would have called it patronising and taken not a blind bit of notice. And so on, round and round.

The 1960s generation may have had a dream, but it would seem from the contemporary sixth-former's point of view that they didn't achieve it. It would also seem that they have become dream-bound in relation to their past. Sheila Rowbotham's memoir of the 1960s is an attempt to redeem the dream from a scornful world that has, according to her, lost its dreaming capacity, though I confess that her title whirls me back to a Disney world of Snow Whites and Sleeping Beauties. Surely, *Promise of a Dream* was warbled by one of those over-articulating sopranos while Cinders waltzed in the arms of her prince-to-be? Oh no, it was 'A Dream Is a Wish Your Heart Makes', which is in much the same sentimental ball-park. In keeping with the drippy title, Rowbotham's text is fuelled by a complaint of misunderstanding and, familiar enough from our own youth, accusations of simplification:

> as the hopeful radical promise of the 1960s became stranded, it was variously dismissed as ridiculous, sinister, impossibly utopian, earnest or immature. The punks despised the Sixties as soppy, the Thatcherite Right maintained they were rotten, the 1990s consensus was to dismiss them as ingenuous. Dreams have gone out of fashion ... A sanitised 'Sixties' were to re-emerge, glossily packaged as the snap, crackle and pop fun times, to be opened up periodically for selective nostalgic peeps on cue: the pill, the miniskirt, the Beatles, Swinging London, Revolution in the Streets. As if anything were ever so simple!

Yet there is something special about the 1960s generation: we have managed not to change the system, but to keep the 1960s, our 1960s, all aglow or at least aglimmer in the world out there. The young, in addition to despising us, envy us, as well they might, since whatever our form of Sixties activity, it was done in the sure and certain knowledge that when we had finished there would be jobs to go to. We had a great time, listened to good music, wore a uniform of our own invention, played like children among the drugs and light-shows, fucked copiously, took to the streets, and seriously frightened the horses in Grosvenor Square, and all the while felt righteous, that we were blowing away the dust of the world. The overt promise was that very shortly we would be the governing generation, and look at us, hippies, radicals, scorning tradition and hypocrisy, how could we not run the world as it was meant to be, as we meant it to be? The underlying promise was that after we had dropped out, we would be able to drop back in, get the work, education and stability that we had thrown up in the name of putting things to right. Certainly, for most, the latter promise came true. As to the rest of it, our generation is now reaching retirement age; this is the world we were going to make. One of our number is President of the United States, another Prime Minister of the UK, many are academics, teachers, publishers, writers and broadcasters, others must be policemen, industrialists, engineers, city planners, civil servants. If we want to take the credit for an improvement in the lot of women and gays, who do we blame for Thatcher, privatisation, the power of the multinationals, the failure of education, the grinding poverty of large parts of the world, the arms industry? According to Sheila Rowbotham, the hopeful radical promise of the 1960s became stranded. She doesn't tell us why. Her book is, in fact, no more than a rather pedestrian memoir of youthful engagement, a reminiscence, the very nostalgia she accuses those who came later of committing. It actually ends before the first Women's Liberation conference, before her own serious historical research into women's history began.

Rowbotham moved from a middle-class Tory Methodist upbringing in the West Riding to a London whose streets were paved with Marxism-Leninism in the approved manner of the times. A restrictive girls' boarding school where she read extra-curricular Sartre and Kerouac and practised being Juliette Gréco in her time off, the Sorbonne and a first boyfriend who took her provincial style in hand and then left her, to Oxford, to Aldermaston, and via Edward and Dorothy Thompson, to the watering hole of the New Left at the Partisan in Carlisle Street in Soho. It's a fair geography of the early 1960s. People had begun wandering about, and unless you stayed put, you were bound to meet them. They were delighted to discover that you had read the same books, and even suggested new ones, you were amazed they enjoyed your company, that they let you into their groups. Being introduced to radical London was like starting at nursery school, scary, but with the assurance of finding your way to your peers.

It was odd that parents like the Rowbothams who were considered hopelessly hidebound let their daughters go off to Paris accompanied only by a girlfriend. The times were changing even before we changed them.

Rowbotham stolidly records her sexual progress and problems as she goes: the uncertainty about whether she could be said to have lost her virginity when she hadn't had an orgasm, whether she would ever have one, and when she does, if orange is the right colour for the lights that lit up in her head. Answers to this question and others (birth control, the importance of the clitoris, an introduction to a circle of socialists – Robin Blackburn, Gareth Stedman Jones, Perry Anderson – who challenged her acceptance of Edward Thompson's non-sectarian New Left, the frivolity of mascara) came from Bob Rowthorn, who became Rowbotham's adviser and long-term – oh I don't know – boyfriend. The seeds of 1970s feminism were a long way from flowering. Political revolution was a boy's game. Women were lovers, secretaries, tea-makers, but co-revolutionaries only when they behaved like the boys. Feeling powerless at the lack of cultural change, Rowbotham resorted to what she calls 'guerrilla outrages' and while in a restaurant with Bob and his mob, being left out of the hard-edged political conversation, she noticed a man in a window opposite changing his clothes. She began a monologue on his state of undress. 'It took a while for the table to notice, they were so preoccupied with their intellectual debate. Perry regarded me with distaste, referring to me henceforth as "that girl".' Class credentials were an allied problem:

> On reflection I decided that a lot of my problems with the working class came from my being an outsider. You're a rough-looking twot,' said a Leeds voice as I marched through Briggate in my beatnik outfit. I decided I would try and modify my clothes a bit. I couldn't just be an impersonal socialist.

In the late 1960s, Rowbotham was tempted by druggy hippie culture, which prompts recollections of acid trips and the 14-Hour Technicolor Dream at Alexandra Palace, but it was a short-lived flirtation. Edward Thompson wagged an avuncular finger at her:

> I think it is neither better nor worse than other forms of psychic self-mutilation – but worse at the moment because it belongs to a culture so excessively self-absorbed, self-inflating and self-dramatising. *Very* like Methodist revivalism, self-examining hence v. unhappy and not v. good at mutuality . . . the involuted culture you paddle in – that isn't 'you' . . . do try to talk a bit about other worlds.

Luckily she was drawn back into the Young Socialists (not self-absorbed, self-inflating and self-dramatising?) by the forthcoming anti-Vietnam demonstration in Grosvenor Square, and a plan to drop the slogan 'Oxbridge paddles while Vietnam burns' over a bridge during the Oxford and Cambridge boat race, 'thus catching the TV cameras and millions of viewers'.

And so it goes on. The boyfriend problems (the relationship with Rowthorn became 'open'), the political struggles (the battles within the *Black Dwarf* collective), the dogged leafleting and marching (Spies for Peace, Grosvenor Square), the attitudes to women (should she walk naked down a flight of stairs for Jean-Luc Godard? 'Don't you think I am able to make a cunt boring?' exclaimed the auteur). Sexuality became political when the International Socialists decided to expel her. '"You've been fuck-ing with a Stalinist," hissed a man in Hornsey, pinning me against the wall at a party.' Was this the beginning of the Women's Movement? Rowbotham began to get involved in a Women's Liberation consciousness-raising group. 'I was convinced that women could make a unique contribution to radical thinking about behaviours, responses, everyday existence and consciousness.' The problem of the personal versus the political would not go away. She recorded the dilemma in her diary. Was

> the prevailing culture of masculinity . . . *only* a consequence of capitalism or was there some underlying structure which we were to call 'patriarchy'? Second, I wanted to know whether we should concentrate on changing the attitudes and behaviour of the revolutionary Left or try 'to reach women in general'?

The rest is history, though it looks as though we shall have to wait for volume two for her account of it. But if the loss of a capacity to dream is the issue she wishes to address here, Rowbotham's angst-ridden earnestness is not likely to set a new generation dreaming. The young (and some of the old) will probably find her sketch of 1960s radicalism and the first stirrings of the Women's Movement as embarrassing as hearing their parents speak of their own engendering. What, for example, are they (or any of us) to make of her resignation from the editorial board of *Black Dwarf*? After pro-vanguardist Fred Halliday had dismissed her discussion paper 'One Law for the Lion and the Ox is Oppression' with 'I disagree with you 100 per cent,' she couldn't face the next discussion on her paper 'Cinderella Organises Buttons'. She cowered in the pub lavatory to escape Anthony Barnett, who had been detailed by the board to fetch her, while he stood outside demanding that she come out and discuss her article 'rationally and politically'. A week later the board received her letter of resignation, which suggested that 'they sit round imagining they had cunts for two minutes in silence so that they could understand why it was hard for me to discuss what I had written on women'. After Tariq Ali read it aloud to the assembled group, there was a silence, finally broken by Anthony Barnett exploding: 'This is outrageous.'

In her introduction, Rowbotham claims that 'many obvious questions about the Left in the 1960s have simply never been asked and many areas of political and social experience have been curiously ignored.' You may doubt this, but in any case her personal account adds little to the debate that hasn't been heard already. It is most likely to be read avidly by the names she drops, to confirm or outrage their own recollections. The stranding of the dreamy Left is never dealt with. Someone less attached to the myth of their youth will have to see to that.

In our declining years, it seems that we are going to do what generations before us have done and huddle together with our memories to offer each other comfort or keep the old adventures alive. Rowbotham's suggestions for further reading include no end of trips down memory lane: Sara Maitland's *Very Heaven: Looking Back at the 1960s*, Richard Neville's *Hippie Hippie Shake*, Michelene Wandor's *Once a Feminist: Stories of a Generation*, Tariq Ali's *Street Fighting Years*, Nigel Fountain's *Underground: The London Alternative Press 1966–74*. Can you doubt that even now more manuscripts are being produced by those in their fifties recounting the glory days of their late teens and twenties? They are essentially for each other, for why should the young bother with self-regarding recollection? It is as if when we were nearing twenty in 1965, we were offered a deluge of memoirs set in the late 1920s. If we discover that the young regard the 1960s as a flare-up of style and little else, we are finding only what each generation finds, which is that being young is to be opposed to the old who have had their chance. It does seem to be that everything has to be done again, much the same but in a different style relearned more or less from scratch. The tiresome thing about getting older is that you hear and read the same things over again. Stuff you know already is given out as news. The young discover global capitalism, sexual freedom, social restraints, and the old discover that they are bored, opening newspapers to read articles they read thirty years ago, listening to revelations that were new to them decades past. And on and on. So we turn in on ourselves, like our parents' generation did, and mutter about the banality of movies, TV programmes, magazines. We begin to decide that these things aren't made for us, and instead of trying to find a way to engage with and exchange ideas outside our own generation, we start to write memoirs like retired generals from some long forgotten war, or decide that it's just as well we're old because the world has failed to understand what we have done for it and it is no longer good enough for us.

A Human Being

Karl Marx by Francis Wheen. Fourth Estate 1999

Adventures in Marxism by Marshall Berman. Verso 1999

They say, and it does seem to be true, that we get the prime ministers and presidents we deserve. Now, it looks as if each generation is going to get the Karl Marx it deserves. There are advantages in watching the process of a Marx revived again and again according to the perceptions of social pundits: with each recasting and each self-appointed recaster of Marx representing the texture of current thought, we'll have a chance to observe something about our state of mind, while, if we were there before, we can comfort ourselves with the notion that *our* Marx – naturally – was the real Karl. Right now, columnist, game-show pundit and biographer of Tom Driberg, Francis Wheen is here to tell us that all the previous practitioners and theoreticians of Marx's work – both the governments and the academics (in economics, history, geography, sociology, literature) who professed themselves Marxists – have 'calamitously misinterpreted' his thought. The academics and zealots have had their day apparently, and it is time, Wheen says, 'to strip away the mythology and try to rediscover Karl Marx the man'. If your immediate response is 'why?', you've probably been off-planet for a few years. The biographical obsession, personality-bound cod analysis, has got everywhere. We prefer to see the portrait of the man, rather than think about his thoughts. The retreat in search of lively personal origins as a form of explanation is less demanding than the perpetual examination of ideas and their development. In October 1998 the *New Yorker* named Marx as 'the next great thinker' (possibly following on from the author of *The Little Book of Calm*). Marx the Movie is surely just around the corner, and not long after we can – oh please can we? – expect the musical 'Carbuncle!'; maybe, if we get very lucky, Disney will animate lovable, hairy Karl, or as Wheen describes him 'squat and swarthy, a Jew tormented by self-loathing' (voiced undoubtedly by a frantically guttural Robin Williams) scribbling *The Communist Manifesto* at his desk while a chorus of comically evil creditors sing a hummy hymn to capitalism, 'We've got nothing to lose but our claims.' Oh, what an exciting new century we have to look forward to.

Wheen wants to retrieve Marx the man and exonerate him from responsibility for what has been done in his name. Marxism is not Karl Marx, it is true, any more than Darwinism is Charles Darwin. You may not be astonished by this thought. 'What neither his enemies nor his disciples are willing to acknowledge is the most obvious yet startling of all his qualities: that this mythical ogre and saint was a human being.' Perhaps such an admission is so obvious, not to say banal, that neither enemies nor disciples thought it worth taxing their readers' patience making the point. Wheen, however, feels the time is ripe for delivering this thought to the world, and perhaps, in a deeply dispiriting way, he is right.

The McCarthyite witch-hunt of the Fifties, the wars in Vietnam and Korea, the Cuban Missile Crisis, the invasions of

Czechoslovakia and Hungary, the massacre of students in Tiananmen Square – all these bloody blemishes on the history of the 20th century were justified in the name of Marxism or anti-Marxism. No mean feat for a man who spent much of his adult life in poverty, plagued by carbuncles and liver pains, and was once pursued through the streets of London by the Metropolitan Police after a rather over-exuberant pub crawl.

I can't say whether your heart races with eager curiosity at that list of devastating world events, or at the promise of learning more about Marx's carbuncles and pub crawls, but my heart sinks at the idea that we are in a period when it's these which are thought to have the greater claim on our attention and even to bear some serious relation to 20th-century history. We've had Protestantism blamed on Luther's flatulence, and evolutionary theory dependent on Darwin's neurotic bellyaches, why not Marxism on Karl's carbuncles? Certainly, the life is interesting, and a biographer might, as several have, set out to discuss the way in which the dynamics of Marx's life and psychology articulated with his work. No one, however, as far as I know, has suggested until now that a study of Marx's daily life might clear up all confusions and errors that past and present students and interpreters of the work have fallen into.

Wheen's crusade is to redeem Marxist thought for those who imagined that the demolition of the Berlin Wall signalled the end of the Marx project. It is a book for those who fear Marx is on the scrap heap of defunct ideas – those who might be feeling a little glum at the prospect that history has come to its conclusion. It is fair enough to be glum: there are not so many ideas in the world that we can afford to shred the more interesting ones, nor so many committed and vivid thinkers that we should allow them to sink into obscurity. But I wonder whether presenting the thinker as a godless Job afflicted with boils and a taste for liquor is quite the best way to do the job. Doubtless there will be those who say it doesn't matter how it's done, let the author of *Capital* and the *Communist Manifesto* become a cuddly old curmudgeon, so long as it keeps the ideas afloat. But a safe and cosy revolutionary is merely a new kind of mythologising. Perhaps it's just a matter of taste. Me, I like my radicals roaring.

Wheen's taste, if his style is anything to go by, seems to be of the boys' boarding-school variety: this is Marx as his story might have been written by Billy Bunter's friend Cherry, or Jennings and Darbishire – tongues out, pencils poised, after stocking up in the tuck shop. If it is an attempt to repackage difficult Marx in popular language, Wheen's timing is out by several decades. It is very bizarre to read that young Karl pestered his otherwise neglected mother by trying 'to wheedle money out of the old girl', and to be told how surprising it was that a young woman born into the Prussian ruling class (Jenny von Westphalen) 'should have fallen for a bourgeois Jewish scallywag'. The 'I say, Jeeves' language continues with such antique treasures as Marx mixing with 'the most reactionary boobies in Prussia', Engels writing 'squiffy letters after lunch', Marx and Engels composing *The German Ideology* 'theorising like billy-o', and Marx forming 'opportunistic partnerships with some pretty rum coves'. Rum coves? New revelations that Marx and Engels were funded by liquor smugglers? There must be an entire generation who would need access to a dictionary of historical slang, and certainly my spell-checker failed to recognise 'squiffy' and 'billy-o', neither of which, I confess, I added to its baffled dictionary. But then Wheen is no devotee of literary style. In a recent column in the *Guardian* he railed against the Booker committee for failing to include Posy Simmonds's unremarkable cartoon parody *Gemma Bovery* in the shortlist of best novels of the year. Apparently, 'each of Simmonds's beautifully observed drawings is worth at least a thousand words of descriptive prose' – not an encouraging thought as you approach the start of Wheen's own four hundred pages. Still, it depends whose prose one is talking about. Wheen unfortunately did not invite Posy Simmonds to draw his life of Karl Marx and save his readers the bumpy journey through his own descriptive prose. This is not just an aesthetic complaint: it is strange to set out to re-present Marx as contemporary and relevant, and then use the defunct language of the British prep school to try to achieve it.

The fact is that the texture of Marx's life is portrayed as vividly, movingly and elegantly as anyone could want in the first volume of Yvonne Kapp's life of Eleanor Marx, written in 1972. Nothing in Wheen's biography supersedes her insights and asides on the family life in relation to the work or, as Wheen also points out with a smug sneer, the paradox of a man driven to overspend in order to get his daughters properly educated and acceptable for bourgeois English society, while analysing the structural flaws underlying that society. This tells us little more than that Marx lived as a man in his time, while envisaging something rather different ('It is not the consciousness of men that determines their standing, but on the contrary, their social-ising that determines their consciousness'). As to the relevance of Marx's writing at the present time, Wheen does not experi-ence Marx's power with anything like the charm and impassioned conviction of Marshall Berman's collection of essays, *Adventures in Marxism*.

Berman's clean, personal prose comes as sweet relief after the dreary O-level-set-text style of Wheen's plodding descriptions of the 1848 revolutions. Berman, now approaching 60, has lived, struggled with and taught Marxism since he was 18, when his professor of religion, Jacob Taubes, told him about a book, only just published in the States, that Marx had written 'when he was still a kid, before he became Karl Marx'. What the young Berman found in the young Marx – i.e. in the 1844 manuscripts – was a passionate description of the kind of American capitalist who Berman felt had betrayed and killed his father. He discovered in the text a reverence for the individual as a worker, creative force and even lover that places Marx in the company of 'Keats, Dickens, George Eliot, Dostoevsky, James Joyce, Franz Kafka, D.H. Lawrence'. Marxist thought and the Modernist tradition converge for Berman, as both try to grasp and confront the modern experience: Marx's 'new-fangled men . . . as much the invention of modern time as machinery itself'; Rimbaud's 'il faut être absolument moderne.' His adolescent discovery led him towards 'Marxist humanism', far removed from the orthodox Marxists 'who have at best ignored Modernism, but all too often worked to repress it, out of fear, perhaps, that . . . if they kept looking into the abyss the abyss would start looking back into them.' Berman was part of the New Left, which he now pronounces the Used Left, and his preference for the early 'humanist' texts puts him in contention with more theoretical, but less sentimental Marxist thinkers. 'Reading *Capital*,' Berman insists, 'won't help us if we don't also know how to read the signs in the street.' In response to a critique by Perry Anderson of his book *All That is Solid Melts into Air*, he declares his position: 'Another reason that I've written so much about ordinary people and everyday life in the street . . . is that Anderson's vision is so remote from them. He only has eyes for world-historical Revolutions in politics and world-class Masterpieces in culture; he stakes out his claim on heights of metaphysical perfection, and won't deign to notice anything less.' Wheen, too, reads the work as a vivid analysis of contemporary Western life, but he feels the need to spin the philosopher back into favour. Marx, he would have us know, was an ironist.

Irony is one of those words that I feel we might do well to put in storage for a while until we have recovered an understanding of what it actually means. Irony, at the fag end of the 20th century, has come to signal nothing much more than 'cool' represented to the Baby Boomers of the Sixties. If it's 'ironic' we can breathe easy, it's OK, we can laugh knowingly, while knowing nothing much, and thinking even less. Ironic chic has been with us since Woody Allen set us all smiling smugly in the cinemas, but lately it has got out of hand. TV's *Eurotrash* gives permission to wallow in silicon-enhanced breasts and cultural impoverishment with an ironically raised Gallic eyebrow. Chat-show host and DJ Chris Evans announces quite regularly that what he does is 'ironic', whereas those not hypnotised by the word know that 'vacuous' is a better description. If you suspect something you have produced is poor and pandering, just call it 'ironic' and the queues will snake around the block, happy to be seen as part of the cunning plot. Irony is quite the thing, de rigueur, so I worry when I'm told that I can admire Marx, after all, because he is a master of irony. Never mind the collapse of the Soviet Union, feel the irony. 'To do justice to the deranged logic of capitalism, Marx's text is saturated, sometimes even waterlogged, with irony – an irony which has nonetheless escaped almost every reader for more than a century.' Wheen proves his point with Marx's satire on the productive usefulness of the criminal: 'The criminal . . . produces the whole of the police and of criminal justice, constables, judges, hangmen, juries, etc; and all these different lines of business, which form just as many categories of the social division of labour, develop different capacities of the human mind, create new needs and new ways of satisfying them.' According to Wheen, this bears comparison with Swift's *Modest Proposal*. And in spite of his contention that the world has been blind to Marx's irony, Edmund Wilson, he tells us, managed to see it, calling Marx 'certainly the greatest ironist since Swift'. In 1976, S.S. Prawer, in *Karl Marx and World Literature*, noted 'Marx's witty disquisition on the "productive" nature of crime'. Word does seem to have got about. Nor have Marx's style and wit escaped Marshall Berman's attention:

The irony of bourgeois activism, as Marx sees it, is that the bourgeoisie is forced to close itself off from its richest possibilities, possibilities that can be realised only by those who break its power . . . the bourgeoisie have established themselves as the first ruling class whose authority is based not on who their ancestors were but on what they themselves actually do . . . they have proved that it really is possible, through organised, concerted action, to change the world.

Not merely ironic, but, if that is what you are after, inspiring stuff.

One problem for those who set about redeeming a 19th-century reputation is that they are liable to be required to justify to the present day the mores of the time. Wheen wants to rescue his 'squat and swarthy' Jewish hero from accusations of anti-semitism. A tough one this, given Marx's second essay on the Jewish Question:

What is the secular basis of Judaism? Practical need, self interest. What is the secular cult of the Jew? Haggling. What is his secular God? Money . . . We therefore recognise in Judaism the presence of a universal and contemporary anti-social element whose historical evolution – eagerly nurtured by the Jews in its harmful aspects – has arrived at its present peak, a peak at which it will inevitably disintegrate. The emancipation of the Jews is, in the last analysis, the emancipation of mankind from Judaism.

This quote, according to Wheen, has been taken out of context: 'From Judaism, *nota bene*, not from the Jews. Ultimately, mankind must be freed from the tyranny of all religions, Christianity included.' Not anti-semitic so much as secular socialist – and as such, rather more palatable. What then, later in Wheen's book, when Marx takes issue with the *Daily Telegraph*'s editor, Joseph Moses Levy? 'But what does it profit Levy to attack Mr D'Israeli and to change 'I' to 'y' when Mother Nature has inscribed his origins in the clearest possible way right in the middle of his face ... Levy's nose provides conversation throughout the year in the City of London.' Or when he describes Ferdinand Lassalle as 'Lazarus', 'Baron Izzy' and 'the Jewish nigger'? There's really not much to be done about this except to sigh that times were different then. Berman, while attempting to redeem Marx's anti-semitism by calling it a passing phase, takes the same quote on the Jewish Question more seriously than Wheen. It seems, he says, that the primal Jewish sin, for Marx, is a sense of self, as in 'practical need, self-interest'. He connects this directly with the legacy of Platonism and Christianity, where self is evil and virtue becomes self-sacrifice. 'In the 20th century this cliché would be reinvented by Stalinist Communism.' Berman allows himself doubts, but opts in the end for optimism: 'Did Marx himself ever believe anything like this? I can't swear he didn't, but if he did, it wasn't for long. Very soon, and in all his great works, he would affirm practical need and self-interest as primal forces that make life go on.' The Jewish question remains unresolved and painful in Berman, but I can live with it better than I can with Wheen's unconvincing gloss.

Of course, the great paradox of Marx's life, as everyone, Berman and Kapp, as well as Wheen, recognises, is the disjunction between the theory and the driving poverty, or lack of thrift, that provides a perfect example of alienated labour. Wheen recognises, as Kapp did before him, that while the Marxes failed to live on relatively handsome sums either inherited from time to time, or donated by the angelic Engels, Marx himself was trapped by bourgeois standards into the social requirements of a family man with three daughters to marry off. The girls needed the accomplishments offered by South Hampstead School as well as extra drawing and music lessons, and a decent address to bring their friends home to.

In this, as in the rest of the book, Wheen works his way through the life and works of Karl Marx as others have done before him. Clearly, he has done his research, but much of what he quotes and comments on in the work is standard stuff that will be familiar even to those with only an elementary knowledge of Marxism. And it is astonishing to read Wheen's crowing claim that on the subject of Marx's analysis of the alienation of the worker 'no Marxian scholar or critic has drawn attention to the obvious parallel with Mary Shelley's *Frankenstein*', which, he tells us helpfully, is 'the tale of a monster which turns against its creator'. Look no further than Berman in his original essay 'All That is Solid Melts into Air', written in 1978: 'Marx's bourgeois sorcerer descends from Goethe's Faust, of course, but also from another literary figure who haunted the imagination of his generation: Mary Shelley's Frankenstein. These mythical figures, striving to expand human powers through science and rationality, unleash demonic powers that erupt irrationally beyond human control, with horrifying results.'

Perhaps, if you're starting from scratch with Marx, you might read Wheen and get the basic facts, but I'd rather put Berman's slim, thoughtful book of essays into any enquiring hand to feel that Marx the thinker's future was assured.

Without the Benefit of Hindsight

The Last Days of the Jerusalem of Lithuania – Chronicles from the Vilna Ghetto and the Camps, 1939–1944 by Herman Kruk. Edited & Introduced by Benjamin Harshav. Translated by Barbara Harshav. Yale University Press 2003

Herman Kruk was a man of 42 and the director of the Yiddishist Grosser Library at the Cultural League in Warsaw when in September 1939 war broke out and he, along with other Jewish men who were in danger of being snatched off the streets, fled the city. After a month of wandering, hiding and failing to escape to the East, he arrived in Vilna, then under Lithuanian control, along with twenty thousand other Jewish refugees from Poland. Vilna already had a Jewish population of 60,000, with a thriving modern secular culture where the YIVO, a research institute in the Jewish humanities and social sciences, an academy of language and centre of cultural policy, had been founded in 1925 and whose governing board included Sigmund Freud. The YIVO moved to New York during the war, and was responsible for compiling, editing and translating Kruk's diaries into Yiddish during the decade after they were found during the first days of liberation.

A diary is a compulsive read because it is an innocent account of the diarist's times, written, that is, without benefit of hindsight. Hindsight belongs to the reader, who knows how the hopes and fears of the diarist turned out and whether the weight and interpretation given to events day by day was appropriate or wide of the mark. The knowingness of the reader gives her an edge which in reading fiction and even historical analysis is usually absent – with a diary she is closer to the role of an author: she knows how the story ends, she can assess the reliability of the writer's attitudes to and judgement of events, characters and possible outcomes against what actually happened. In the case of Herman Kruk's diary, written in Vilna before and throughout the existence of the Vilna Ghetto and in the labour camps of Estonia up until the day before the Russians liberated them, his conscious (and extraordinarily conscientious) daily witnessing is always coloured by the tragic hindsight the reader brings to it. Like Anne Frank, Kruk was not informed by any knowledge either of his own future or of Hitler's intentions towards the Jews (information comes erratically as rumour, often wrong), but unlike Frank, Kruk was a political activist, overwhelmingly concerned as a party man – a member of the Socialist Jewish Bund – about the destruction of the intricate social and cultural life of European Jewry which had built up over the previous thousand years. His private fears, the loss of his family, friends and comrades, the terrors of the unknown occasionally break through – 'Two years ago, I still had my normal social activity, my job, my home, and my wife next to me, my brother, his child, and all my near and dear ones . . . [Two years ago, I didn't] yet think how soon I would be a refugee and didn't understand the situation. Now I understand, I understand.' – but in general he subordinates them to his passionate interest in saving or mourning an entire people's established way of life. For him, and his party, the Jewish Diaspora *is* the Jewish homeland, the idea of *doikeyt* (hereness) expresses the feasibility of creating an autonomous Jewish

327

culture within Poland, while still being citizens of the state. It's an idealism he never relinquished: the belief that socialism and culture would rally and unite all groups against the forces of fascism. In his daily concerns he seems often to be more opposed to right-wing Zionists in the ghetto than to the German enemy, because he believed that the Yiddishist Diaspora was already a Jewish nation and already in the process of being destroyed by ghettoisation and socially-excluding anti-semitic decrees. His aim was for the nation of Eastern European Jewry to survive and continue. As the editor of this volume, Benjamin Hashav explains:

> There was a dense network of Jewish activities [in Eastern Europe], competing ideologies and political parties, youth movements and sports clubs, literature in several languages, publishing and translations of world literature into Yiddish and Hebrew, newspapers and libraries, separate Jewish trade unions and educational systems – a secular, modern, European-type, autonomous Jewish nation – though without power over any territory – that emerged in the nineteenth and twentieth centuries and perished in the Holocaust.

This is what makes Kruk's diary so unusual. It is an account of another holocaust, not often in the forefront of the personal histories written later by those who survived the devastation, and certainly not given its rightful due by those Israelis who claimed and continue to claim the Holocaust as an imperative for the military occupation of Palestine and the devastation of the freedom, livelihood and culture of its people. In his introduction Hashav suggests that there were two holocausts that were rendered into a single catastrophe by a manipulation of language. Pre-war Eastern European Jewry lost their way of life as well as their lives. In Yiddish culture the Holocaust was called by the Hebrew word

Churban meaning 'total ruin, destruction'. It was the term for the destruction of the first and second temples in biblical Palestine, and was used to describe the extermination of Jewish communities in the past such as the 'Churban Ukraine' in 1919. It was not by accident, says Hashav, 'that the Zionist establishment in Israel did not want to dignify the death of European Jewry with the term that denoted the end of a Jewish independent nation in the past'. *Shoah*, the Israeli Hebrew word used in preference to *Churban*, means 'a natural disaster, an external catastrophe rather than a pivotal historical event in the life of a nation'. Although over time it came internationally to assume the other meaning, this discrepancy between the Yiddish Diaspora and Hebrew-promoting Zionists is a thread that runs through the whole of Kruk's diary. He never allowed his political position on the nature and place of Jewish identity – the loss of history – to be overshadowed by the fear and suffering he also considered it his duty to recount.

Kruk describes the early days of Vilna filling up with refugees: a community being overwhelmed by terrified people who have lost their homes and families, and then organising itself to provide aid to the refugees – elementary living space, and food, but also a children's book publisher to provide textbooks for the collapsing school system. 'Nevertheless, the general mood of the faculty is good. They all believe that the school will develop again and show new achievements. And they all believe in the attachment of the Jewish masses to the Yiddish language.' His socialist, Bundist optimism is a kind of bold faith in the face of despair which appears again and again. Where the orthodox Jews had God to turn to or blame, Kruk had socialism and his belief in the Jewish masses.

Two years later, in June 1941, when Vilna was under the control of the Soviets, the Germans invaded the city. Again the Jews tried to escape, but Kruk remained in Vilna. His decision to stay was the result of weariness and fatalism but also the beginnings of a determination to endure, along with a reason for endurance.

329

No more strength to take the walking stick in hand and set out
again on the road . . . The heavy shoes are off, the rucksack is
unpacked – I'm staying . . . And right away, I made another decision: if I'm staying anyway and if I'm going to be a victim of
Fascism, I shall take pen in hand and write a chronicle of a city.
Clearly, Vilna may also be captured. The Germans will turn the
city Fascist. Jews will go into the ghetto – I shall record it all. My
chronicle must see, must hear, and must become the mirror and
the conscience of the great catastrophe and of the hard times.

(Given this determination, the remarkable survival of the
diary and its value as an historical source, it is a great pity that the
publishers of this first English language edition couldn't have
honoured it with a sewn rather than a glued binding. My copy
separated from its spine and broke in half while I was in the
middle of reading it.)

By the time the Jews were forced into the ghetto in September
1941, 40,000 Jews from Vilna and its locality had been killed by
the Germans. The remainder were concentrated into two ghet-
tos – the smaller of which was soon liquidated and its inhabitants
executed. Where 4,000 Jews had lived on seven streets, there
were now 29,000, according to Kruk's estimate, trying to find
shelter, food and a living. Instantly, he says, an apartment became
a street, and a street a whole city. But within days of their con-
finement, Kruk is telling of the formation of the *Judenrat* to
administrate the ghetto, the beginning of the Post Office, the
distribution of bread cards, the work of doctors and nurses on the
streets and the organising powers of emerging criminals and
traders. Kruk himself was originally made deputy chief of the
Jewish Police but resigned, refusing to work with the chief Jacob
Gens whom he quotes as declaring, 'Beatings. We have to have
beatings, otherwise they won't listen to us.' Already the bureau-
cracy of the ghetto was finding the distinction between

collaboration and survival to be narrowing. Gens was to become the leader of the *Judenrat* and import his friends on to the committee, which sets off a major theme in the diary of disgust and complaint about the conduct of the Jewish ghetto authorities against its own people with Jacob Gens as a continuing villainous and cowardly presence. Gens had been an active Zionist Revisionist Party member, a right wing group, thought of by the Left as fascists before the war because of their contacts with Mussolini's Italy. (It had a paramilitary brown-shirted youth movement, Betar, hostile to the Diaspora and socialism, whose last commander was Menachem Begin who, like Kruk, had fled to Vilna in 1939, but unlike him was detained by the Soviets and then made his way to Israel where he fought with the Zionist underground and eventually became a militantly right wing prime minister, a precursor of the present one.) The *Judenrat* and Jewish police were responsible for making selections of Jews for transportation or death demanded by the Germans. Gens' justification for complying was that he saved more Jews in the long run than he sent to their death – perhaps true in the short term, but in Kruk's (and hindsight's) view, simply enabling the German plans to proceed more smoothly. Kruk expresses his contempt for Gens and his party with heavy sarcasm. On January 1st 1942, Kruk notes: 'Il Duce of the ghetto, the Revisionist police chief Gens, held a New Year's Eve party, attended by 25 persons, in his apartment. At 12 o'clock at night, Il Duce took the floor and said that despite the hard year this was and despite his hard work, he recalls how he stood at the gate and saw Jews taken away . . . nevertheless, he thinks he has done important work . . . What this important work consists of, we have written about quite often. Who knows how many times we will have to write about it [Kruk means the selections and rounding up of Jews] . . . But in fact, Gens spoke, the women cried, and what the chief said was received with great "understanding".' Gens' wife 'admitted to

331

some women that she knew that people have great resentment for her husband, that he is suspected of ugly things. But she "guaranteed" that he is a decent man and is doing important work. And not in vain did she wander like a beaten dog outside the ghetto walls whenever she knew an Aktion was going on in the ghetto.'

He is deeply concerned when edicts come from Gens about the ghetto schools and their 'reformed program' reinforcing the study of Hebrew and the special study of the geography of Palestine, along with Bible studies and the introduction of Hebrew in the primary schools and kindergartens. A leading article in the official ghetto magazine, Kruk notes, 'says that Yiddish study is a Vilna speciality, that Vilna has not gone along with the Jewish nationalist stream, etc.'. Even in the ghetto, even facing the death of their children, feelings are fierce on the issue of ghetto, even facing the death of their children, feelings are fierce on the issue of nationalism. 'Friend Kozik will not allow his child's head to be confused by teaching him Hebrew . . . Now he shows me the letter where it says that his son must study Hebrew, and he asks me what to do. I advise him to remain silent because this is how the matter has been received here – one is silent . . .'

Kruk's is firstly a diary of political life which merges into increasingly urgent questions of survival, though he never loses sight of the demolition of the culture he prizes. He was ambivalent about the Communist partisans inside the ghetto and those who ran off to fight with organised groups in the dense forests of the area. He admired their action and their bravery, but he feared for the survival of the overall group – for him the diminishing society of the Vilna ghetto which was all that remained of Eastern European Jewish culture. At times he knew that the death of Jewry was inevitable and then he agreed with the secret arming of the ghetto, 'Recently everything has pointed toward one thing – tremble for tomorrow . . . No, we will not be

taken like sheep! No, we will not let them.' It is better, he concluded, to die fighting the Germans than to be led away and
shot. But he wavered. His fears, even at the very end, that an
uprising would cause the entire ghetto to be liquidated, that
something might happen, that liberation would come, overrode
his support for the partisans, and he counselled patience. His
realistic despair ('Where to flee? Where can you flee? . . . Thus
the Vilna Jewish masses are waiting in line. The noose is thrown
around their neck and they wait for the hangman to come and
pull it . . .') alternated with the Yiddish saying 'You can't know a
thing', the title of a play put on in the ghetto, which the translator notes as implying among other things: '"Who knows? You
never know. Don't be so sure, it may still turn out well."' In
March 1943, Kruk writes, '. . . I'm still alive and want to live – a
lot – and hope to get out of here and perhaps enjoy my near and
dear ones – those, of course, who are alive . . . Maybe, maybe . . .'

It is this inextinguishable but faint hope – where there's hope
there's life? – that causes Kruk repeatedly to think each time
something murderous happens to tell him the truth about the
Germans' intentions, that if only the Jews endured they would
survive. The prize of Jewish survival in Europe was everything,
and included the simple possibility of personal survival. Fatalistic
heroism always took second place in this dilemma. And in a way
he was right – liberation *was* just around the corner. He might
have survived, the Jews might have survived and the chance of
living was better than the certainty of dying. At each stage there
was a resistance to believing the truth which slowly emerged – as
why wouldn't human beings resist the truth of the Final
Solution? The meaning of Ponar – a nearby forest – grows fear-
fully in Kruk's account. At first just whispers and wild surmise
and then more definite information, until finally a handful of
escapees return to the ghetto (to what future?) and tell the facts
about the tens of thousands who were supposedly taken away to

work camps, but were actually marched into mass graves in a clearing of the forest and shot. In the Estonian work camps Kruk was sent to, the Allies got closer and the Germans knew the end was coming. Kruk indicated that he was aware of their likely reaction. 'The Germans themselves are terribly depressed and confess that they are jealous of the Jews. "Soon you will be liberated. And our lot is bad. They will slaughter us with no mercy."' Even so, he did not run, as others did, and join the partisans in the forests. He waited, maybe with hope, perhaps with a fascination to see things through to the end, whatever – or perhaps simply with that disbelief in one's own death that flutters around us all under all circumstances. With each Allied success, Kruk asked if this was good or bad for the Jews. Each triumph that brought liberation closer was also potentially lethal to the ghetto and the camps. Such assessments of events were also a feature of life in the ghetto. When people were taken away in transports, when local shtetls were liquidated and more Jews crammed into the ghetto, when an order for uniforms came in and meant another two months' work for the tailoring workshop, the response was always to wonder what it meant for the whole community's likely life or death. An order surely was good – they would not be executed for two months at least; the meaning of the influx from the surrounding area was unknowable – were they concentrating the Jews to kill them all or because they needed them in one place for labouring? Even an *aktion* was seen in this way. When eighty old and infirm Jews were taken off and shot, people asked each other if it was good or bad for the ghetto. Endurance includes becoming inured, to some extent. 'The ghetto grows more tired and, especially, more indifferent from day to day. Just recently 67 Jews of Biala Waka have fallen on the altar of our time. The ghetto had many loved ones there but went through the case as if nothing had happened. People swallowed it, and life goes on . . . The ghetto is cold and indifferent to everything.'

But survival was not entirely all of it. In Klooga, Kruk's first camp in Estonia, which lacked washing facilities or beds for workers who tried to live on 33 decagrams of bread a day, an idea emerged to set up a meeting-group of intellectuals. 'Gathered around a full table, covered with a white tablecloth and self-brewed coffee, the assembled people tearfully honoured their fallen colleagues and praised the great event of being able to sit together, look at the white tablecloth, and talk to each other like human beings . . . And the human beings suddenly felt like humans! . . . True, all of them were hungry . . . but all those intellectuals devoured the fine table, the white tablecloth, the festive gathering, and the atmosphere, which was so far from Klooga and even farther from reality . . . Everything here is built on sand . . . The fear of meeting. The great risk and small return . . . All of it was pointed out: the group of intellectuals would die before it was even born.'

Though he would not risk the loss of the remnants of culture that was the Vilna ghetto, Kruk took risks with his own life. His ghetto job was salvaging material from the Vilna libraries for the Rosenberg Task Force, which planned to ship the books back to Germany for that most Wonderland of proposed German institutions, *Judenforschung ohne Juden* – the Institute for the Study of Jewry without Jews. He used his freedom of movement to steal and smuggle Jewish secular and religious texts to safe hideouts where some of them were to survive the war. Without alerting the German head of the task force, Kruk ran a small cultural resistance movement all of his own. He was also in charge of the ghetto library and declared a public holiday to celebrate when the hundred thousandth book had been taken out. And, of course, he kept his diary, even under the impossible conditions of the work camps, after a sixteen hour, undernourished day building defences for the German front line. 'I bury the manuscripts in Lagedi, in a barrack . . . right across from the guard's house. Six persons are present at the burial.' This was part of Kruk's last entry on 17th September 1944, the day before he and all the other inmates of the camp were shot and their bodies burned on a pyre of logs they themselves had been forced to build. The following day the Red Army reached the area and the only survivor of six witnesses dug up Kruk's buried diary.

After the war the notion of a Jewish Diaspora as a legitimate and vivid trans-European culture died. All that remained of the old Diaspora became a memorial remnant, a useful excuse which militant nationalist Israelis appropriated for their own use.

BIBLIOGRAPHY

These articles appeared in the following publications:

A VIEW FROM THE BED

A View from the Bed, *Guardian Weekend*, 1999.

Every Mother Prays, *Hairstyles and Fashion: A Hairdresser's History of Paris 1910–1920. Edited by Steven Zdatny, Berg 1999*, London Review of Books, 2 March 2000.

Being 50, *Welcome to Middle Age! (And Other Cultural Fictions). Edited by Richard Shweder, Chicago 1998*, London Review of Books, 15 October 1998.

Both Feet Firmly on the Ground, *Guardian Weekend*, 1999.

Reading the Labels on the Marmalade Jars, *Jewish Chronicle*, 1998.

Ice Fishing Huts, *Independent on Sunday*, 1999.

Fashion Statements: *Archaeology of Elegance 1980–2000. Edited by Marion de Beaupré et al. Thames and Hudson 2002*, London Review of Books, 14 November 2002.

DIFFICULT CHAPS

Did Jesus walk on water because he couldn't swim? *The Children of Noah: Jewish Seafaring in Ancient Times by Raphael Patai. Princeton 1998*, London Review of Books, 20 August 1998.

A Life, Surely? *The Ossie Clark Diaries, edited by Henrietta Rous. Bloomsbury 1998*, London Review of Books, 18 February 1999.

The People's Tycoon, *Branson by Tom Bower. Fourth Estate 2000, London Review of Books*, Vol. 22 No. 22 6 November 2000.

The Daddy of All Patriarchs, *Abraham on Trial – The Social Legacy of Biblical Myth by Carol Delaney. Princeton University Press 1998. London Review of Books*, Vol. 20 No. 24 10 December 1998.

The Lights in the Land of Plenty, *Beautiful Losers/The Favourite Game by Leonard Cohen. Penguin 2000. Previously unpublished article.*

VISCERAL STUFF

Get It Out of Your System, *The Anatomy of Disgust by William Ian Miller. Harvard 1997. London Review of Books*, 8 May 1997.

Oh, Andrea Dworkin, *Misogyny: The Male Malady by David Gilmore. Pennsylvania 2001. London Review of Books*, 6 September 2001.

Feel the Burn, *Pain: The Science of Suffering by Patrick Wall. Weidenfeld 1999. London Review of Books*, 30 September 1999.

AWKWARD DAMES

Someone Else's Work, *The Girl from the Fiction Department – A Portrait of Sonia Orwell by Hilary Spurling. Hamish Hamilton 2002. London Review of Books*, Vol. 24 No. 8 25 April 2002.

Perfectly Human, *Lillie Langtry: Manners, Masks and Morals by Laura Beatty. Chatto 1999; Véra (Mrs Vladimir Nabokov): Portrait of a Marriage by Stacy Schif. Random House 1999. London Review of Books*, 1 July 1999.

A Slut's Slut, *Dangerous Muse: A Life of Caroline Blackwood by Nancy Schoenberger. Weidenfield & Nicolson 2002. London Review of Books*, Vol. 23 No. 20 18 October 2002.

Turn the Light Off, Please, *A Slight and Delicate Creature: The Memoirs of Margaret Cook. Weidenfeld & Nicolson 1999. London Review of Books*, Vol. 21 No. 5 4 March 1999.

HEART'S DESIRE

One, *New Statesman* and *Observer*,2000.

Two, *Observer*, 2000.

Three, *Observer*, 2000.

Four, *Observer*, 2000.

Five, *Observer*, 2000.

Immobility, previously unpublished article, 2001.

HOW IT IS

Keeping Up, *The Dictionary of New Words, OUP 1998, London Review of Books*, 1998.

Getting It, *E=mc2 by David Bodanis. Pan 2001. London Review of Books*.

The Family Way, *Guardian*, 2 July 2003.

Caramel Apples and Cotton Candy, *The Celebration Chronicles: Life, Liberty and the Pursuit of Property Values in Disney's New Town by Andrew Ross. Verso 2000; Celebration, USA: Living in Disney's Brave New Town by Douglas Frantz and Catherine Collins. Holt 1999. London Review of Books*, Vol. 22 No. 16 24 August 2000.

Movie Monk, *The New Biographical Dictionary of Film by David Thomson. Little, Brown 2002; Nobody's Perfect: Writings from the 'New Yorker' by Anthony Lane. Picador 2002; Paris Hollywood: Writings on Film by Peter Wollen. Verso 2002. London Review of Books*, 24 January 2003.

Get On With It, *The Knox Brothers by Penelope Fitzgerald. Harvil 1990. The American Scholar*, Autumn 2000.

SEX . .

Good Vibrations, *Solitary Sex – A Cultural History of Masturbation by Thomas W. Laqueur. Zone Books 2003, LA Times Review of Books*, March 16 2003.

Pot Noodle Moments, *The Sexual Life of Catherine M. by Catherine Millet. Serpent's Tail 2002. London Review of Books*, Vol. 24 No. 14 25 July 2002.

My Little Lollipop, *The Truth at Last: My Story by Christine Keeler with Douglas Thompson. Sidgwick & Jackson 2001. London Review of Books*, 22 March 2001.

Larkin's Lesbian Period, *Trouble at Willow Gables and other fictions by Philip Larkin, edited by James Booth. Faber and Faber 2002. London Review of Books,* Vol. 24 No. 10 23 May 2002.

. . . AND SHOPPING

Supermarket Sweep, *Observer Style and Travel*, 18 April–17 October 1993.

ANGRY-ON-A-SOFA

Election Diary 1, *New Statesman*, 21 May 2001, Vol. 14 Issue 657.

Election Diary 2, *New Statesman*, 4 June 2001, Vol. 14 Issue 659.

Election Diary 3, *New Statesman*, 11 June 2001, Vol. 14 Issue 660.

A Long Forgotten War, *Promise of a Dream: A Memoir of the 1960s by Sheila Rowbotham. Allen Lane 2000. London Review of Books*, 6 July 2000.

A Human Being, *Karl Marx by Francis Wheen. Fourth Estate 1999; Adventures in Marxism by Marshall Berman. Verso 1999. London Review of Books*, 25 November 1999.

Without the Benefit of Hindsight, *The Last Days of the Jerusalem of Lithuania – Chronicles from the Vilna Ghetto and the Camps, 1939–1944 by Herman Kruk. Edited by Benjamin Harshav. Yale University Press 2003. London Review of Books*, Vol. 25 No. 10 May 2003.

STRANGER ON A TRAIN
Jenny Diski

'We were on a train, out of the way of our lives; any of us could tell anything we liked. We were, for the time being, just the story we told.'

In spite of the fact that her idea of travel is to stay at home with the phone off the hook, Jenny Diski takes a trip around the perimeter of the USA by train.

Somewhat reluctantly, she meets all kinds of characters, all bursting with stories to tell, and finds herself brooding about the marvellously familiar landscape of America, half-known already through film and television. Like the pulse of the train over the rails, the theme of the dying pleasures of smoking thrums through the book, along with reflections on the condition of solitude and the nature of friendship and memories triggered by her past time in psychiatric hospitals.

Cutting between her troubled teenaged years and contemporary America, the journey becomes a study of strangers, strangeness and estrangement – from oneself, as well as from the world.

Now you can order superb titles directly from Virago

The prices shown above are correct at time of going to press. However, the publishers reserve the right to increase prices on covers from those previously advertised, without further notice.

Virago

Please allow for postage and packing: **Free UK delivery.**
Europe: add 25% of retail price; Rest of World: 45% of retail price.

To order any of the above or any other Virago titles, please call our credit card orderline or fill in this coupon and send/fax it to:

Virago, PO Box 121, Kettering, Northants NN14 4ZQ
Fax: 01832 733076   Tel: 01832 737526
Email: aspenhouse@FSBDial.co.uk

☐ I enclose a UK bank cheque made payable to Virago for £ . . . .
☐ Please charge £ . . . . . . to my Visa/Access/Mastercard/Eurocard

Expiry Date ☐☐☐☐   Switch Issue No. ☐☐

NAME (BLOCK LETTERS please) . . . .

ADDRESS . . . .

. . . .

. . . .

Postcode . . . . Telephone . . . .

Signature . . . .

Please allow 28 days for delivery within the UK. Offer subject to price and availability.

Please do not send any further mailings from companies carefully selected by Virago ☐